New Perspectives in German Studies

General Editors: Michael Butler was Emeritus Professor of Modern German Literature at the University of Birmingham and Professor William E. Paterson OBE is Professor of European and German Politics at the University of Birmingham and Chairman of the German British Forum.

Over the last twenty years the concept of German studies has undergone major transformation. The traditional mixture of language and literary studies, related very closely to the discipline as practised in German universities, has expanded to embrace history, politics, economics and cultural studies. The conventional boundaries between all these disciplines have become increasingly blurred, a process which has been accelerated markedly since German unification in 1989/90.

New Perspectives in German Studies, developed in conjunction with the Institute for German Studies and the Department of German Studies at the University of Birmingham, has been designed to respond precisely to this trend of the interdisciplinary approach to the study of German and to cater for the growing interest in Germany in the context of European integration. The books in this series will focus on the modern period, from 1750 to the present day.

Titles include:

Matthew M.C. Allen
THE VARIETIES OF CAPITALISM PARADIGM
Explaining Germany's Comparative Advantage?

Peter Bleses and Martin Seeleib-Kaiser
THE DUAL TRANSFORMATION OF THE GERMAN WELFARE STATE

Y. Michal Bodemann (*editor*)
THE NEW GERMAN JEWRY AND THE EUROPEAN CONTEXT
The Return of the European Jewish Diaspora

Michael Butler and Robert Evans (*editors*)
THE CHALLENGE OF GERMAN CULTURE
Essays Presented to Wilfried van der Will

Michael Butler, Malcolm Pender and Joy Charnley (*editors*)
THE MAKING OF MODERN SWITZERLAND 1848–1998

Paul Cooke and Andrew Plowman (*editors*)
GERMAN WRITERS AND THE POLITICS OF CULTURE
Dealing with the Stasi

Beverly Crawford
POWER AND GERMAN FOREIGN POLICY
Embedded Hegemony in Europe

Wolf-Dieter Eberwein and Karl Kaiser (*editors*)
GERMANY'S NEW FOREIGN POLICY
Decision-Making in an Interdependent World

Anne Fuchs
PHANTOMS OF WAR IN CONTEMPORARY GERMAN LITERATURE, FILMS AND DISCOURSE
The Politics of Memory

Karl Christian Führer and Corey Ross (*editors*)
MASS MEDIA, CULTURE AND SOCIETY IN TWENTIETH-CENTURY GERMANY

Axel Goodbody
NATURE, TECHNOLOGY AND CULTURAL CHANGE IN TWENTIETH-CENTURY GERMAN LITERATURE
The Challenge of Ecocriticism

Jonathan Grix
THE ROLE OF THE MASSES IN THE COLLAPSE OF THE GDR

Gunther Hellmann (*editor*)
GERMANY'S EU POLICY IN ASYLUM AND DEFENCE
De-Europeanization by Default?

Dan Hough, Michael Koß and Jonathan Olsen
THE LEFT PARTY IN CONTEMPORARY GERMAN POLITICS

Margarete Kohlenbach
WALTER BENJAMIN
Self-Reference and Religiosity

Charles Lees
PARTY POLITICS IN GERMANY
A Comparative Politics Approach

Hanns W, Maull
GERMANY'S UNCERTAIN POWER
Foreign Policy of the Berlin Republic

Alister Miskimmon
GERMANY AND THE COMMON FOREIGN AND SECURITY POLICY OF THE EUROPEAN UNION
Between Europeanization and National Adaptation

Caroline Pearce
CONTEMPORARY GERMANY AND THE NAZI LEGACY
Remembrance, Politics and the Dialectic of Normality

Christian Schweiger
BRITAIN, GERMANY AND THE FUTURE OF THE EUROPEAN UNION

James Sloam
THE EUROPEAN POLICY OF THE GERMAN SOCIAL DEMOCRATS
Interpreting a Changing World

Ronald Speirs and John Breuilly (*editors*)
GERMANY'S TWO UNIFICATIONS
Anticipations, Experiences, Responses

Henning Tewes
GERMANY, CIVILIAN POWER AND THE NEW EUROPE
Enlarging Nato and the European Union

Maiken Umbach
GERMAN FEDERALISM
Past, Present, Future

Roger Woods
GERMANY'S NEW RIGHT AS CULTURE AND POLITICS

New Perspectives in German Studies
Series Standing Order ISBN 0–333–92430–4 hardcover
Series Standing Order ISBN 0–333–92434–7 paperback
(*outside North America Only*)

You can receive future titles in this series as they are published by placing a standing order. Please contact your bookseller or, in case of difficulty, write to us at the address below with your name and address, the title of the series and the ISBN quoted above.

Customer Services Department, Macmillan Distribution Ltd, Houndmills, Basingstoke, Hampshire RG21 6XS, England

---

The New German Jewry and the European Context

The Return of the European Jewish Diaspora

Edited by

Y. Michal Bodemann
Professor of Sociology
University of Toronto, Canada

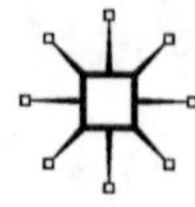

First published 2008 by
PALGRAVE MACMILLAN
Houndmills, Basingstoke, Hampshire RG21 6XS and
175 Fifth Avenue, New York, N.Y. 10010
Companies and representatives throughout the world

PALGRAVE MACMILLAN is the global academic imprint of the Palgrave Macmillan division of St. Martin's Press, LLC and of Palgrave Macmillan Ltd. Macmillan® is a registered trademark in the United States, United Kingdom and other countries. Palgrave is a registered trademark in the European Union and other countries.

ISBN-13: 978–0–230–52107–0 hardback
ISBN-10: 0–230–52107–X hardback

This book is printed on paper suitable for recycling and made from fully managed and sustained forest sources. Logging, pulping and manufacturing processes are expected to conform to the environmental regulations of the country of origin.

A catalogue record for this book is available from the British Library.

A catalog record for this book is available from the Library of Congress.

10 9 8 7 6 5 4 3 2 1
17 16 15 14 13 12 11 10 09 08

Printed and bound in Great Britain by
CPI Antony Rowe, Chippenham and Eastbourne

Contents

Notes on the Contributors

Olena Bagno, originally from Donetsk, Ukraine, is a PhD candidate at the University of Tel Aviv and a lecturer in the Department of Political Science at Ben-Gurion University, Be'er Sheva. Her research interests focus on Political Behaviour, International Migration, EU Migration Policies, and Methodology. She has conducted extensive research on the Russian-speaking migration from Ukraine in Israel and Germany. She has also carried out research on Soviet war veterans in Germany.

Y. Michal Bodemann teaches sociology at the University of Toronto and has studied at the Universities of Munich, Heidelberg and Mannheim. His major publications include *Jews, Germans, Memory: Reconstructions of Jewish Life in Germany* (editor), and two volumes in German: *Gedächtnistheater: Die jüdische Gemeinschaft und ihre deutsche Erfindung* (Theatre of Memory: the Jewish Community and its German Invention) which was listed on the German book critics' list of ten best non-fiction books; and *In den Wogen der Erinnerung: Jüdische Existenz in Deutschland* (In the Sea of Memory: Jewish Existence in Germany). His book, *A Jewish Family in Germany Today: an Intimate Portrait*, a monograph on an extended Jewish family living in Germany today, appeared in 2005. With Gökce Yurdakul, he has edited two volumes: *Migration, Citizenship, Ethnos: Incorporation Regimes in Europe and North America*, Palgrave Macmillan (March 2006); and *Citizenship and Immigrant Incorporation: Comparative Perspectives on North America and Western Europe* (Palgrave Macmillan, 2007).

Dan Diner is Professor at the Hebrew University of Jerusalem (Department of History) and Director of the Simon Dubnow Institute for Jewish History and Culture at Leipzig University. He is the author of numerous articles and books on the history of the twentieth century, the history of the Middle East and German history, especially the history of National Socialism and the Holocaust. Recent books include: *Versiegelte Zeit: Über den Stillstand in der islamischen Welt*, Propyläen Verlag Berlin, 2005; *Gedächtniszeiten: Über jüdische und andere Geschichten*, Verlag C. H. Beck, München, 2003; *Feindbild Amerika: Über die Beständigkeit eines Ressentiments*, Propyläen Verlag Berlin, 2002; *Raccontare il Novecento: Una Storia Politica*, Garzanti Libri Milano, Italy, s.p.a. 2001, 278 S; and *Beyond the Conceivable: Studies on Germany, Nazism, and the Holocaust*, Berkeley, 2000.

Sander L. Gilman is a distinguished professor of the Liberal Arts and Sciences at Emory University, where he is the Director of the Program in Psychoanalysis as well as of Emory University's Health Sciences Humanities Initiative. A cultural and literary historian, he is the author or editor of over seventy books. His Oxford lectures *Multiculturalism and the Jews* appeared in 2006; his most recent edited volume, *Race and Contemporary Medicine: Biological Facts and Fictions*, appeared in 2007. He is the author of a basic study of the visual stereotyping of the mentally ill, *Seeing the Insane*, published by John Wiley and Sons in 1982 (reprinted 1996) as well as the standard study of *Jewish Self-Hatred*, the title of his Johns Hopkins University Press monograph of 1986.

Olaf Glöckner holds an MA and is a historian who specializes in Jewish studies; he works at the University of Applied Science Potsdam (Germany). Currently, he is preparing a comparative analysis of Russian Jewish elites in Israel and Germany.

Judith Kessler is a social scientist and journalist who received her MA in philology and literature in East Germany, and in social science, psychology, and political science in West Germany. She has been involved in studies and publications on Jewish contemporary culture and Soviet-Jewish emigration, including: 'From Aizenberg to Zaidelman: Jewish Immigrants from East Europe and the Jewish Congregation Today' (1995); 'Jewish Emigration from the Former Soviet Union since 1990: a Study on 4000 Immigrants' (1996); 'The Search for Identity and Subculture: Experiences of Welfare Work in the Jewish Congregation' (1999); and 'The Cultural and Religious Self-image of Berlin Jews: Results of the First Congregational Survey' (2002/3).

Leslie Morris is Associate Professor of German and Director of the Center for Jewish Studies at the University of Minnesota. She is the author of a book on history and memory in Ingeborg Bachmann's poetry, and co-editor, with Karen Remmler, of *Contemporary Jewish Writing in Germany*. She has also co-edited, with Jack Zipes, *Unlikely History: the Changing German-Jewish Symbiosis*. She has written articles on the poetics of exile, diaspora, translation, sound and memory. She is currently completing a book entitled *The Trans-Jewish: Translating Jewish Memory in Germany Today*.

Jeffrey Peck is a Professor in the Program in 'Communication, Culture and Technology' at Georgetown University and is a Senior Fellow at the American Institute of Contemporary German Studies in Washington,

DC. He currently holds the two-year DAAD Walter Benjamin Chair in Jewish Studies at Humboldt University. In 2004, he edited an AICGS report on 'The Jewish Voice in Transatlantic Relations' and in 2005 published an essay for AICGS on 'American Jews in an Evangelical America'. In 2006, he published *Being Jewish in the New Germany* with Rutgers University Press which addresses the growth of and influences on the Jewish community in Germany since 1990 in a global context.

Diana Pinto is an intellectual historian and writer living in Paris. The daughter of Italian Jewish parents, educated in the United States and a resident of France, she is equally at home in all three cultures. She is a *Summa cum Laude* graduate of Harvard University where she also obtained her PhD in Contemporary European History. She has written widely on transatlantic issues and on French and Italian politics. She is the author of *Contemporary Italian Sociology* (1981) and *Entre deux mondes* (1991). She is currently the Director of a pan-European Ford Foundation sponsored project 'Voices for the *res publica*' at the Institute for Jewish Policy Research, London.

Julius Schoeps is Professor of Contemporary Jewish and German History at Potsdam University (Germany) and the Director of the Moses Mendelssohn Centre for European Jewish Studies, Potsdam. He initiated a series of empirical investigations on the early Russian Jewish immigration to reunified Germany. He specializes on the history of Zionism, Jewish history in Berlin, anti-Semitism and restitution for Holocaust survivors.

Liliane Weissberg is the Christopher H. Browne Distinguished Professor in Arts and Science at the University of Pennsylvania, and Professor of German and Comparative Literature. Among her publications in the field of German-Jewish literature and culture are the critical edition of Hannah Arendt's *Rahel Varnhagen: the Life of a Jewess* (1997), and the anthology *Cultural Memory and the Construction of Identity* (with Dan Ben-Amos, 1999). She has just completed a new book entitled *Approaching Gentility: Early German-Jewish Autobiography and the Quest for Acculturation.*

Gökçe Yurdakul (PhD, University of Toronto) is Lecturer in Sociology at Trinity College Dublin. She is also Adjunct Professor at Brock University, Canada. Her teaching and research interests include immigration, citizenship, race and ethnicity, gender and women, focusing on Turkish migrants in Germany and Islam in Europe. Dr Yurdakul is the editor of two books: *Migration, Citizenship, Ethnos* and *Citizenship and Immigrant*

Incorporation: Comparative Perspectives on North America and Western Europe (both with Michal Bodemann, 2006, 2007, New York: Palgrave Macmillan). She has published and has forthcoming articles in edited books and scholarly journals, such as the *Annual Review of Sociology, Journal of Ethnic and Migration Studies, Soziale Welt* and *Violence Against Women*. She is currently working on a project which has recently been awarded a Social Sciences and Humanities Research Grant: 'Jews and Turks in Germany: Immigrant Integration, Political Representation and Minority Rights'.

Introduction: the Return of the European Jewish Diaspora

Y. Michal Bodemann

This book is going to print in less than auspicious times. In the Middle East, we see the implosion of Palestinian and Israeli society; large-scale corruption and civil war in Palestine, in Israel, large-scale corruption as well, political disaffection on the Left with the collapse of the peace movement, collapse of the party system as we know it and an ominous resurgence of the far Right that seeks the 'transfer' of the Israeli Arab population. In Israel the Right is supported in part by the new Russian-speaking immigrant vote and in the US by conservative political forces, from President Bush to the Christian Fundamentalists, as well as by major sections of the Jewish establishment itself. Meanwhile, the settlements on the West Bank keep growing.

These developments in Israel have been evolving since the assassination of Yitzchak Rabin and the failure of Oslo. Among significant sections of the Jewish Diaspora, however, they have brought about considerable disaffection with Israeli politics. Many, especially in the younger generation, are taking issue with the persistent violation of human rights in the occupied territories and elsewhere and in recent times have voiced their objections to these policies in public: especially so in Britain, Germany and the US. In Britain in 2007, a distinguished group of Jews voiced their concern about human rights violations in Israel. In the US, an angry controversy erupted over an article by Alvin Rosenfeld, published by the American Jewish Committee, which linked 'liberal Jews' to anti-Semitism.[1] In Germany in 2006, where political correctness over Israel is the order of the day and where Jews historically have been hesitant about voicing their dissent, over seventy well-known Jews signed a petition, expressing their concern about Israeli policies – ignored, in large part, by the German press and roundly attacked, in this case as well, by the Jewish establishment. Much of this was spearheaded by the articles on the 'Jewish Lobby' in the US by

John Mearsheimer and Stephen Walt and Tony Judt's much discussed essays.[2]

These developments have brought to the fore a substantial polarization in the Jewish Diaspora, in North America and in Europe. For many, Israel has become a country (almost) like any other. It is no longer the exclusive centre of the Jewish universe, and the Holocaust is not the focal point of their version of Jewish history; unlike the discourses that were central to Jews since the post-war period and which remain central to the Jewish establishment where dissent is strongly sanctioned. This daring new insistence on the centrality of Diaspora as the essence of Jewish cultural life was articulated first perhaps by Daniel and Jonathan Boyarin who have questioned the Zionist project altogether: 'The solution of Zionism – that is, Jewish state hegemony, except insofar as it represented an emergency and temporary rescue operation – seems to us the subversion of Jewish culture and not its culmination. Capturing Judaism in a state transforms entirely the meanings of its social practices.'[3]

In the spirit of the Boyarins' ground-breaking article, 'Generation: the Ground of Jewish Identity', this new generation has moved away from Holocaust commemoration as a negative civil religion and is reinventing 'positive' diasporic Jewish traditions in new religious and secular forms. This new interpretation of Diaspora includes a group of mostly younger historians such as Ivan Marcus or Frank Stern who, while not ignoring the catastrophe of the Shoah and the persecutions through the centuries, have departed from a 'lachrymose' (Salo Baron) version of Jewish history which especially after the Shoah had served as further justification for the establishment of the State of Israel.[4] That earlier version of Diaspora history could see little else but waves of persecution.

Many of these reinventions are coming from the Jewish periphery and have brought about a greater visibility of Jewish women in Jewish affairs with new energy and creativity in religious services and community work at large. They have also led to a rise of egalitarian religious services, to an alternative Jewish community and emotional support sought by lesbian and gay Jews, but also by intermarried couples, non-halachic (patrilineal) Jews and converts to Judaism who are seeking full acceptance via Reform Judaism or other, largely local, institutional frameworks. Often we see that diversity develop outside the big established centres of Jewish life, first and foremost outside Israel itself. One such periphery in Jewish terms is Germany and perhaps Europe at large, and used by Israelis and North American Jewish artists, scholars and writers as a laboratory to experiment within their respective fields. Klezmer groups such as *Brave Old World* fit into this category, as do the large number of visiting Israeli and Diaspora

Jewish scholars and writers. Yet by many, Europe and Germany in particular are dismissed as riddled with anti-Semitism and as uncritical partisans of the Palestinian side and generally following an appeasement strategy in relation to Israel's, or the Jewish people's enemies at large.[5]

Indeed, while there is a growing gap between Diaspora Jews and Israel,[6] the gap between the million Jews in Western and Central Europe on the one hand and those of the North American Jewish Diaspora and Israel on the other is astonishing. Part of it can probably be explained, as Diana Pinto has suggested, by the memories of oppression and persecution that Jewish immigrants to North America have conveyed to later generations. In the American Jewish consciousness therefore, and to a large extent, Europe does not really exist as a Jewish environment, and American and Israeli Jewish travel to Europe, as most poignantly with the 'March of the Living' for younger Jews, is largely still an excursion into Jewish death rather than Jewish life. In the American Jewish consciousness, there is an Israel–US axis outside of which Jewish life is not really conceivable.[7]

Diana Pinto's contribution in this volume addresses some of these observations. Her starting point is the reconciliation between Germany and France that was accomplished after the Second World War, and the question is whether and how such a reconciliation can be accomplished between Jews and European society. Pinto takes us back to the broader constellation of European Jewry on the one hand, and American Jews and Israel on the other. Israel and the US are the two new poles in the Jewish world, as successors of – in their imagination at least – obliterated European Jewry. They imagine Europe as being anti-Jewish, between appeasement and indifference in relation to Jewish matters. The Jewish world, she argues, absorbed in an increasingly 'exclusive and intolerant memory', has become autistic and destabilized which explains its, at times, aggressive behaviour;[8] Europe, on the other hand, excluding Germany perhaps, has largely failed to seriously address the Holocaust and to reconcile itself with the Jewish world.

As far as American Jewry and Israeli intellectuals are concerned, there are some interesting developments nevertheless, and not everyone there shares Charles Krauthammer's views about Europe which Pinto refers to. Many younger North American Jews have begun to rediscover contemporary European Jewish culture in Britain, Italy, France, Poland, Prague and Berlin and are interested in European Jewish history beyond, before and after the Shoah. The fact, for example, that the Jewish museum in Berlin is one of the most visited sites in Berlin speaks to this point. Similarly, we should take a closer look at the developments among the Israeli intellectual elites, in contrast to what we see in Israeli political attitudes towards Europe. Pinto points to Europhile authors such as Amos Oz, A. B. Yehoshua or David Grossman as examples. In the past two decades especially, Israeli elites have seen a notable turning away from an almost exclusive orientation towards the US. They have rediscovered Europe and found European interlocutors. Even the average middle-class Israeli has discovered that Berlin is the place to visit. Moreover, they had also long ago begun a dialogue with the Arab-Muslim world, far ahead of their counterparts in Europe and America.

Israel and American Jewry, however, cannot simply turn all European nations into guilty accessories; an exclusive and intolerant memory will lead to further alienation between Jews and others. Both Jews and Europeans at large must pursue universal values, not narrow particularisms. In the US and elsewhere outside Europe, it is seen as a proof of European decadence that it seems unable to integrate its immigrants and deal effectively with anti-Semitism. These two points are linked, of course, because most of the new anti-Semitism comes from Arab/Muslim immigration. Finally, Pinto calls on European Jews to take full part in the *res publica* rather than retreating and shutting themselves off from the world. It is my contention that a return to and revalidation of Diaspora is more likely to accomplish this opening towards the *res publica* than an exclusive fixation of European Jewry by Israel and the United States.

Echoing Hannah Arendt in some ways, Dan Diner's essay advocates a rereading of history from its fringes. Diner suggests that we should take a closer look at Europe's borders, epitomized here today by the question of the admission of Turkey to the European Union, and the great symbolic significance of Turkey's membership. Admission of Turkey is not only opposed by German (and other European) politicians, but even by some of the most distinguished German historians – and one might add, by much of the educated middle classes and intellectual elites at large. The question Europeans have been addressing then is, 'who is fitting in?' especially in terms of religion; this refers not only to the Turks, but the Jews too may be at risk here of not quite fitting in. As a pan-European population par excellence, and for a long time, Jews have not always fit well into the system of European nation-states, in contrast to the previous imperial structures.

The Jews, Diner argues, are simultaneously modern and pre-modern; reluctantly, they had to abandon their unique corporatist status during imperial times in Germany, France, Poland and elsewhere, in exchange for an individualized religious 'confession'. Subsequently, they had to abandon much of their transnationalism, still present in the early nineteenth century, in exchange for a position as nationalized Jewries. Nevertheless, they have continued to lead a trans-territorial, 'somewhat pre-modern diasporic existence'.

The deep structures of European (and of German) history, then, reverberate into our time and determine the shape of European unification. Here Diner suggests a promise, as well as a danger, in which European Jewry finds itself today: while their transnational and trans-territorial heritage should make them exemplary European citizens, the new religion-based exclusions, the racialized campaigns against Islam and the insistence on a Christian Europe may harbour great dangers for the other non-Christian minority, and it is not clear today to what extent the European nation-states will recede in favour of an integrated Europe.

While Diner takes the question of Turkish membership into the past in order to understand the present, Sander Gilman takes us from the past one step closer to the present time. He argues that there are indeed parallels between seventeenth-, eighteenth- and nineteenth-century Judaism (and one may add, Christianity) and twentieth-century Islam. Here, too, past patterns and historical experiences are being replayed in a contemporary context. Just as in earlier times, when Germans and other Europeans had called on the Jews to either abandon their religion or reshape it as a modern Judaism in a secular state, we are seeing today European calls upon Muslims to abandon their faith, or at least demands for a modern Islam in a 'secular' Europe. To Islam, not accustomed to being a diasporic religion, that challenge is even greater, and much of the friction on account of Islamic fundamentalism has its roots in this diasporic experience. It is rarely recognized, however, and as Gilman also points out, that this 'secular' state, then and now, is a form of secularized Christianity. Those who propagate a multicultural state must ask themselves whether even a multicultural society might not function as a form of exclusion. With Bourdieu and Waquant we see, moreover, that multiculturalism more often than not serves as a screen that hides class relations.

Nevertheless, it is the multicultural discourse that permits minorities to relate to one another and to use each others' integration as a model for their own integration in the context of the new environment. This is also the basic argument of the chapter by Bodemann and Yurdakul. We have attempted to pursue this train of thought in our more detailed analysis of the ways in which German Turks have begun to incorporate into German society and to evolve from an immigrant group into an ethnic minority. We argue that Turks use Jewish narratives of Jewish religious practice, communal organization and of the Holocaust in order to make claims against the German state. The German-Turkish presence in Germany and its practice of claims-making, moreover, has brought about an entirely new constellation. Germany today is no longer confronted with the Jewish community as the only significant ethno-national group. Today, Germans must face the Turkish community as well. This, in turn, has resulted in a triadic relation, and it suggests possible coalitions between the historically and the numerically most significant minorities in Germany.

Indeed, whether they like it or not – and ambivalences naturally prevail between both groups – Jews and Turks are forced into alliances both in their claims against the German state and in their struggle against neo-Nazism and racism/anti-Semitism in German society. Here, both Gilman's and our own contribution point to the insightful thought of the German-Turkish author Safer Senoçak. In his work, the study of Jewry is based on the notion of reconstructing a 'lost tradition' – which raises the questions of whether, in the long run, this might not also apply to the German-Turkish case and of the possibility of a reconstructed history of (Ottoman-) Turkish and European relations.

Part II of this volume looks specifically at the place of Jewish culture and memory. Here, we address the question of how the revival of Jewish culture and of the Jewish Diaspora in Germany and elsewhere in Europe has become possible – in light of past history and the small number of Jews living there. I would argue that this revival – whatever one may think of it – is unthinkable without what I would describe as a Judaizing milieu: a broad periphery of non-Jews interested in or fascinated by Jewish traditions and religion. Only where sizeable markets and audiences are available for Jewish culture and those who perform it is such a revival possible: with non-Jews acting as a stand-in for an absent Jewish audience. Jewish audiences alone could never have produced a sustainable 'Jewish' milieu, in light of their small numbers.

In Part III, Liliane Weissberg takes us back, first to the history of Jewish studies in Germany, notably the famed *Hochschule für die Wissenschaft des Judentums*, a tradition which was destroyed by Nazism. After the war, and after a long silence on Jewish culture at large, Weissberg notes with considerable ambivalence how Jewish studies have begun to flourish at German universities – because much of these Jewish studies are being pursued by non-Jewish Germans. In contrast to Jewish studies in North America, Jewish studies at German universities are completely separated from the Jewish community itself, and therefore lack the authenticity and vitality that comes from an exchange between the academy and everyday Jewish life. Some non-Jewish Germans, moreover, are seeking these studies as a route to conversion. Jewish studies in Germany, argues Weissberg, are studies on virtual subjects by virtual Jews, contemplations of ruins of what has been lost.

It is exactly this 'contemplation of ruins', of what has been lost, that is the theme of W. G. Sebald's work, and Leslie Morris guides us in fine detail through his writings which incidentally have received far more attention outside rather than within Germany. She points out that Sebald was awarded a literature prize from a Jewish foundation, thereby associating his work to Jewish writing, and the question is, 'how Jewish is it?' Morris, for good reason, does not supply us with a clear-cut answer. Sebald and his work, I would argue, present a form of liminality that is common with the Judaizing milieu that I have addressed earlier. Morris sees Sebald inhabiting space between Jewishness, being British, being German, and his writings are permeated by themes and tropes of shifting, blurring and travel; his narrators assume images of pre-Shoah European Jews: as flâneurs, wanderers, cosmopolitans. He is a perfect example, in my view, of what Pinto has described as the new 'European Jewish space'.

No book on contemporary German Jewry could avoid addressing the Russian-speaking migration to Germany and this brings us to the final section of this volume. Interestingly, Russian/Soviet-Jewish migration has prefigured and mirrors the expansion of the European Union into the East. It began in the late 1970s and came into full swing in 1989–90. Without that influx, the community of German Jewry which has by now been more than quadrupled would have been nearly obliterated. The extraordinary transnational character of that migration, the central focus of Judith Kessler's contribution, has linked German Jewry, previously quite marginal, more closely to Jewish communities elsewhere: from Eastern Europe, Ukraine and Russia to Israel and North America.

What is apparent from all three essays of this final section is that there is great uncertainty and disagreement about the actual numbers of Jews in Germany. All we know is that the number of individuals registered with the *Gemeinden* has increased from under 30 000 to somewhere around 100 000 – with an additional 100 000–200 000 'Jewish' immigrants who are not Jewish according to *halacha*, and who declined to become members of the community either due to lack of interest or conviction or because they are the non-Jewish dependants of Jews. The chapters by Julius Schoeps and Olaf Glöckner, and Judith Kessler and Michal Bodemann seek to address aspects of this phenomenon: it is at the very least questionable whether this new development by itself could bring about a long-term reflorescence of German-Jewish culture. On the other hand, it will clearly produce a drastically revised *Ortsbestimmung* for German Jewry, away from the one that took shape in the agonies of the post-war period.

The most important issue emerging from this large-scale migration, however, is its demographic anomaly. Due to the skewed age structure, and despite the substantial size of this influx, Germany today constitutes a big Russian-Jewish nursing home. Most immigrants are elderly, 35 per cent of the population is over 60 years of age and 70 per cent is unemployed. From there, one must conclude that, barring unforeseen developments, the size of community membership within the next thirty years will shrink back to little over 50 000 or 60 000 members. The ways in which the community at large, including the non-members, will constitute itself in the long run – as a Jewish, as a Russian-Jewish or plain Russian ethnos – remains an open question as well. All three essays in Part IV give us some ideas as to where this development may lead, as well as addressing the ongoing role of Holocaust memory, the relationship to the Ukrainian or Russian or Baltic 'home', to Israel and to Germany itself.

This volume traces its origins to a conference held in Toronto in late February 2005. We are grateful to the Friedrich Ebert Stiftung and Dieter Dettke, its erstwhile Director, the DAAD New York, the Goethe Institute Toronto and Edith Klein at the Joint Initiative in German and European Studies (JIGES), University of Toronto, who have all provided marvellous support without which this volume would not have been possible. With Jeffrey Peck and Derek Penslar I have discussed the issues presented here over many years. We wish to thank Elina Yagudayev for her extensive research assistance. Particular thanks go to Nadine Blumer for her painstaking, excellent editorial assistance throughout this process.

Notes

1. See Alvin H. Rosenfeld (2006), *'Progressive' Jewish Thought and the New Anti-Semitism*, New York: American Jewish Committee; Patricia Cohen (2007), 'Essay Linking Liberal Jews and Anti-Semitism Sparks a Furor', *The New York Times*, 31 January; David Harris (2007), 'AJC Statement on Professor Rosenfeld Essay', *AJC News*, 1 February.
2. John J. Mearsheimer and Stephen M. Walt (2006), 'The Israel Lobby and US Foreign Policy', *Middle East Policy*, 13, 3, pp. 29–87; Tony Judt (2003), 'Israel: the Alternative', *New York Review of Books*, 23 October.
3. Daniel Boyarin and Jonathan Boyarin (1993), 'Generation: the Ground of Jewish Identity', *Critical Inquiry*, 19, 4, pp. 693–725. In a broader framework, Barbara Kirschenblatt-Gimblett (1994) has helped bring about a new positive evaluation of Diaspora, away from notions of displacement and dispersal. 'Spaces of Dispersal', *Cultural Anthropology*, 9, 3, pp. 339–44.
4. Ivan G. Marcus (2002), 'A Jewish-Christian Symbiosis: the Culture of Early Ashkenaz', in David Biale (ed.), *Cultures of the Jews: a New History*, New York: Random House, pp. 448–516; Frank Stern (2003), *Dann bin ich um den Schlaf gebracht. Ein Jahrtausend jüdisch-deutscher Kulturgeschichte*, Berlin: Aufbau

Verlag. See also my review of this, together with Amos Elon's *The Pity of it All*, in *Süddeutsche Zeitung*, 27 May 2003.

5. Many, like Rosenfeld or Markovits, forget that there are various expressions of anti-Semitism in the US and Canada as well and that surveys on anti-Semitic attitudes in North America do not produce radically different results from those found in Europe. For the US, Rosenfeld positions alleged anti-Jewish and anti-Zionist attitudes on the 'radical' intellectual fringe and mentions broader anti-Semitic sentiments there in passing; in Europe, however, they merit detailed attention. See Andrei S. Markovits (2007), *Uncouth Nation: Why Europe Dislikes America*, Princeton: Princeton University Press.
6. Survey data regarding this can be found in Gabriel Sheffer (2005), 'Is the Jewish Diaspora Unique? Reflections on the Diaspora's Current Situation', *Israel Studies*, 10, 1, pp. 1–35.
7. In their otherwise fine recent book celebrating Jewish diasporic life, Caryn Aviv and David Schneer ignore European Jewry outside Moscow completely, and in a chapter on Jewish museums and Holocaust memorials – a largely US- and Israel-centred analysis – the major sites in Berlin and elsewhere in Western and Central Europe are not discussed at all. One reason why the book features a chapter on Moscow, apart from Schneer's knowledge of Russia, may be that Moscow was a European terrain not touched by the Shoah. Caryn Aviv and David Schneer (2005), *New Jews: the End of the Jewish Diaspora*, New York: New York University Press. See also the informative article in *The Economist*, 'Second Thoughts About the Promised Land', 13 January 2007. Discussions on this subject have proliferated since the publication of this article. See, for example, 'Emanizpation der Diaspora' ('Emancipation of the Diaspora') in *Die Tageszeitung*, 6 March 2007. Some of the ideas presented here on the German Diaspora resonate with Jeffrey M. Peck (2006), *Being Jewish in the New Germany*, New Brunswick, NJ: Rutgers University Press, a comprehensive look at contemporary German Jewry.
8. This can also be seen in many North American histories of the Shoah. Many of these accounts accuse Germans and other Europeans and especially the churches (correctly) of remaining silent in face of the genocide; they fail to deal, however, with the unwillingness of the rest of the world, notably the US, to take any action, even though the knowledge of the mass murders was widespread.

Part I

A European Jewish Space?

1
Can One Reconcile the Jewish World and Europe?

*Diana Pinto**

'Entry into Europe no longer interests me. I have no desire to be part of an entity which hates Israel and is anti-Semitic.' This is how one of the most important Jewish personalities of the Czech Republic answered my greetings. It was the end of April 2004 and I had turned to him to congratulate him on his country's then imminent entrance into the European Union. This highly cultivated man, committed to the strengthening of Czech democratic life, had nothing in common with the Eurosceptics close to President Vaclav Klaus. He belonged to the world of Vaclav Havel and had awaited the Brussels 'consecration' with great impatience. His instant negative reply, devoid of any nuance or appeal, thus rang all the more harshly in my ears. It invalidated everything towards which I, as a European Jew (but also he), had worked for: the creation of a positive Jewish presence inside a Europe that was finally reconciled with all of its pasts. Above all, his answer stood as a troubling warning to all of Europe, announcing, if not actually sealing, the *return* of an intrinsic incompatibility between 'being Jewish' and 'being European'.

Incompatibility?

One must speak of a 'return'. For this incompatibility was not new. In the poisoned atmosphere of the first half of the twentieth century, it was *de rigueur*. Those who evoked 'Europe' and its 'new order' after the First World War were most often anchored either in the new corporatist and nostalgic circles seeking the return of a militantly organic Christian order or in the growing swamps of a racial anti-Semitism. These pre-war advocates of a 'pure Europe' perceived 'the Jew' – whether capitalist or communist, and in both cases cosmopolitan – as the greatest enemy. Only 'after', in a cultivated cosmopolitan and nostalgic imagination, so well incarnated by Stefan Zweig's legacy, were the Jews presented as great 'Europeans'. The only ones, along with the highest nobility, whose lives made a mockery of existing borders. But this European Jewish identity, the glorious fruit of a *Mitteleuropa* and a Russian empire, both of which were orphans of Western political democracy, had nothing in common with the idea of 'Europe' which had brought the continent to its catastrophe, by conceiving it as a civilized rampart against both the Bolsheviks and the Americans. One need only read the memoirs of Amos Oz to see that the 'Europe' so constantly evoked by his parents was a Europe of polyglot *Luftmenschen*, not of citizens.[1] This Europe was destroyed by the Holocaust and was therefore absent from the post-war ideal of a twelve-starred Europe, born in the Western sphere of the continent, in those countries where the Jews had been fully-fledged citizens and proud patriots.

The Czech Jew's refusal of the new enlarged European Union of 2004 was anchored in this troubled past once again brought to life by two contrasting sentiments: those of loss and of return. The loss (or rather the non-renewal) of those truly borderless humanistic values that had incarnated Europe's glory, values now seemingly replaced by the truncated borderlessness of nationally based contingents in Brussels' Europe. The return, tinged with black, of a Europe with anti-Semitic and pacifist accents and with indifference, if not towards its own Jews, then towards Israel and a Jewish world now perceived as 'foreign'.

This double verdict seemed to confirm inside the European Union what had already become standard fare after the Holocaust in the two new poles of the Jewish world: America and Israel. These poles defined themselves as the successors of what was perceived (wrongly) as a monolith: a destroyed European Jewry. Since 2000, a new existential anguish, the fruit of the second Intifada, of a world anti-Semitism which, after Durban, no longer hid behind the mask of anti-Zionism, and of a new Western fragility after 11 September 2001, has only confirmed, beyond any doubt, this very black American-Jewish and Israeli reading of Europe.

I am not sure that the vast majority of non-Jewish Europeans have fully understood the depth and gravity of these new anti-European judgements. Spontaneously seeking to condemn the appearance or the return of an old/new anti-Semitism or strongly encouraged (when not obliged) by the Jewish world to do so, the intellectual and political elites of this new 25-member Europe have diligently applied themselves, in many a conference and forum, to a core challenge: how to isolate and destroy the anti-Semitic 'beast'. But in their mind such a beast resembles a tree: its ancient roots burrowed in the subsoil of each nation's past, but with leaves and fruits that are the product of an exogenous grafting stemming from a new Muslim immigration. No one in Europe is prepared to accept that such an anti-Semitic beast could actually thrive at the very heart of the post-war European project. And until recently, one could confidently assume that Europe's own Jews shared such a reading. But is this still the case today? Or was the Czech Jew's judgement premonitory?

In the European reasoning post-war European construction incarnated in its hopes the most beautiful example of a 'never again' transformed into a moral imperative. This vision of a Europe 'after', sketched out even before the end of the Second World War, consolidated in the face of the post-war rubble and of the concentration camps, lay at the origins of the Council of Europe with its triple core values: human rights, the rule of law and democracy. Such a vision subsequently moved to the practical realm when the ancestor of the EU, the European Economic Community, prodded the reconciliation between nations through economic interpenetration and cooperation and through the abolition of borders. This post-war Europe was not and could neither be considered anti-Semitic nor anti-Israel. The corridors of the Council of Europe still harbour today photos of David Ben Gurion, Israel's first prime minister, sitting comfortably, more than once, in the front row among many heads of government of the Council's member states: a slightly geographically eccentric and even personally eccentric (because without a tie) cousin in a family reunion in Strasbourg. Nor could one accuse the new Europe being built in Brussels of being anti-Semitic or anti-Israeli, neither in its symbols (the 1979 election of Simone Veil, an Auschwitz survivor, as the first president of a directly elected European Parliament) nor in its concrete accords (the bevy of particularly privileged economic, commercial, cultural and scientific links that still tie the Jewish state to the European Union).

Indeed, during the entire post-war period, the Jews of Western Europe who were not communist felt entirely at ease with this European project, even with the European ideal, perceived as the logical end point of their commitments as citizens of their respective states. This ideal was full of promise and in no way seemed to threaten the symbolic ties that bound them to the State of Israel. The fall of the Berlin Wall from this point of view allowed the Jews from the 'other Europe' to integrate into this enlarged European space, because they too belonged to that 'kidnapped West' evoked by Milan Kundera in the 1980s. Often the sons and daughters of post-war communist dignitaries, this new generation fully participated in the movements of national renewal in the ranks of *Solidarnosc*, within Charter 77, in the alternative circles of Hungary, as in the construction of a fragile civil society in the Balkans.

An anguished Jewish world

It goes without saying that since 2000, the Jews of Europe, like the rest of the Jews of the world, have felt destabilized and rendered fragile, but with a difference. Even the Jews of France who with particular alarm denounced the French authorities for the slowness of their reactions in the face of the resurgence of anti-Semitic attacks, did so from within in order to convince them to change their policies, and not from without as actors preparing to leave the country. What was true with respect to each country was even truer with respect to Europe. The Jewish voices expressing their acute malaise chastised the media for being biased against Israel and slow in treating the topic of anti-Semitism. They rose up against those civil society activists who prodded the boycott of Israel and who had representatives even within the European Parliament and inside the NGOs working on behalf of human rights, while condemning the ongoing financing of the Palestinians at the hands of a European bureaucracy still following a policy formulated in the Oslo-driven 1990s. But throughout the years that followed the second Intifada of 2000, even the most pessimistic Jews did not rise up against the European ideal and the idea of European deepening and enlargement. The European 'never again' still appeared to be compatible with their hopes and values.

This no longer appears to be the case today. 'The Jews', through the ongoing debates over Europe's anti-Semitism, have become, without any necessary malevolence on the part of their fellow citizens, a distinct and homogeneous group. A group which increasingly feels 'apart' even though it remains a fully-fledged actor in all societies. The result of this psychic transformation has been the rapprochement of the official European Jewish institutions with their American counterparts as well as with the official government line of Israel, through the sharing of a common sense of anguish and an exacerbated sense of identity.[2]

For the first time, Europe's Jews are beginning to have doubts concerning the true novelty of the post-war setting. The European 'never again' has been replaced by a Jewish 'never again to us'. Europe is no longer perceived as a 'plus' with respect to the sum of its member states, but as a 'minus' which must be monitored, controlled and even, if necessary, maintained because it is dominated by the logic of the smallest common denominator. This negative vision is not false when it is applied to concrete dossiers in the realm of political and economic policy. But it seems totally unjust when it comes to the founding principles of a Europe subsumed under the European Court of Human Rights. For these values are not negotiable. But for an anguished Jewish world, everything in

Europe appears to be unstable and changeable ... everything except its indifference to the Jews, the result of Europe's eternal anti-Semitic 'essence'.

On this count, we are experiencing a major conceptual rupture. In many Jewish circles across the continent one no longer speaks about 'anti-Semitism in Europe' but, influenced by American Jewry, about an 'anti-Semitic Europe'. In a terrible semantic shift, what belongs to a conjuncture has now been transformed into an essence. Honed in the context of the Iraq war, the American Jewish reading of Europe increasingly equates the continent with the 1938 Munich appeasement, with eternal anti-Semitism and with an equally proverbial indifference.[3] In so doing, the American interpretation comes together with the Israeli vision of Europe as a continent eager to dispense teachings about the Middle East without, however, ever having confronted the horror of its own past. It was such an interpretation which led an Israeli editorialist to comment on the birth of the euro, as the birth of a 'debased coin', not in economic but in moral terms.[4]

The disenchantment of the Czech Jew who contemplated the European flag, not unlike the child proclaiming the emperor to be without clothes, was grounded on such a double reading. It is now Brussels' Europe which appears to be naked in terms of its political institutions, its research centres, and its technocratic corridors. This Europe is not under accusation in Jewish eyes for its own intrinsic weaknesses, but as the living symbol of a far more ancient Europe with its attendant cultural and political stigmata. Alas, in front of such a historical compression of identities, yet another round of conferences on anti-Semitism will solve nothing. Nor will the proliferation of working groups run by self-conscious European officials on the defensive. On the contrary, each encounter aggravates misunderstandings by adding its share of 'bad vibrations' to a climate of suspicion, especially when international Jewish organizations invite themselves in the role of tutors for all the endangered 'little' Jews lost in a Europe gone astray.

The open breach

The breach thus opened between Europe and the Jewish world is extremely dangerous for reasons that are rarely invoked explicitly. Such a chasm renders fragile both actors, who by interacting as opposing parties, only strengthen their worst penchants. The struggle *around* the whole question of anti-Semitism in Europe (as opposed to the necessary struggle against anti-Semitism) is destroying the legitimacy of a continent which has proclaimed itself a haven of peace, historical reconciliation and unity, and which instead appears, in Jewish eyes, to be selective in its hypocrisy. But this struggle is also aggravating the autism of a Jewish world now convinced of having been abandoned (with America as the sole rampart) in the face of a structurally hostile world of which Europe is the harbinger.

Europe today appears in Jewish eyes as a monster with multiple archaeological layers. A murderous anti-Semitic past. A technocratic, politically indecisive present, except when it comes to manifesting its coldness towards Israel and towards Jewish emotions. A future half-way between appeasement and indifference. Appeasement towards the new European Muslim populations whose voices in the different body politics never cease to grow, thus inevitably influencing governmental choices already conditioned by the neighbouring Arab world. Indifference towards omnipresent Jews both as a collective entity in international terms and as an 'over-represented' group among the elites of a barely pluralist continent.

For the Europeans instead, the Jewish world or the 'Jews' give the impression of having being seized by an irrational rage and by a historical blindness, both pushing them to make inadmissible comparisons with the 1930s. These fears are aggravated by an almost paranoiac egocentrism which has made the Jews lose all sense of justice towards others and all respect for international norms, the best proof of this blinding being the Jewish abandonment of the universal connotations of the 'never again'. In France this tension is particularly exacerbated because it stems from the double heritage of a single man: René Cassin. One can only wonder whether the author of the Universal Declaration of the Rights of Man who was also the President of the *Alliance Israélite Universelle* could still feel at ease in both worlds today, for they no longer seem to understand each other.

This dialogue of the deaf is worrisome because its consequences go well beyond the purely 'European and Jewish' sphere. These tensions are conditioning the transatlantic dialogue and poisoning the Western world as a whole. The disdain for Europe that is so widespread in American neo-conservative circles, as well as within Israeli power circles, is anchored in a vision of Europe as faithful to its eternal self, a Europe that is a veritable cabinet of horrors. As for the coldness the European world displays vis-à-vis Israel, it is not uniquely the fruit of an inherent anti-Semitism. It is linked to a growing malaise vis-à-vis a country that, in the name of the exceptional suffering of the Jewish people, and in the name of an increasingly self-defensive, and also anachronistic ethnic-religious national identity, has often proclaimed itself above all international legal parameters, not unlike a lone wolf. This double identity of Israel, recognized as legitimate in the immediate wake of the Holocaust, is perceived as being no longer in tune with the pluralist democratic principles of today's Europe. All the more so, in that these principles have been reinforced in the wake of 1989, both East and West, by the new demands made by Europe's minorities, particularly the continent's own Jews, in their desire to live fully with their multiple identities. Without evoking the slightest equivalence (Israel hardly living in the middle of the European oasis) many Europeans note the growing discrepancy between the rights Jews possess across Europe and the rights non-Jews possess in Israel. This discrepancy has contributed in an important manner to the slow erosion of the capital of sympathy which Europe and the Europeans had with respect to the Jewish state.

Breaking the silence

What can one do to fill this breach that is becoming wider by the day? It seems to me that we must all have the courage to break the insidious silence that is settling in and to lift the taboos that surround the whole issue of 'Jews and Europe'. The time has come to push for reconciliation, in the formal sense of the term. A reconciliation that would require that on both sides there be a new willingness to address, not the usual set of political, diplomatic and economic dossiers, all bogged down in a swamp called the 'Middle East', but a new set of topics centred on intellectual, cultural, identity and even psychological issues. This implies that Europeans display the same capital of sympathy with respect to the Israeli past which they fully exhibited in the 1990s, and still continue to exhibit, with respect to the long Jewish past both before and during the Holocaust. To do so, Europeans must fully integrate the weight of the Shoah in the birth of the State of Israel, a coupling that was long refused by Israel's own founding fathers and by Zionist 'orthodoxy'.

It goes without saying that such a reconciliation between the Jewish world and Europe will not be simple to carry out. For it will be very different from the previous reconciliations (German–Czech, German–Russian, and now Polish–Ukrainian) which have been inaugurated in the wake of 1989 along the lines of the original post-war Franco–German reconciliation. For such a European–Jewish reconciliation to occur, one will have to overcome an impressive set of historical and psychological obstacles. The dialogue between the Jewish world and Europe will only improve when American Jews and Israelis (but also the North African

Jewish immigrants to France, and those of the former Soviet Union to Germany) become fully aware of the massive amount of will and work that went into the continent's reconciliation with itself. It is important that they realize the degree to which the European ideal of reconciliation is neither an ideal of the 'weak' nor a pacifist symbol of idle luxury. It took a lot of effort to transcend the wounds of history and its cortege of hereditary conflicts, to overcome the geography of sealed borders deemed protective, and to trust the institutions of another state, particularly the police and the judiciary in an ever growing European cooperation. Nor was it easy after 1989 to engage in a set of more symbolic reconciliations between countries and within each of them, thus attacking the deepest layers of national emotions in the name of relativized suffering. To consider all of this work as the amusement of Venus at a time when what is needed is the clear-cut power of Mars is a great and myopic injustice.[5]

It will not be easy to convey such a reconciliation lesson to the Jewish world. For a simple reason: the 'mother' of all reconciliations, the Franco–German one, arrived too late: after the Holocaust when there were no more German Jews to welcome it on the other side of the Rhine. One can only dream about what such a reconciliation would have prevented if it had taken place after 1919 rather than after 1945, when it would also have reconciled the German Jews proudly wearing the pointed helmet with the French Jews proudly wearing the red pants of their respective armies. One obviously cannot rewrite the history of the past but one must still go on writing history's new chapters. Reconciling the Jewish world with Europe can constitute today the first step in the eventual integration of Israelis (and therefore by extension all Jews) in a historical narrative which cannot remain forever shattered by the Holocaust.

It will take time, a lot of time, for this to happen, at least several generations before the Jewish anguish related to this abyss finally begins to heal. But such a future healing cannot even begin if Jewish pessimists are convinced that the Holocaust has already slipped, is slipping or will slip out of the radar screens of an indifferent Europe. Contrary to their belief, the Holocaust is not about to be forgotten in a European civilization whose very essence is historical, for this is the continent of the Muse Clio. Like the French Revolution, the Holocaust is also destined to become a reference point endowed with its own independent life separate from its original actors and victims. The French Revolution, at its onset, had announced a new planetary hope. The Holocaust, instead, announced an equally planetary doubt and despair. And on this count, it is destined to remain (Israel's vicissitudes being part of its own trajectory) the subject and the object, the reference and the silence, the motor and the backdrop, the measure and the counter-measure of our collective political struggles and our universal ideals ... but also of our cultural anguish and spiritual fears.

For any reconciliation to take place, Europe's non-Jews cannot think exclusively of the Holocaust as a universal paradigm while the Jews experience it, again, as the pain of amputation combined with the fear for Israel's survival. Europeans must understand the deeply ingrained historical reasons which underlie these Jewish misgivings towards a continent where a third of their own was exterminated just sixty years ago (a mere batting of an eyelid in terms of *la longue durée*) and to take a first step towards a Jewish world that has become ever more aggressive because it is, despite the outward appearance of force, totally destabilized. In order to do so, Europeans must overcome a partially understandable 'Jewish fatigue' linked to the almost excessive centrality of Jewish references in the 1990s and the over-mediatized tensions concerning the 'new anti-Semitism' of recent years.

We now have to live with the consequences of a tragically coincidental calendar. The barely covered wounds of the Holocaust only came to the fore fifteen years ago when the 'other Europe' where the Holocaust was implemented was brought back into the European circle with the demise of communism. These wounds were still very much exposed when a brand new twenty-first century inflicted a whole new set of wounds on the Jewish body politic. The Jewish world could only fuse the wounds of the past and those of the present into a highly anguished psychic over-determination, based on this simultaneity. It did so precisely at the same time when non-Jews had the (justified) impression of having accomplished their 'duty to memory', thus meriting a catharsis of sorts. In acting on this justified impression, by turning to other victims and priorities, Europeans aroused in the Jewish world an equally justified feeling that Europe, now basking in a newly found indifference based on self-righteousness, once again seemed to be turning its back on Jewish anguish and tensions – emotions which did not simply belong to the dark past alone but to a burning present.

It is this discordance of time and sentiments which must be confronted head on by both sides. To do so, Europeans who are not Jewish must transform their own concept of reconciliation so as not to fall into the trap of believing that no such effort is necessary on behalf of the Jewish world for a series of convenient alibis based on the following 'because': because Europe never declared war on the Jews, the Jewish state did not exist during the Second World War, and because Hitler's war against the Jews had no territorial basis and was not even recognized by the Allies, there can be no reconciliation between Europeans and Jews along the classical lines of those between former enemies. This is all the more so because the Jews of each European country are fully-fledged citizens, and reconciling them with their own country would not make much sense. This logic is further reinforced by two technicalities: the fact that Israel is not within Europe and that its society is ever less influenced by its European origins.

Problematics of reconciliation

A European–Jewish reconciliation can take place only if one touches on other problems and issues. And once established, such a new type of reconciliation could very well also inaugurate a new cycle of other non-territorial symbolic reconciliations, particularly throughout Europe's ancient colonial world. But this implies changing references. Throughout the 1990s and to this day, when Europe thinks of reconciliation with the Jewish world, it thinks of offering its 'good and loyal services' to promote peace between Israelis and Palestinians. But Europe will never be able to play any significant role in the Middle East unless it is first reconciled with the Jewish world.

It would be wrong to assume that only non-Jewish Europeans must rethink their world. American Jews and Israelis must also overcome their own historical blindness. Coming from two countries which defined themselves as historical exceptions with respect to a despised old Europe, they have not known at first hand the European experience of conflicts and hereditary wars with its neighbours. In the American case, there was no need to come closer to weaker neighbours which had been 'domesticated'. In the Israeli case, there was no possibility of making a true peace with Arab neighbours, since all reconciliations presuppose a full society-wide recognition of the other. These historical differences help us understand why Europe's reconciliations, seen from America, appear to be only a passing 'detail' in the history of a continent that was formerly the theatre of the Cold War and now a simple Western periphery. An increasingly irrelevant detail, almost as though Florence and Pisa had celebrated their 'reconciliation' at the end of the Renaissance as an important symbol of a new 'Italian Union' in the making, destined one day to also include Venice, Genoa … and Naples, at the very moment when Europe's balance of power abandoned forever the Italian peninsula to move towards France and Spain.

For the Israelis instead, after the failure of the Oslo peace process, Europe's reconciliations seem also anachronistic but in a tragic manner. Israelis perceive them as irrelevant for two sets of painful reasons: because inapplicable in the Middle East and all too successful on a continent that had chased the Jews from its midst. Seen in this light, Israel is little more than a piece of Europe returned 'home' to its land only to be abandoned to new predators by its old 'European headquarters'. Europe's self-satisfaction and epiphany over its enlargement at the very moment when Israelis are trapped in their worst internal and external existential struggle is experienced by most Israelis as the last blow that Europe has dealt to the Jewish people.[6]

Memory and history

Three other conceptual obstacles mark the different paths taken by the Jewish world and Europe after the Holocaust. The first is the use of Memory as an antithesis to History. The second is the weight of contradictory geographical imperatives. And the third is the difficult reconciling of parallel sufferings and memories. Yosef Yerushalmi in his classic, *Zachor*, underscored that the Jewish people by tradition were the people of Memory and not of History. The calendar of its collective interests practically never coincided with the calendar of the other peoples, makers of history, in whose midst the Jews lived. When the Jews began thinking in historical terms, they had already bitten the forbidden fruit of assimilation, thus losing their collective identity as one people. It seems to me that this conflict between Memory and History is once again relevant in two crucial realms: Holocaust commemoration and the relations of Israel with other nations. In both cases, Memory as a source of emotion has often carried the day over History as a source of healing. On this specific count, the divergence of calendars seems to be increasing, since the Jewish world has still been unable to reconcile its quest for normalcy with its desire to keep its particularist essence.

The same is true for the desire to surmount the constraints of geography. Before the Holocaust, the Jews of Europe dreamt of living with open borders. Not only the small caste of cosmopolitans, but also the Eastern European ultra-orthodox and unassimilated populations, who, often without having ever left the village of their birth, became citizens at first of different empires and, after the First World War, of different nations. Even among the assimilated and patriotic Jewries of Western Europe, family networks often transcended national borders. History's tragic irony ensured that when, after the Second World War, Europeans discovered the importance of relativized and even abolished borders, few Jews cared to take on their role as precursors in this realm. Europe's geography lost its importance for a Jewish world reconstituted elsewhere. That geography was replaced by a far more existential geography on the razor's edge of Israel's threatened fate. But the geography of the Jewish state, at the crossroads of biblical spaces and security spaces, has not yet produced viable borders. That is why the Jews have transformed themselves into an ever more ethnic people seeking to strengthen a Jewish state inside ever more secure borders: the absolute opposite of the European dynamic.

The third obstacle to be surmounted is that centred around the notion of parallel memories and the historical taking into account inside each country of all those 'others' who were not present at the origin of each national epic. For the Europeans, the decade of the 1990s was the decade when the parallel memory of the Jews, essentially built around the commemoration of the Holocaust, reached its apex. This memory, formerly absent from the *memento mori* of each nation, attained its virtual core, replacing what had been a heavy silence. The coming home of the Holocaust to Europe as a whole should have (logically) reinforced the ties that bound together Jews and Europeans. And indeed this was the case for many, especially for the generation of the survivors. But for the majority of the Jewish world who had not actually experienced the Holocaust, the opposite happened. The return of the Holocaust in the 1990s was experienced as little more than a belated and unsatisfactory reparation. For America's Jews, as for those of Israel, the pan-European commemorations merely sealed a dead past rather than inaugurating another chapter for the Jewish world within a renewed Europe. Since 2000, this past-oriented reading has given way to a far more pessimistic interpretation. The public evocation and commemoration of the Holocaust is now perceived as nefarious because it rendered banal the horror and above all because it convinced Europeans that they had paid their debts vis-à-vis the Jewish people. Europe, thus cleared of its own guilty record on the Jewish front, could devote itself to other memories of past suffering. Among these, those of the Germans now defined as victims of their own war and above all those of the Palestinians defining themselves as the victims of the 'ex-victim' now presented as a perpetrator, particularly galled many Jewish activists. The very idea of making the Holocaust 'soluble' inside other parallel memories of suffering implied in their eyes a certain tolerance of those who played a direct or even indirect role in the Jewish tragedies (which now include Israel). And yet, the Jewish world must understand that all reconciliations among peoples go through such a painful recognition of the wounds and sufferings of others, even when they seem far smaller in comparison.

The Holocaust commemorations of the 1980s and 1990s had another unintended consequence. They rightfully showed just how many little 'normal' people, as opposed to monsters, were necessary for the effective unfolding of the Holocaust: active collaborators, willing followers of orders, passive witnesses and simple people who claimed to know nothing. But in so doing, these commemorations effectively turned all European societies into guilty accessories to the Final Solution with the exception of a few Just individuals and most (but not all) Resistants. The result was the unleashing of a constantly growing shadow across the entire continent – the very opposite of the healing process that was originally envisaged. The outcome has been more than problematic. Every European, in the anguished eyes of post-2000 Jews, has been turned automatically into a potential culprit, not only in the past, and in the present, but even more so in the future vis-à-vis what most Jews judge to be the most insidious and unspeakable crime of all: indifference.

Furthermore, for the great majority of Jews who no longer live in Europe, the memory of the Holocaust has become a fossilized and hijacked memory. A frozen memory for American Jews who continue to integrate it in a Europe which no longer exists. A burning memory for the Israelis who have transposed it to the heart of their own national anguish. Used in such a manner, this displaced Holocaust memory is fast becoming at the planetary level an increasingly exclusive and intolerant Jewish memory. The result is highly troubling. Thinking of themselves as eternal victims, the majority of Jews and of their institutional representatives do not feel concerned about any possible Jewish 'duty of memory' towards others. They do not feel obliged to transcend their own pain in order to facilitate the birth of healed and reconciled parallel memories in the name of any larger collectivity, be it national, European or global. One can therefore speak of a perverse effect. Holocaust commemorations have not brought Jews closer to the 'others', and even less to 'Europe'. On the contrary. They have alienated them even further. The vast majority of Jews who no longer live in Europe would find no interest in the equivalent of a Jewish Truth and Reconciliation Commission at a European level, whose content would not be political but cultural and symbolic, and would also have Europe's new immigrants in mind.

One must add yet another paradox to all the preceding ones. During the 1990s, the Jewish world did manage to reconcile itself with almost all of the countries of Europe, but it did so at a political and economic level, particularly with respect to exchanges with the State of Israel. Yet, despite these pragmatic successes, Jews still seem unable to reconcile themselves with 'Europe', most likely because this term does not evoke a continent but a Rorschach ink blot revealing their own millennial anguish. In order to surmount this psychological 'blocage', it will be necessary to rethink two key concepts of European history: the idea of a Judaeo-Christian tradition and that of the Enlightenment. One must assess the Jewish presence, but also counter-presence, as well as absence in this double underpinning of the European ideal. For the adjective 'Judaeo-Christian' has always possessed highly ambiguous connotations, and it has become even murkier now that some Europeans use the term to define the continent with respect to a Muslim threat. Similarly, the concept of 'Enlightenment', with its implication of a Jewish elevation through the loss of its obscurantist particularisms, but also with its promise of luminous universal values, has not been properly re-examined. All reconciliations imply an honest squaring of accounts, but over these highly complex topics a lot of openness will be required, not an easy task in our identity-prone epoch.

The last great obstacle

The last great obstacle that must be overcome for an effective reconciliation is to be found in the political realm and is, as such – given the fact that all sides are inside the same Western family of nations – a taboo topic. At stake is the extremely complex relationship which many Jews have with respect to democracy. Jews believe in democracy but they oscillate between an idealistic faith in its principles and a great wariness towards its practice. This ambiguity is grounded in an ancestral fear of an uncontrolled *vox populi* lashing out against Jewish populations across Europe. All the more so in that the Jewish world remembers, as if it were yesterday, that Hitler came to power democratically before unleashing his terrifying hordes against the Jews. Since 2000, this ambiguity vis-à-vis democracy has been revived. The Jewish world fears the new Muslim minorities across Europe for they are at least ten times more numerous than the Jews on the same continent. This fear is strengthened by American Jews, fervent believers in the beauty of the democratic ideal but also equally fervent believers (just like their American non-Jewish peers) in the extreme fragility of this democratic flower. In their eyes, it can only truly exist in a very specific microclimate (essentially the US and Britain). Israelis on principle do not worry about such intra-democratic distinctions. Zionism has taught them that any Jew in the Diaspora is sooner or later at the mercy of non-Jewish priorities, even in the most democratic of regimes. In the Israeli vision, Jews can only be safe in their own homeland. Since the delicate question of the 'diasporic' nature of American Jewry cannot be addressed directly given the strategic needs of the Jewish state, it is Europe which has become the lone inheritor of this double American and Israeli wariness vis-à-vis democracy as an ideal and as a practice. For the experience of the Holocaust tragically proved beyond a shadow of a doubt the degree to which the *Rechtsstaat*, so worshipped by German and Mitteleuropean Jews, just as *La République*, so loved by its French Jewish elites, disappeared through a simple stroke of the pen.

In the current crisis of confidence of the Jewish world towards Europe, the ancestral past and the Holocaust weigh infinitely more than all the democratic guarantees which a responsible European Union can legitimately claim as a track record. Europeans must thus become aware of a very simple, yet disturbing, fact. For the majority of American Jews and Israelis, Europe remains the equivalent of an alcoholic who has stopped drinking, but who can at any moment relapse into his old habits, in this case ... anti-Semitism. And in this tribunal grounded on psychological criteria, it is up to the accused to furnish the proof of his innocence.

Israel, the Jews and Europe

The 'proofs' since 2000 seem, in the eyes of the most anti-European Jews, very weak indeed. America's neo-conservatives have thus re-baptized the new post-war Europe built around the Franco–German reconciliation as the 'old Europe'. Its refusal to participate in the Iraq war was immediately attributed to Europe's 'obvious' links to its ancestral past. This attitude has revealed an equally worrisome trait of today's America: its remarkable lack of confidence in its own post-war policy-making vis-à-vis a continent it helped rebuild through the Marshall Plan. This historical doubt is tragically ironic. It took hold at the same moment when America's policy-making intellectuals began to draw up grandiose plans, devoid of any historical or cultural grounding, for a 'new democratic Middle East'. A Middle East whose basic ingredients were even more doubtful than those of Europe's pre-war past. Europe's glorious civilization (incidentally, fully appreciated even by the most anti-European of American Jews) was built around the spaces of liberty and of counter-power forged throughout its long history. It was these spaces of liberty that allowed the Jewish Diaspora to live, and even to develop, in Europe for two millennia, and which are totally absent today from the Arab-Muslim world. But for the Jewish world, such a distinction is meaningless, because even though Israel is in a highly hostile neighbourhood, it is 'protected' from it by its status as a state and by the US. Let us hope that this Jewish faith in the Hobbesian regalia of sovereignty does not reveal itself to be as unfounded as the old Jewish faith in the *Rechsstaat*.

In the realm of pure politics, beyond all idealistic good intentions, it is in the interest of the Europeans to commit themselves to a reconciliation with the Jewish world if they really want to play a role in the Middle East. But it is also in the interest of the Israelis if they want to attain one day that 'normality' among nations which was the primary objective of the political Zionism of Israel's founding fathers. The European error up to now has been to believe that they could be heard by 'exporting' their recipe for reconciliation to the Israelis and to the Palestinians. As long as the Jewish world has not reconciled itself with Europe and the Israelis with the continent of their constitutive nightmares, Europe will never be able to play seriously in the arena of power politics. It so happens that the Middle East is the only dossier that lies at the very heart of its bi-millennial past, the only one in which Europe can prove its future vocation as an important international actor.

Conversely, Israelis and America's Jews have also erred by assuming that it was enough to have the support of the most powerful state in the world in order to be protected. Such a reading contains the echoes of an old Eastern European Jewish reflex. Jews always chose (understandably) to be on the side of tolerant empires against nations built along ethnic criteria. In doing so, however, they only aggravated their apartness, thus further feeding national anti-Semitisms. This dialectic is still true today. For the Jewish world, America is, and justifiably so, the tolerant empire. But this leads to a logical consequence: Europe in the post-2000 Western order is now perceived as the equivalent of that Eastern Europe which in the nineteenth century had missed the train of democratic modernity. The best proof of Europe's fall into backwardness is its inability to integrate its immigrants and deal with anti-Semitism. Given this reading, the bad relations between Europe and the Jewish world can only appear as self-evident. They furnish a supplementary (or is it a final?) proof of the decadence of a continent that has lost, as so many declining historical settings before it, 'its' Jews.

Are Europeans aware of the fact that what lies behind the ever-recurring and often tedious debates over 'transatlantic tensions' or the 'Middle Eastern peace process' is a sub-text full of innuendoes over nothing less than the 'final' decline of Europe as a civilization? A decline which is really more rooted in the meta-historical reflections of a Toynbee or a Spengler than in the social science analyses of a Huntington? And that such a decline finds its most powerful 'proof' in the loss of Jewish confidence in Europe? Let there be no mistake. Asking such a question in no way implies giving new life to the crazy spectre of a 'Jewish conspiracy' that would be behind Europe's decline, a Europe 'obliged' to give in to some kind of

Jewish blackmail. On the contrary. A reconciliation between Europe and the Jewish world can only strengthen both. Israel needs Europe in order to return to the normal give and take of history among others. Europe needs Israel and the Jewish world to be faithful to its own idealized image, for it would be difficult for the continent to celebrate its own renewal and the ideals of its civilization if the historical victims of its old religious and racial intolerance continue to shun it.

What is to be done?

Who can actually carry out such a reconciliation, which for the time being has not even begun? Inside Israel's moderate left very well-known voices such as those of Amos Oz, A. B. Yehoshua or David Grossmann are beginning to evoke 'Europe' in less negative terms. But they turn towards the continent in a utilitarian manner as one would turn towards a distant judge who could best help the Israelis divorce from the Palestinians. Europe, in the eyes of such Israelis, can prove useful precisely because of the capital of confidence it enjoys in the Arab world. At a time when the US has become too close to the current government of Israel, the old continent is better equipped to play a more equitable role in fostering the divorce.[7] This more neutral reading of Europe is already a step forward compared to the anti-European stances of the Jewish world. But it is only a small step and not necessarily in the direction of reconciliation. For such a rapprochement can also rest on a far blacker judgement. Israel not being able to carry on two wars at the same time, its imperative priority lies in the finding of peace with the Arab world. Not only because Arabs are its neighbours but because in the long run the ties between 'Semitic' cousins will be far stronger than those with the Christian continent where the Holocaust unfolded, a continent in which Jews will never be able to be at peace.[8] Such a reading, in many ways fascinating but also terrifying in its double cultural and political syllogisms, is far more widespread than one may believe.

Will one be able to count on the Jews of the US in order to make progress on the reconciliation front? Even those who hate the Bush administration and who rose up in indignation against the conditions at Guantanamo, and who found some truth in the reservations of 'old' Europe against the war in Iraq, or who even appreciate a certain type of multilateralism, cannot do away with a visceral anti-European streak when one touches their Jewish 'soul'. How could it be otherwise for a community whose vast majority is the offspring of those Jews of Eastern Europe who fled a continent of misery and of anti-Semitism at the end of the nineteenth century and the very beginning of the twentieth? These American Jews have not only adopted the prevailing American ambiguity towards the 'old world' that is shared by all immigrants of European descent. But in the light of the Holocaust they could only measure the intelligence of their forefathers who chose to emigrate, for without it, they, today's post-war American Jewry – and it is their *hoc credo* – would not have seen the light of day.

In the end, only Europe's own Jews, in their double heritage and identity can reconcile the European and Jewish worlds, along with a 'coalition of the willing' from the other parts of the Jewish world. For having lived in Europe as fully-fledged citizens they are the only Jews that know that this continent with all of its defects and its even more egregious weaknesses has nothing in common, in terms of the reality of lived life, with its pre-war predecessor. To argue the opposite is to insult the memory of the Holocaust victims. If only because of the absence of that racial anti-Semitism which killed the six million Jews, of that religious anti-Semitism which taught scorn towards the Jews, of that anti-Semitism of the elites which shunted most Jews into very specific spaces of society thus rendering them more vulnerable, and of that intellectual anti-Semitism which gave so much importance to the notion of a 'pure' Europe. If only because of the role now accorded to Jews as individuals, but also as communities inside European societies and as a culture increasingly interwoven in general culture. It is important to remember that all of these transformations only reach back to 1989 for the European continent as a whole. But just like the oxygen in the air that one does not notice until one lacks it, Europe's Jews who share the anguish of the wider Jewish world seem to be forgetting these fundamental truths. They must latch onto them once more so that they can at last fully take part in the battles to come between those who adhere to universal values and those who instead prod increasingly narrow and exacerbated particularisms.

But in order to play such an intermediary role, Europe's Jews should still believe in a European ideal as an absolute 'plus' rather than as a relative 'minus'. They should believe in the pedagogical and integrationist capabilities of their democracies officially bound by universal values and the 'duty of memory' as they attempt to integrate their new immigrants. They should continue to believe that Europe's 'never again' is still valid for them and not just for the new victims of a continent undergoing profound mutations. They should believe that their voices count despite their weak numerical weight because, both in their fears as in their hopes, they convey a message that is valid for the entire *res publica*. And, because they are willing to subscribe to the above, they should want to implicate themselves as citizens and as Jews in the future of the continent. They 'should' ... The list is long and the answers not clear in our troubled democracies. All the more reason for Europe to rise to the challenge for it lies at the heart of its promising positive identity. The dice are still not cast. But the warning of the Czech Jew is there to tell us that time is running out. For all of us.

Notes

* Author's translation of a text which was originally written in French and published in *Commentaire*, 107, Paris (Autumn 2004).

1. Amos Oz (2004), *A Tale of Love and Darkness*, London: Harcourt.
2. The cleavage became fully apparent during the seminar on anti-Semitism which the EU Commission organized on 19 February 2004 in Brussels with the participation of the World Jewish Congress (WJC), which took place after many psychodramas between the President of the Congress, Edgard Bronfman, and the President of the Commission, Romano Prodi, who was accused by Bronfman of being anti-Semitic. On the day of the seminar the *Financial Times* published two articles under the evocative title 'Is Darkness Falling On Europe Again?' Prodi's reply was 'No'; Bronfman's was a clear-cut 'Yes'. Bronfman's article was co-signed by Kobi Benatoff, President of the European Jewish Congress, a satellite of the WJC. Kobatoff claimed to speak on behalf of Europe's Jews and was totally aligned against Prodi. *The Financial Times* (19 February 2004).
3. Charles Krauthammer, one of the most important neo-conservative intellectuals, gave a speech on 7 May 2003, days after the Iraq war was proclaimed to be officially 'over', at the annual meeting in Washington of the American Jewish Committee. This speech contained some of the most virulent anti-European statements. Europe in this case was defined as the continent returning to its 'norm' after an artificial post-war parenthesis, the norm being the 'millennial hatred of the Jews'. The audience gave Krauthammer a standing ovation after his speech. For another take on this anti-European sentiment see Leon Wieseltier (2002), 'Against Ethnic Panic', *The New Republic*, 27 May.
4. For the Israeli version of this anti-European critique see Fania Oz-Salzberger (2002), 'Europe Should Step In and Look Israelis In the Eye', *The International Herald Tribune* (29 March), where the author contrasts Germany's treatment of the Jewish past with Brussels'. The most total critique was that given by the editorialist, Ari Shavit, who considered the euro 'debased' because it incarnated a continent which like Medea had devoured its Jewish children, while always refusing to confront the crime. 'Our Good Mother Medea', *Haaretz* (28 December 2001).
5. An obvious allusion to Robert Kagan's (2003) *Paradise and Power: America and Europe in the New World Order*, New York: Atlantic Books.
6. Fania Oz-Salzberger (2003), 'Europe Forgets Israel's Origins', *International Herald Tribune*, 27 June.
7. This is the position of Amos Oz. See his interview in the *Nouvel Observateur*, 4–10 March 2004 and his short essay, *Aidez-nous à divorcer! Israël Palestine, deux états maintenant*, Paris: Gallimard, 2004.

8. A. B. Yehoshua presented this view while speaking at the Third General Assembly of the European Council of Jewish Communities during a plenary session in which I also participated, held on 21 May 2004 in Budapest. It was highly significant that the public of more than one thousand Jewish leaders from all over Europe could understand Yehoshua when he announced that he was not a European and did not want to become one, but that they were surprised when Yehoshua called for Europe's help in order to save Israel.

2

Residues of Empire: the Paradigmatic Meaning of Jewish Trans-territorial Experience for an Integrated European History

Dan Diner

Let me open the historical inquiry on the paradigmatic meaning of the Jewish experience for an integrated European history by taking a somewhat indirect approach to the subject. The indirect approach relates to a more current view on the European project proper. It appears to be widely accepted that the European Union is smoothly continuing its predisposed way of accelerated integration. With common institutions, a unified currency, further enlargement into the realm of East-Central Europe, an anticipated constitution and even a joint foreign as well as a prospective security policy, Europe is becoming – as some would like to see it – a new and emerging superpower. Everything seems to be feasible, except the answering of one quite essential question: where are Europe's borders? Who will ultimately belong to the European Union and who will not? Who will be further admitted and who will not? Will its boundaries be of an institutional, political, cultural or of a geographical nature? Is, or shall Europe be by and large a Christian commonwealth, although evidently and obviously fundamentally secularized?

This latter question is still pending, and today focuses on the admission of Turkey. Can Europe's political, cultural and institutional architecture withstand the inclusion of Turkey, a country at the continent's further periphery and predominantly Muslim by religion? Surprisingly, leading and left-leaning German historians have voiced very strong opinions about the admissibility of Turkey and its possible integration into the European community. These historians, highly prestigious scholars like Hans-Ulrich Wehler and Heinrich-August Winkler, believe that the accession of Turkey to the European Union will jeopardize the very fabric of integration achieved hitherto, that the inclusion of Turkey will endanger the European project, disrupt its composition, and undermine its very texture.

It is necessary to appraise this judgement carefully. We must first ask why these German historians are so upset. What do they have in mind when they scrutinize the project of European integration, that is, of Europe's unification? I suppose that both Wehler and Winkler speak from a peculiar perspective strongly infected, if you like, by their specific *déformation professionelle*. After all, both are obviously focusing on the nineteenth-century process of German unification, its preconditions, its development and its predicaments. Indeed, Wehler and Winkler are outstanding historians of the German nation-state. Could it be – and this is my cautious, my precautious query – that the very processes and patterns of integration which led to the historical unification of Germany, shape their understanding of Europe's unification – as if it were the invisible hand of the political imagination? It is a process inaugurated with the *Zollverein* of 1834, that is, the abolition of tolls and tariffs in the framework of the *Deutsche Bund*, and continued into German Confederation, all the way to the establishment of the German Reich in 1871.

It seems that in relation to EU issues, Wehler and Winkler may indeed have the modes and patterns of a traditional territorial and quite cohesive nation-state in mind: the European Union as an enlarged nation-state, even comparable to a unitary body politic like the USA, even its counterpart. However, I have severe doubts. These doubts evoke the query: does not the very fabric of Europe, its historically moulded variety and diversity, allow us to imagine a political composition, which is constructed more or less according to institutional patterns, reminiscent of a nation-state; a nation-state with a delimited territory and strictly regulated institutions which will allow it to make decisions especially in the domain of potential future emergencies? And yet the unique web of Europe seems to demand a somewhat different scheme of integration, an integration based on softer incorporations and more flexible institutions. I detect institutional patterns, which point rather to the experience of formerly existing, pre-modern empires, and less at the hard modes characteristic of nation-states: nation-states that are cohesive, homogeneous, *une et indivisible*.

Paradoxically, German history in particular – not the history of the German nation in the course of modern history, but its pre-modern precursor, the *Alte Reich*, the imperial framework dismantled by Napoleon in 1806, with its more open, less regulated institutions, negotiable domestic power-broking beyond strict majority vote, and flexible borders – seems institutionally more suitable for the European project than the modes and patterns of the nation-state regardless of how they have been transformed. The admission of Turkey, or more specifically, the long process of its admittance, will make the structural dilemma of Europe's integration obvious: imperial or national, soft or hard, open or sealed? The legacy of the nineteenth century reminds us that it is the Eastern Question which defines the realm of Europe; or, evoking while altering a famous coinage by Carl Schmitt: *Europa ist die orientalische Frage als Gestalt.*

What does all this have in common with the Jews and Jewish experience? Aside from the fact that – as somebody once ironically claimed – everything, or nearly everything, is or can be associated with the Jews, this association is indeed serious. The Jews are a ubiquitous population, that is, ubiquitous in time as well as in space. By their very nature the Jews were a European population, indigenous Europeans *avant la lettre.* What features made their lives so very European, in opposition to the forms and norms of the nation-state? The answer lies close to hand: they were obviously non-territorial, transnational, multilingual, mostly urban, and compared to others unusually mobile. And what makes them and their experience so exceedingly important for a new perspective of Europe's past and Europe's future? The answer is equally obvious: their very life-worlds on the continent were situated beyond, beside, or above that form of body politic which is generally denominated as the nation-state. The Jews as a diasporic population fit quite well into the frameworks of multinational empires and less obviously into homogeneous and therefore compulsory – and however liberal they may have been – assimilatory nation-states. Indeed, they and especially their institutions, their forms of social intercourse, had a strong pre-modern leaning. The Jews were somehow represented remnants of pre-modern *nations*, remaining residues, a duplication of social estate in modernity.

This sounds like a forthright repeal of everything which is generally approved, namely the undisputed assumption – made by Horkheimer and Adorno among others in their 'Dialectics of Enlightenment' – that the Jews were pioneers *of* modernity, while here they are reversely portrayed as distinctive agents of remaining pre-modern patterns *in* modernity. True, as individuals the Jews were evidently pioneers of modernity. The whole history of innovations in the nineteenth and twentieth centuries is dominated by Jews. But what about the Jews as a collective? At the level of collectivity, did pre-modern patterns indeed prevail? The history of Jewish integration into modernity – the history of emancipation, of citizenship, of Jewish institutions, of Jewish representation – can be read or re-read through the angle of pre-modernity.

Why and how does this story relate to the European project, the establishing of European integration and its institutions beyond, above and besides the nation-state? It may sound somehow surprising, but prevailing legacies of pre-modern forms and norms, institutions and identities – imperial identities, so to speak – still lingered at the core of the European idea after 1945. Let us focus on the significant markers of belonging embodied by the leading persons and personalities at the cradle of the new Europe: Konrad Adenauer, the German Chancellor, Robert Schuman, the French Foreign Minister, and Alcide de Gasperi, the Italian Prime Minister. All three of them had some significant and unique features in common. First and foremost it was always highlighted that they were Catholics by faith. It is true that their intimate relations to the Catholic Church were undoubtedly an important source of communality. Yet, they had even more specific features in common. And these features go deep in time as well as in space, representing former life-worlds – imperial residues of sorts. It is obvious and indeed striking, that all three were extreme latecomers to their proper nation-states. Actually, all three originated from their respective countries' peripheries. The Rheinländer Konrad Adenauer, even at the time of the Weimar Republic, stood aloof from the German-Prussian nation-state – despite the fact that political Catholicism had achieved its cultural and institutional goals, enshrined in the Republic's constitution and largely integrated in the national fabric without restrictions. Nevertheless in 1919 Adenauer was infamously suspected of having plotted with the French for a secession of the *Rheinland* from Germany. Robert Schuman, the French Foreign Minister, was born in Luxemburg, brought up and educated in German Alsace, and in the Second World War he had been enlisted as captain in the ranks of the Imperial German Army. De Gasperi originated from an irredentist region, from Trentino. Until 1918 he had been a deputy at the Old Austrian Diet in Vienna, the *Reichsrat*. Each of these three men can be perceived as a remnant of the nineteenth century, residues of imperial pasts. And among themselves they spoke German – an imperial, as well as a cosmopolitan language. Thus, at the cradle of the European idea there lingered the legacy of empire.

As mentioned above, the Jewish experience as a definitive experience of a non-territorial, non-national and diasporic population may be perceived as an intriguing angle of interpretation, of re-interpretation for a so-called integrated, Europeanized European history beyond the nation-state. Thus, it is perceived not as a further effort in the established mode of entangled histories, nor as an enterprise of *histoires croisées*, but as one history, one and undivided – situated by its very definition above and beyond that venture which gave birth to historical narration in the nineteenth century: the adventure of the nation-state. While the notions and concepts of pre-modernity that were being transformed into modernity are obviously crucial, the disclosure of the intriguing affinity of pre-modern and post-modern forms is even more interesting. Indeed, the concept of empire gets an epistemological meaning for historical re-conceptualization – beyond the nation-state and for the historical period of the nation-state: reinterpreting the new through the life-worlds of the old. We are dealing in fact with the still unrevealed potentialities of the history of the Jews for general historical investigation.

Unravelling our subject from the early modern period to the high-days of the nation-state means starting from Jewish institutional autonomy, and this by and large from an Eastern perspective. Indeed, in the beginning was the *va'ad arba aratsot* – the Jewish Council of the Four Lands – the synod of Jewry in the realm of the Polish Kingdom. The Four Lands were the provinces of Greater Poland with Poznan at the centre; Smaller Poland with Cracow; the area of Lvov; and the province of Volhynia. The synod represented the form of a corporate social order of Polish Jewry in the imperial context of the Polish-Lithuanian Commonwealth. The synod embodied a degree of autonomy and self-administration that was unattainable elsewhere for Jews in their diasporic life-worlds. Its origin can be traced back to a royal charter, a privilege obtained in 1551 from King Sigismund (August). This privilege was derived from the poll tax the Jews had to pay collectively. And this collectively demanded requirement and liability gave rise to a whole network of self-administering Jewish institutions, in particular for legal regulation in almost all affairs of the social, the religious, the personal spheres, including the election of rabbis and judges. It was no accident that Simon Dubnow, the Russian-Jewish historian writing in the late nineteenth and the early decades of the twentieth century, and the foremost protagonist of a modern, trans-territorial autonomy of the Jews in the Russian empire and beyond, would come to celebrate the royal charter of 1551 as the 'magna carta' of Jewish independence. This system and its regulations are somehow reminiscent of the Ottoman *millet* system, intertwined with the principle of collective tax liability headed by the respective supreme cleric – in case of the Jews, the *haham bashi.* Taking the structural non-simultaneity of development in the different political cultures in East and West into account, the Ottoman Jews as other recognized ethno-religious groups in the framework of the last Muslim empire continued to function according to corporate modes reformed constitutionally in 1865, comprising their own *majlis umumi*, their own Jewish national council, until it was dissolved, as well as the institutions of other ethno-religious groups, by the Young Turk revolution of 1908.

The Council of the Four Lands in Poland-Lithuania, a network of self-administering institutions which was dissolved in 1764, drew upon the institution of the *kahal*, the communal council, which according to Dubnow was akin to the 'nucleus' of the cultural autonomy of the Jews that he himself later propagated. At a time of increasing integration, unification, rationalization and homogenization, the communal institution of the *kahal*, itself formally abolished in Russia in 1844, led to all manner of speculations about, and hostility towards, Jewish autonomy. The emancipation of the Jews promoted by the French Revolution was absolutely dedicated to that homogenizing equality which detested any difference in the body of the nation – or the residues of a pre-modern order of privileges which preserved such difference. The attitude of the Revolution in its anti-corporate agenda was completely and unambiguously clear in this regard. As individuals, as *citoyens*, the Jews were to be granted everything, but as *natio*, as a vessel of pre-modern, residual emblem of collective belonging, as *corps de nation* embodied in the structure of the Old Regime, they were to be granted nothing whatsoever. Tellingly, Clermont-Tonnerre declared that 'They [the Jews] should not be allowed to form in the state either a political body or an order.'[1] The taking of the civic oath involved the renunciation of all privileges and exceptions. Autonomy had come to an end.

It was not the French Revolution alone – with its concomitant individualization of the person as citizen on the basis of a horizontal geometry of legal equality as the greatest single change in the previous vertical social order – that challenged corporate Jewish autonomy. It was the absolutist state that already intervened in autonomous and corporately regulated spheres and this in order to subjugate them to its ever more centralized regime of integration, welfare, surveillance and control. The Habsburg Emperor Joseph II, for instance, decreed in 1782 that business documents written in Hebrew or Yiddish were not admissible as evidence in the courts. Moreover, he abolished group responsibility for toleration money and subjected the Jews to all the political, civil and juridical processes of the land. The Austrian emperor was resolved even to grant the Jews equal rights, but only when their political separation had been terminated and when no more than religion remained to distinguish them from their compatriots. The self-governing community must go.

This ongoing process of transformation from the previous vertically composed social order to a horizontally moulded formal equality entailed the internalization and privatization of religion as *confession*, as denomination. Previously the sacred had permeated holistically almost all spheres of human activity by means of religious law. And by the ubiquitous application of religious law the presence of the sacred could be sensed nearly everywhere. Now it was successively neutralized by the ongoing universal process of distinction, demarcation and separation of the spheres of social intercourse – split into the spheres of intimacy, of the private, of the public. By this, the realm of the sacred was reduced first and foremost to the domain of ritual and liturgy. This transformation from an all-embracing religion into mere faith can be perceived as a kind of 'secondary conversion'. It was a secondary conversion in that the maintenance of one's own belief altered faith and rendered it compatible with the communicative forms required by modernity. Indeed, Judaism was rendered protestant.

What resulted was the following: by stripping the Jewish communities of their corporate formation and self-administration, a transformation of the emblems of belonging was engendered. While in the West faith could have become internalized and made invisible, in the East ethno-religious markers of belonging became externalized and therefore visible. The result was an increase in differentiation of internal Jewish identities and their continuous rationalization. One of the modes in rationalizing ethnicity was the emergence of a nationally oriented Jewish historiography in the later nineteenth century as proposed by Simon Dubnow on the basis of the concept of the *kahal*. It was not the *kahal* as a valid institution, but the *kahal* as paradigm and the subject of intellectual quest grounded on the concepts of a non-territorial Jewish autonomy. When rendered into historical thought it appears as a fundamental mode in the construction of former Jewish life-worlds. The vanishing political-religious corporate form is literally converted into the narration of a collective consciousness beyond territoriality and ethnic homogeneity. In this way, the *pinkasim*, the protocols of the organs of Jewish self-administration, advanced to become the central source for a modern Jewish historiography centring on the Jews as a collective and as a nation, that is, an ethnicity beyond and above the nation-state.

The ubiquitous process of the further differentiation of the Jews on the basis of distinctive national citizenships and their associated loyalties to the various nation-states they were living in, ran counter to the trans-territorial and transnational strands which infused imperial Jewish diasporic existence. That is amply demonstrated by forms of Jewish diplomacy at the time. In order to comply with the newly re-established mode of international order based on the principle of the balance of power and its regulation in the wake of the Congress of Vienna in 1815, the received traditional means of the pre-modern conduct of intercession by Jewish notables with access to courts and chancelleries, of *shtadlanuth*, if you like, was successively transmuted into a common 'European Concert of Jewry'. Its aim was to obtain legal equality for Jews that would comprise civil rights. At the Congress of Vienna, and in order to safeguard the rights formerly obtained by the Napoleonic reforms, the interpellation of Jews, including those from Frankfurt/Main, Lübeck, Hamburg and Bremen was on the agenda of the Congress and was supported by Hardenberg, the Prussian, and Metternich, the Austrian, the chief negotiators. In 1840 the Damascus Affair, a ritual murder or so-called blood-libel charge, was widely discussed in the newly evolving European public sphere, communicated by the emerging culture of a widely circulating press. It struck in the midst of the already heated discourse on the emancipation of the Jews, the so called *Judenfrage*, the Jewish Question, where figures of prominence became involved, among them Heinrich Heine and Karl Marx. The Damascus Affair instigated something of a common Jewish realm of political awareness and solidarity – encompassing the Jews of the West, the Jews in the East and the Jews in the Orient. In the wake of this seminal event in Jewish consciousness at the temporal watershed from the pre-modern to the modern, the kidnapping and compulsory baptism of a Jewish child in Rome in 1858, the notorious *Mortada* case, brought the *Alliance Israëlite Universelle* in 1860 into being. The Paris-based *Alliance* was an organization, which – apart from its intervention on behalf of persecuted Jews – was involved in the dissemination of French language and culture as heralds of emancipation and humankind. In 1878 Jewish individuals and Jewish organizations, including the *Alliance*, were considerably involved at the Congress of Berlin, a conference summoned by Bismarck aimed at internationally regulating the results of the just concluded eighth Ottoman-Russian war, and this in order to attain equal rights for the Jews of Romania. That was by and large the last international conference of importance orchestrated by the Great Powers. At this point, the common European imperial space of international order, formerly based on the principle of balance of power, fell apart.

The so-called revolution of alliances of the European state system, successively emerging in the 1870s, while increasing its destructive dynamism in the 1880s and culminating finally in the establishment of two opposing blocs based on rivalry and enmity – a tendency of dualistic opposition, which brought about the seminal catastrophe of the First World War – substantially narrowed the scope and latitude for Jewish diplomacy. The structural prerequisites for a shared Jewish political commonality and common diplomatic action were by and large undermined. After the loss of internationalism inherent in the previous system of balance, the Jews were even more obliged to accommodate themselves to the increased demands of different national loyalties. The predicament of British Jewry at the eve of and especially during the First World War is notorious. The year 1907 brought about a resolution of conflict between liberal England and autocratic Russia – a resolution which paved the way for further alliance. This association not only contradicted Britain's own parliamentary tradition, but was also clearly opposed to its fundamental political orientation throughout the entirety of the nineteenth century. Such an unholy alliance required British Jewry to remain silent for *raison d'état*; despite the restrictive policy pursued by the Tsar towards the Jews and in contrast with British Jewry's long-held scepticism towards imperial Russia. This tendency accelerated after the irreversible downfall of continental empires in the wake of the First World War and the formation of myriads of nation-states. All this served to augment expectations of loyalty, further impinging on the manoeuvrability of Jewish diplomatic action and initiatives – a quandary that would impose its dramatic consequences on the Jews especially in East-Central Europe between the two world wars.

The increasing tendency towards the nationalization of empire in the nineteenth century as well as the centrifugal shifts such nationalizations generated, led conversely – and this in an attempt to safeguard the imperial integrity – to conceptual provisions of extra-territoriality in preserving the multinational fabric of empire. In order to neutralize the dismembering effects brought about by the combination of democratic representation on the one hand and the politicization of language and culture on the other, obviously resulting in a break-up of the imperial domain in metastasizing territorial entities, a quasi-corporate concept beyond democratic majority rule was required. Among these corporate institutions beyond and above majority and minority relations was the Austro-Marxist principle of national-personal autonomy put forward by Karl Renner and Otto Bauer for the preservation of the multinational composition of the empire. It was probably more than a mere irony of history that Austrian Social Democracy, by objecting to secession on the basis of nationality, had no other option than to preserve the imperial fabric and, by implication, the monarchy. Social Democracy attempted to combine the principle of majority rule, anchored in arguments of democracy and demography and based on horizontally buttressed equality, with a cultural and linguistic autonomy that bore corporate traits and was indifferent to the respective numerical relations of majority and minority. Such a vision seemed to mesh well with Jewish intentions to reconcile liberalism grounded in formal equality and citizenship, while at the same time recognizing diversity. However, in the specific Austrian case, Social Democracy recognized neither the one and a quarter million Jews as a distinctive nationality, nor Yiddish as a collective Jewish language. With some instructive exaggeration one can arrive at the conclusion that the most convenient anchor for the Jews happened to be the Emperor, the *katechón* of the remnants of pre-modern life-worlds as well as of multinationality, which was enshrined in the monarchy.

The make-up of imperial Social Democracy in the Habsburg monarchy can be deciphered through the later events of February 1934. In these days of turmoil of the First Republic the socialists rose in arms against the authoritarian, the so-called Austro-fascist regime of Dollfuss. The uprising was doomed to failure first and foremost because the socialists of the republic were by and large confined to the residual domain of former empire – to the monarchical metropolis of Vienna, a veritable *lieu de l'empire*.

When in the wake of dismemberment of empire and the looming territorialization of nationalities the Russian-Jewish historian Dubnow – proceeding from the historical memory of the *kahal* – developed his concept of a non-territorial Jewish autonomy, he was in fact poorly informed about the ideas that Karl Renner and Otto Bauer articulated at the century's close. When he became fully aware of this mode, he expressed his surprise and excitement at how close his concept of de-territorialized cultural autonomy came to the notion of national-personal autonomy promulgated by the Austro-Marxists. While Dubnow espoused the liberal approach to cultural autonomy among Russian Jews and beyond, a socialist and social revolutionary variant of this idea was championed by the Jewish Workers League in Poland and Lithuania, that is, by the *Bund*. The reception of the ideas of Bauer and Renner in the ranks of the Bund entangles a revolutionary *Zeitgeist*, which tended to neglect collective group rights in favour of the universally constructed working class, with the pre-modern Jewish tradition of the *kahal*. This generated at the time what could today be viewed as a form of multicultural pluralism.

The principle of nationality accomplished in 1918/19 a dubious victory over that of empire in Central and East-Central Europe. It became increasingly obvious that the new and expanded nation-states established on the ruins of the old empires were no less multiethnic than the empires they had so gladly consigned to the graveyard of history. In order to paper over the evident gap between the newly established nations and their various minorities, the Paris peace conference stipulated a degree of minority protection for those new and enlarged states, while limiting their sovereignty. The protection of minorities entrenched in the peace treaties and enshrined in the constitutions of the different new or enlarged states in Central, East-Central and South-eastern Europe, was attributed primarily to the efforts of Jewish organizations, individuals and institutions at the peace conference – especially the previously established *comité des délégations juives*, headed by and large by persons and personalities of East and East-Central European imperial origin. However, the Jewish diplomatic impact was highly exaggerated in public opinion as well as in historiography. The regulations of minority protection were meant primarily for the safeguard of ethnic Germans. The German Reich had suffered considerable losses in territory and population especially in its eastern lands, and Germans – ethnic Germans as well as former citizens of the Reich – had to accommodate themselves to the unusual condition and state of being a national minority.

However, a significant distinction has to be introduced: an ethnic minority is not just an ethnic minority. One can observe a noteworthy difference between those populations turned into ethnic minorities as a result of the secession of territories, newly established minorities carved out of a formerly majority population by dint of political readjustments, minorities instigated by political circumstances and thus obviously situational by character – and such minorities whose very formation was historical. The latter never experienced any other condition than that of territorial dispersion, that is, living within a surrounding majority and without any proper chance of acquiring territorial permanence. These 'new' minorities were imperial nationalities because they emerged from pre-modern and multinational empires without any ambition to control or exercise sovereignty over national territory – such as Jews, Baltic Germans, Armenians or Greeks in the Russian empire. For the sake of the argument, it includes the estate of the aristocracy as well.

The historian Dubnow, who closely followed the deliberations in Paris, assumed that the notions and concepts of minority protection contained basic outlines of the *kahal*, the pre-modern form of Jewish communal self-administration. After all, the institution of minority protection seemed to have been designed especially for such populations, which formerly lived within an imperial framework and were endangered by politics of ethnic homogenization pursued by newly established and enlarged nation-states. The minorities, historical as well as situational minorities, all in all in between 35 and 40 million people, established in 1925 a joint institution called the Congress of European Nationalities in Geneva in order to safeguard their semi-corporeal rights enshrined in the respective treaties. This forum was led by personalities who had experienced the ethnic multitude of formerly existing empires, especially the Jewish international politician Leo Motzkin and the Baltic Germans Ewald Ammende and Paul Schiemann; it remained active up to the day when Nazi policy on the Jews in Germany brought this cooperation to an end. The minorities were divided and driven apart by revisionist political schemes and anti-Jewish politics. Non-dispersed/compact minorities such as Germans and Magyars, living near redrawn borders in compact settlements, sought their salvation in irredentism, while 'imperial' minorities, mostly scattered or of urban background, could not aspire to an effective attachment between ethnos and territory; this includes Germans from the Baltic or the Banat for instance, and most especially Jews. That was the very condition Hannah Arendt had in mind, when – in her seminal *Origins of Totalitarianism*, the iconic treatise on the cataclysmic twentieth century – she reflects on what she calls the 'Aporia of human rights' pessimistically relating to the historical experience of the 1930s. Stripped of his former citizenship by de-nationalization or simply by dissolution of empire, the stateless person has never been able to attain the protection of statehood. He or she was stranded in an obscured sphere beyond any possible legal sanctuary. This was the condition awaiting millions of people, suddenly emerging as ethnic minorities in newly established or enlarged nation-states after the First World War.

At first, minority protection had become an issue in the wake of the anti-Jewish pogroms in Eastern Poland in 1918, especially the pogroms of Lemberg and Pinsk. Allegedly the Jews were suspected and blamed for sympathizing with the Bolsheviks. Yet even earlier, especially in the wake of the fourth Duma elections in 1912, they had been regarded by the Polish nationalists as a population that viewed the idea of a Polish nation-state with agnostic reserve. Such an injurious stain had been exacerbated by the consequences of the Russian Revolution, although its roots were of a deeper nature. After the quelling of the Polish January uprising of 1863 and the subsequent Tsarist policy of enforced Russification in Congress Poland, ever more Jews emigrated from the Russian areas proper into that realm. The Litvaks, or Litvaki, culturally shaped by the Jewish-Russian Enlightenment and Russian integration politics, were regarded by ethnic Poles as the trustees and compliant heralds of empire; and as such they appeared to have little enthusiasm for the prospects of Polish independence. Furthermore the Litvaks favoured Russian as an imperial, thus cosmopolitan language, facilitating a far greater prospect and scope for education, communication and integration.

The attraction Jews felt for an imperial fabric, its traditions and institutions, aroused suspicion among those who regarded the supranational empires exclusively as hothouses of repression. With the establishment or 'restoration' of Poland after the First World War, the former pre-modern expanse of the Polish-Lithuanian Commonwealth was claimed as the proper territorial frame by a new Polish nation-state. This led to the largely forgotten Polish-Soviet war of 1920, a confrontation at Europe's eastern periphery, at the so-called borderlands, which encompassed national, imperial as well as class ingredients. As the Soviet forces under the command of Tuchatshevski advanced on Warsaw, Jewish soldiers and officers of the Polish army as well as Jewish nurses in the hospitals were suspected of disloyalty. The idea that the Jews would almost certainly support the Russian Bolsheviks was only one of the arguments. The Jewish military personnel were removed and interned in different camps. The most notorious one was the camp of Jablonna, actually established for Soviet POWs.

The advance and acculturation of Jews took place in the nineteenth century largely in imperial languages. That was particularly obvious in the case of collectives based on estate, ethnicity and religion whose security and advancement presupposed the non-national context of empire. By contrast, local vernaculars were held in far less esteem. They hindered social and spatial mobility, functioning more to serve the purposes of communication in familiar local domains, such as the nearby market or the immediate workplace. In any case, they were of little use for education and the universal and cosmopolitan cultures of science and learning.

German, most particularly the German language of the Habsburg monarchy, can by virtue of its dominant position be qualified as an imperial language. Along with its importance as a major cultural and academic language, it was likewise the linguistic medium of administration, justice and the military. Though it neither differed in grammar, syntax nor in any other form from the German spoken and written in the German Reich, it evidently did in its application. When, where, by whom, with whom and under what circumstances was German spoken – at home, in public, for specific functions? In order to understand the dialectics of language and belonging, Felix Pollack should be quoted – the Austrian émigré, poet and translator of German classics into English, and later librarian at the University of Wisconsin in Madison. He distinguished ironically and accurately between Germans and Jews: 'Es ist immer das gleiche,' he concludes, 'die einen sind Deutsch und die anderen können es' – that is, distinguishing between those who are German and others who know German.[2]

The changes which the application and the use of German by Jews underwent in Prague are particularly clear. And this not only in the wake of the literary legacy of Franz Kafka, whose biography, as well as his opus, reflects the experienced transformation, the successive conversion of the employment of the German language by ethnic Germans on the one hand and by German-speaking Jews on the other. Because of the notorious and ongoing struggle between Czechs and Germans in Bohemia and Moravia, the German-speaking Jews – wedged between both ethnicities – continuously withdrew their use of German, an imperial German, from the sphere of the public into the realm of the private, successively accepting Czech as a public tongue. Kafka's close friend, the Jewish poet Oskar Baum, was permanently blinded in a scuffle with Czech school children because of his German schoolbooks. According to Kafka, he lost his eyesight as a German, something he in fact never was and never accepted himself as being. Kafka, who spoke the Czech language fluently, was sent by his father on at least three occasions to negotiate with angry Czech employees in their homes. The father's Czech was simply not good enough to moderate a conflict in an allegedly 'foreign' language. Ernest Gellner, who was not born in Prague but was educated there, recollects an embarrassing, even menacing event as a child in primary school, when he dared to provoke his classmates by singing a Czech folksong in German.

The Jewish experience in Prague, the ambit of an imperial culture that was falling apart, while being transformed into exclusive and antagonizing ethnic affiliations, seems to assume an epistemic meaning for a scholarly decipherment of the phenomenon of nationalism. The Czech lands and after 1918/19 the multi-national, yet strongly Czech-leaning Czechoslovak Republic – Czechoslovak with or without a hyphen – became something like an arsenal of memory as well as of future knowledge for the scholarly research on the phenomena of nationalism and ethnicity on neutral ground. This is true for the above-mentioned Ernest Gellner in the fields of sociology and anthropology, true for Hans Kohn in the discipline of history, and true also for the largely forgotten Karl W. Deutsch and his theory of 'Nationalism and Social Communication' in the domain of the political sciences. All three originate from Prague. Karl Deutsch's uncle, Julius Deutsch, had been the commander of the socialist militia in Vienna, the *Schutzbund*, which, as mentioned above, rose against the regime of Dollfus in February 1934.

In its cosmopolitan as well as 'imperial' significance, German served Jews during the nineteenth century successively as a Jewish language of wider communication and even worship. German was after all the language of emancipation, acculturation and knowledge in Central Europe and beyond. And during the era of the transformation of Judaism from religion into denomination, into faith or *confessio*, German was even converted into a liturgical language for the Jews of Central and East-Central Europe. Indeed, German as a Jewish cultural language had been adopted in certain religious currents of Judaism, such as Reform, as a proper medium of worship.

The affinity between the German language and culture and the Jews of Central and East-Central Europe can be traced deep into the crises-ridden interwar period when imperial residues were still ubiquitous in Central and East-Central Europe. For example, when after its admission to the League of Nations in 1926, Germany embarked on its vigorous policy of minority protection directed against Poland, German and Jewish interests seemed to converge. The use of German as the lingua franca at the Zionist congresses as well as the language of communication at the Comintern, the Communist International, evoked the imaginary of Jewish Philo-Germanism and pro-Bolshevism. It would be interesting to examine the notorious presence of national minorities and of members of minority population groups which did not fit in with recognized ethnic attributions assembled in the Communist parties of Central, East-Central and South-eastern Europe during the interwar period. Of these parties, the Yugoslav CP was probably the most significant.

In the late autumn of 1939 Raphael Lemkin, a young Polish lawyer and former state prosecutor in Warsaw, arrived via neutral Vilnius in Riga, awaiting passage to Stockholm and ultimately to the United States. In the Latvian capital he went straight to meet the famous historian Simon Dubnow at his home in Kaiserwald. Dubnow had – because of his liberal and anti-Bolshevik political stand – left Petrograd in 1922 and moved to republican Berlin in order to proceed with his later highly esteemed ten-volume *World History of the Jewish People*. The Bolsheviks despised him and considered him a 'white' political émigré. In 1933 Dubnow had to flee the Nazis and settled down in Riga. During their evening talk Lemkin mentioned that he intended to exert himself to 'outlaw the destruction of peoples'. Dubnow agreed by replying that 'the most appalling part about this type of killing, is that in the past it has ceased to be a crime when large numbers are involved and when all of them happen to belong to the same nationality, or race, or religion'.[3] Lemkin arrived in April 1941 in the US and became noted for having coined the term 'genocide' and continued to campaign for the acceptance of a United Nations Convention on such crimes. Dubnow fell victim to collective destruction in the Ghetto of Riga the very same year.

In the convulsive interwar period, in the twilight of time and in the political space in between – in between Germany and Russia – the futures of minorities, especially stateless historical minorities, remnants and residues of empire, were exposed to the menace of impair. Already in the late 1920s and the early 1930s, when Raphael Lemkin was legally struggling to institute the still nameless concept of collective destruction, critical inquiry could suspiciously anticipate the looming dangers. The state of danger was poetically expressed in the German press in 1929: 'There is in the League's glass palace a dark room in which the light never enters and no sound emerges. This is the place where the protection of minorities is implemented.'[4] Those legal scholars and activists who tried to be on guard between the two world wars while protecting the remnants of empire by the fragile means of a collapsing minority regime, as well as succeeding individually to escape the hell of Europe for the United States, established the Institute for Jewish Affairs in New York in 1941. The institute was directed by Jacob Robinson, an international lawyer, who, after having been released as a Russian POW from German captivity after the First World War became the chairman of the Jewish faction and leader of the minority bloc in the Lithuanian parliament until its dissolution in 1926. He represented Lithuania on several occasions at the Permanent Court of Justice in The Hague and served as a Jewish representative at the pan-European Nationalities Congress in Geneva. Later, in New York, he was involved in the preparations for the UN Declaration on Human Rights and – with Raphael Lemkin – consulted the American chief prosecutor at Nuremberg, Robert H. Jackson. He and his brother, Nehemia Robinson, laid the ground for pressing legal questions of indemnification, reparation and restitution in the wake of an age of destruction.

The prosopography of the institute's researchers and its academic board reveals a vanished past. It is composed mainly of persons and personalities of lost imperial pasts and of times in between: Max Laserson, for example, was formerly Associate Professor of Constitutional Law and Legal Theory at the University of St Petersburg, and in 1917 Deputy Director of the Department of National Minorities in the Provisional (the Democratic) Government of Russia; Mark Vishniak, Professor for Constitutional Law, Moscow, was Secretary-General of the Russian Constituent Assembly of 1918, to be dispersed – as is well known – by the Bolsheviks. In the advisory council we come across the great legal scholar Hans Kelsen, a former Viennese who – although not a socialist – had been close to Otto Bauer and Karl Renner; his *Pure Theory of Law* can be historically interpreted as a late attempt to neutralize the multitude of differences in empire by the most formal normative abstractions possible; and Horace Kallen, the father of American pluralism, as the head of the board of trustees.

The history of the Institute for Jewish Affairs has still to be written. Such an endeavour promises a deep insight into the transformation that historical experiences undergo in order to get converted into the respective arsenals of knowledge – here the patterns, forms and phenomena of empire in dissolution.

Let me conclude my panoramic view of the residual meaning of empire as a means for reading, that is, for *re*-reading European history from the fringes. These fringes are multifold: fringes of time, fringes of space and the fringes of a radical experience undergone by a people or population that – because of its ubiquitous trans-territorial, trans-national and somewhat pre-modern diasporic existence – never fit well into the world of European nation-states. The legacy of the Jews of Europe not only remains as a moral imperative at the heart of the European Union, but also challenges the very understanding of European history – as a history to be written anew beyond, above and besides the fabric of the nation-state.

Notes

1. An extended citation can be found in Lynn Hunt (ed.) (2001), *The French Revolution and Human Rights: a Brief Documentary History*, Boston/New York: Bedford/St. Martin's, pp. 86–8.
2. See Reinhold Grimm (1989), 'Nachwort', in Felix Pollak, *Vom Nutzen des Zweifels*, Frankfurt/M: Fischer, pp. 205–14.
3. Anson Rabinbach (2005), 'The Challenge of the Unprecedented: Raphael Lemkin and the Concept of Genocide', *Jahrbuch des Simon-Dubnow-Instituts/ Simon Dubnow Institute Yearbook*, 4, p. 420.
4. Ibid., p. 410.

Part II

The New Diasporic Field

3

Can the Experience of Diaspora Judaism Serve as a Model for Islam in Today's Multicultural Europe?

Sander Gilman

Two moments in modern history: a religious community in France is banned from wearing distinctive clothing in public schools as it is seen as an egregious violation of secular society; a religious community in Switzerland is forbidden from ritually slaughtering animals as such slaughter is seen as a cruel and unnatural act. These acts take place more than a hundred years apart: the former recently in France, the latter more than a century ago in Switzerland (where the prohibition against ritual slaughter still stands). But who are these religious communities? In France (among other countries) the order banning ostentatious religious clothing and ornaments in schools and other public institutions impacts as much on religious Jewish men who cover their heads (and perhaps even religious Jewish married women who cover their hair) as it does the evident target group, Muslim women. (The law is written in such a politically correct way as also to ban the ostentatious wearing of a cross: 'Pierre, you can't come into school carrying that six-foot-high cross on your back. You will have to simply leave it in the hall.') In Switzerland, even today the prohibition against kosher Jewish slaughter also covers the slaughter of meat by Muslims who follow the ritual that results in Halal meat. These prohibitions impact on Jews and Muslims in oddly similar ways when Western responses to 'slaughter' are measured. Very different is how the meat is used: whether in 'traditional' dishes or in a 'Big Mac'. The question is how did and will these two groups respond to such confrontation with the secular, 'modern' world?[1]

Why should the focus of concern in secular Europe, from the Enlightenment to today, be on the practices and beliefs of Jews and of Muslims? Indeed when the Sikhs in France raised the question of whether their turbans were 'cultural' or 'religious' symbols under the terms of the new regulations the official French spokesperson asked in effect: Are there Sikhs in France? Indeed there are.

Yet in September 2004, two French journalists were seized in Iraq and threatened with death unless the law limiting headscarves was not instituted the following week when school was to begin in France. The reaction was not a sense of support for the struggle for an Islamic identity in France. Indeed, virtually all of the French Muslim institutions, from the official French Council of the Muslim Faith to the radical Union of Islamic Organizations in France (UOIF), spoke out against the outside pressure even though it came from the 'Islamic' world. As Olivier Roy, a leading French scholar of Islam, noted: 'They may disagree on the law of the veil, but they are saying, "This is our fight and don't interfere." This is a pivotal moment.'[2] Indeed Lhaj Thami Breze, the head of UOIF, who had been opposed to the law, proposed a compromise in which a moderate interpretation of the law would permit 'modest head covering'.[3] It might appear that the unity of the Islamic community in France in opposing antagonism to the 'law of the veil' in this form was a sign of the development of a secular consciousness in this religious community. What was striking is that the majority of Muslim schoolgirls did not wear or quickly removed their head coverings the day school began. Only about 200–250 girls, mainly in Alsace, wore their scarves to school and all but about 100 took them off before entering the buildings. These girls were removed from the classrooms and provided with 'counselling' in the schools. For them the *hijab*, which had been seen as 'a way to reconcile modernity, self-affirmation and authenticity', was a sign of the Western rights they demanded as Muslims.[4] These were less central than the rule of law. Three male Sikh students in Bobigny, a Paris suburb, were sent home the first day of class for wearing their traditional head covering. This was true whether they saw the headscarf as a political or an ethnic or religious symbol. The demand that one see oneself as a citizen with the rights of the citizen to contest the claims of the secular state overrode any sense of the primary identification as a member of the *Ummah*, the Islamic religious community. Jacqueline Costa-Lascoux, research director at CEVIPOF, the Political Science Centre of CRNR in Paris, noted that 'the hostage taking has helped the Muslim community in France, mainly the young people, to understand that they can live in a democratic society and still be Muslims'.[5] The operative terms here are 'democratic society' and 'Muslim'. It is the constitution of the modern secular state and the need for religions such as Islam and Judaism to adapt to it that is at the heart of the matter.

Yet what does it mean to be a Muslim in this secular world of modern France? Scratch secular Europe today and you find all of the presuppositions and attitudes of Christianity concerning Jews and Muslims present in subliminal or overt forms. Secular society in Europe has absorbed Christianity into its very definition of the secular.[6] Indeed one can make an argument that 'secular' society as we now see it in Europe is the result of the adaptation of Christianity to the model of secularism that arose as a compromise formation out of the wars of religion following the Reformation. The integration of the Jews into Enlightenment Europe, as Adam Sutcliffe has shown in his *Judaism and Enlightenment*, was an integration into Christian Europe (with Christianity having different textures in England than in Holland or in Bavaria, and so on).[7] The veneer was that of a secular state, a veneer that altered the nature of Christianity itself. Little has changed over the past two hundred years. Recently German, Italian, Polish and Slovakian delegates demanded that the 'Christian heritage' of the new Europe be writ large in the (failed) European constitution of 2005. It was only the post-11 September anxiety of most states that enabled Valéry Giscard d'Estaing, as president of the convention writing the constitution, to persuade the group that such a reference would be 'inappropriate'. The demand was transformed into a reference in the preamble to the 'cultural, religious, and humanist inheritance of Europe'. No one missed what was meant. Judaism and Islam have an all-too-close relationship to Christianity and raise questions that remain troubling in Europe.

It is important not to reduce the relationship between Judaism and Islam to the role that Jewish ideas, concepts and practices did or did not have in shaping the earliest forms of Islamic belief. It is clear that nineteenth-century Jewish scholars in Europe had a central role in examining the 'Jewish roots' of historical Islam. Scholars from Abraham Geiger in the 1830s to Ignaz Goldziher at the end of the century stressed the Judaizing nature of early Islam. These roots, true or not, are not sufficient to explain the intense focus on the nature of Islam in Europe today. Islam is not simply a surrogate for speaking about the Jews in today's Europe because of superficial similarities to Judaism. Among Jewish scholars in the nineteenth century the search for the Jewish roots of Islam was certainly more than simply a surrogate for speaking about the relationship between Judaism and Christianity in the nineteenth century, as Susannah Heschel so elegantly shows in her study of *Abraham Geiger and the Jewish Jesus*.[8] At one moment, the examination or construction of Islam provided one major Jewish scholar with a model for the potential reform of contemporary Judaism. One can quote Goldziher's diaries: 'I truly entered into the spirit of Islam to such an extent that ultimately I became inwardly convinced that I myself was a Muslim, and judiciously discovered that this was the only religion which, even in its doctrinal and official formulation, can satisfy philosophic minds. My ideal was to elevate Judaism to a similar rational level. Islam, so taught me my experience, is the only religion, in which superstitious and heathen ingredients are not frowned upon by the rationalism, but by the orthodox teachings.'[9] For him the Islam he discovered becomes the model for a new spirit of Judaism at the close of the nineteenth century.

It is the seeming closeness of these 'Abrahamic religions' and their joint history that draws attention to the real or imagined differences to the majority religion and its new form: secular society. (This is the newest politically correct phrase: the 'Judaeo-Christian tradition' was the catchword for common aspects shared between Judaism and Christianity after the Holocaust made this an acceptable notion; 'the Abrahamic religions' is the new buzz word including Islam into the Judaeo-Christian fold that has become current only after 9/11. Both phrases attempt to defuse the clearly Christian aspect of modern Western secular society by expanding it, but, of course, only re-emphasize it.) This closeness of Christianity to Judaism and Islam results in what Sigmund Freud called the 'narcissism of minor differences'. Those differences are heightened in this secular society, which is rooted in the mindset (and often in the attitudes, beliefs, social mores and civic practices) of the religious community – in Western Europe – Christianity. Thus in Western Europe there was a radical secularization of religious institutions in the course of the nineteenth century. Marriage shifted from being solely in the control of the Church to being in the domain of the state: but this form of secularization still maintains the quasi-religious aura about marriage, something we see in the debates in France about gay marriage. No secularizing European state simply abandons marriage as a religious institution that has outlived its time as nineteenth-century anarchists and some early twentieth-century radical Zionists claimed.[10] The new minority is promised a wide range of civil rights – including those of freedom of religion – if only they adhere to the standards of civilized behaviour as defined by the secular society (but rooted in the desire to make sure that that society with its masked religious assumptions redefines the minorities' religious practice).

We should now look at the experiences within the various strands of Jewish religious (and therefore social) ritual practice from the late eighteenth century (which marked the beginning of civil emancipation) that parallel those now confronting Diaspora Islam in 'secular' Western Europe. The similarities are striking: a religious minority enters into a self-described secular (or secularizing) society that is Christian in its rhetoric and presuppositions and that perceives a 'special relationship' with this minority. The co-territorial society sees this as an act of aggression. This minority speaks a different secular language but also has yet a different religious language. This is odd in countries that have a national language and (in some) a religious language but not a secular language spoken by a religious minority as well as a ritual. Religious schools that teach in the languages associated with a religious group are seen as sources of corruption and illness. Religious rites are practised that seem an abomination to the majority 'host' culture: unlike the secular majority these religious communities practise the mutilation of children's bodies (infant male circumcision, and, for some Muslims, infant female genital cutting); the suppression of the rights of women (lack of women's traditional education; a secondary role in religious practice; arranged marriages; honour killings); barbaric torture of animals (the cutting of the throats of unstunned animals allowing them to bleed to death); disrespect for the dead through too rapid burial; ritual excess (in the case of the Jews, drunkenness at Purim; feasting during Ramadan in the case of the Muslims); ostentatious clothing that signals religious affiliation and has ritual significance (from women's hair covering such as the Muslim hijab to Jewish sheitels to men's hats such as the Jewish stremil or the Muslim taqiyah); and centrally relating all of these practices: a belief in the divine 'chosenness' of the group in contrast to all others. The demonization of aspects of religious practice has its roots in what civil society will tolerate and what it will not, what it considers to be decorous and what is unacceptable as a social practice. Why it will not tolerate something is, of course, central to the story. Thus Alan Dundes argued a decade ago that the anxiety about meanings associated with the consumption of the body and blood of Christ in the Christian Mass shaped the fantasy of the Jews as slaughtering Christian children for their blood.[11] But it is equally present in the anger in secular Europe directed at Jewish practices such as ritual slaughter with its obligatory bloodletting.

One of the most striking similarities of the process of integration into Western secular society is the gradual elision of the striking national differences among the various groups. Muslims in Western Europe represent multiple national traditions (South Asian in the UK, North African in France and Spain, Turkish in Germany). But so did the Jews in Western Europe who came out of ghettos in France and the Rhineland, from the rural reaches of Bavaria and Hungary, who moved from those parts of 'Eastern Europe' – Poland, the eastern Marches of the Austro-Hungarian Empire – which became part of the West and from the fringes of empire to the centre. To this one can add the Sephardic Jews from the

Iberian Peninsula who settled in areas from Britain (introducing fish and chips) to the fringes of the Austrian Empire. The standard image of the Jews in eighteenth-century British caricature was the Maltese Jew in his oriental turban. By the nineteenth century it was that of Lord Rothschild in formal wear receiving the Prince of Wales at his daughter's wedding in a London synagogue. Religious identity (as the Jew or the Muslim) replaced national identity – by then few (except the anti-Semites) remembered that the Rothschilds were a Frankfurt family that escaped the Yiddish-speaking ghetto. The 'Jews' are everywhere and all alike; Muslims seem to be everywhere and are becoming 'all alike'. Even ritual differences and theological antagonism seem to be diminished in the Diaspora where the notion of a Muslim *Ummah* (or community) seems to be realized.

Now for Jews in those lands that were to become Germany, in the Austro-Hungarian Empire, in France, and in those lands that were to become Great Britain, the stories are all different, different forms of Christianity, different expectations as to the meaning of citizenship. Different notions of secularization all present slightly different variations on the theme of: what do you have to give up to become a true citizen? Do you merely have to give up your secular language (Western and Eastern Yiddish, Ladino, Turkish, Urdu, colloquial Arabic)? Today there has been a strong suggestion in Germany and the UK that preaching in the mosques should be done only in English – for security reasons. Do you have to abandon the most evident and egregious practices: or must you, as the German philosopher Johann Gottlieb Fichte (1762–1814) states (echoing debates about Jewish emancipation during the French Revolution), 'cut off their Jewish heads and replace them with German ones'?[12] And that was not meant as a metaphor, but as a statement of the impossibility of Jewish transformation into Germans.

The question we must address is what Jews thought it possible to change in Jewish religious practice and belief in the eighteenth and nineteenth centuries, what it accomplished within various national states, and what it did not accomplish. That is, what was gained and what was lost, both in terms of the ability of living religions to transform themselves and the clear understanding that all such transformations provoke resistance and such transformations call forth other forms of religious practice in response. All of these changes deal in general with the question of Jewish 'identity' but in a complex and often contradictory manner. For the history of the Jews in the European Diaspora the late eighteenth century called forth three great 'reformers' who took on different reforms in the light of the Diaspora status of the Jews: Moses

Mendelssohn (1729–86) and the followers of the Jewish Enlightenment in Germany (and their predecessors in Holland) who confronted a secularizing world; Rabbi Eliyahu of Vilnius – the Vilna Gaon (1720–97) – in the Baltic who desired to reform the Orthodox tradition to make it more able to function in a self-contained Jewish world; and one of the first modern Jewish mystics (the Hasidim), Rabbi Yisrael, the Baal Shem Tov (1698–1760) (the Master of the Good Name) who fought, like his contemporaries in Berlin and Vilnius, against what he saw as the stultifying practices and world-view of contemporary Judaism. All lived roughly simultaneously. In their wake came radical changes in what it meant to be a Jew in belief and practice. For contemporary Islam all can serve as answers to the pressures found throughout the Diaspora. All offer parallels to the dilemmas faced by Islam in the West today. Thus the list of 'abominations' that secular Europe saw in Jewish ritual practices became the yardstick for the question of what Jews were willing to change in order to better fit the various national assumptions about citizenship. These were as different in the nineteenth century as the debates about Islamic head covering in the twenty-first century in France – opposed because it violates the idea of a secular state in Germany – supportive under the very different meanings of multiculturalism – and in the UK where in March 2005 the courts allowed full traditional South Asian clothing (the *jilbab*) as an exception to the 'school uniform' rule in a predominantly Muslim school where the dress code had been worked out with the parents. These are the themes and their literary echo or prefiguration that we shall explore.

Obviously there are also vast differences between Jews in the eighteenth and nineteenth centuries and Muslims today. There are simply many more Muslims today in Western Europe than there were Jews in the earlier period. The Jews historically never formed more than 1 per cent of the population of any Western European nation. Muslim populations form a considerable minority today. While there is no Western European city with a Muslim majority, many recent news stories predict that Marseilles or Rotterdam will be the first European city to have one. In France today there are 600 000 Jews, while there are between five and six million Muslims, who make up about 10 per cent of the population. In Germany, with a tiny Jewish population of slightly over 100 000, almost 4 per cent of the population is Muslim (totalling more than three million people). In Britain about 2.5 per cent of the total population (1.48 million people) is Muslim. Demographics (and birth rate) aside, there are salient differences in the experiences of the Jews and Muslims in the past and today. The Jews had no national 'homeland' – indeed they were defined as nomads or a pariah people (*pace* Max Weber and Hannah Arendt). They lived only in the *Goles*, the Diaspora, and seemed thus inherently different from any other people in Western Europe (except perhaps the Roma). Most Muslims in the West come out of a national tradition often formed by colonialism in which their homelands had long histories disturbed but not destroyed by colonial rule. And last but not least, with the Israeli-Palestinian conflict over the past century (well before the creation of the State of Israel), the establishment of a Jewish homeland as well as the Holocaust seem to place the two groups – at least in the consciousness of the West – into two antagonistic camps.[13]

Religion for the Jews of pre-Enlightenment Europe and for much of contemporary Islam, which has its immediate roots in majority Islamic states, became for many a 'heritage' in the Western, secular Diaspora. What had been lived experience in a *milieu de mémoire* – environment of memory – to use Pierre Nora's often-cited phrase from 1994 becomes a *lieu de mémoire* – a place of memory – that refigures meaning constantly within the Diaspora.[14] What is it that such memory of ritual and practice can or must abandon? What must it preserve to maintain its coherence for the group? The answer depends on time and place and yet the experience of Jews in the Western European Diaspora seems to offer a model case clearly because of the 'narcissism of minor differences' among the three Abrahamic religions. The Jews maintain, in different modalities, their religious identity, even if the nature of the options explored created ruptures that produced new problems and over time partial resolutions and yet further conflicts and resolutions. Thus the ultra-conservative Sephardic Rabbi Ovadiah Yosef, former Chief Sephardic Rabbi of Israel, today applauds the use of aesthetic surgery to improve the marriageable status of women and men.[15]

The central cultural thrust of the New Europe is not European integration in national terms, but the relationship between secular society and the dynamic world of European Islam. As the Syrian-born, German sociologist Bassam Tibi noted decades ago, it is the struggle within Islam to become a modern religion, whether within the Islamic world or in the Islamic Diaspora in the West, that is central.[16] Recently further voices, such as that of Tariq Ramadan and Feisal Abdul Rauf, have noted the need for a 'modern' Islam.[17] There are certainly moments of confrontation in which Islamic ritual and practices have changed in specific settings. One can think of the entire history of Bosnian Islam from the nineteenth century until its destruction in the past decade and the resultant fundamentalist cast given to Bosnia over the same period. There is, however, a substantial difference between the contexts. Anyone interested in contemporary Europe before 9/11 knew that the eight hundred pound gorilla confronting France, Germany and the United Kingdom – and to a lesser extent Spain and Italy – was the huge presence of an 'unassimilable' minority. The point is strongly made by Samuel Huntington in his recent pronouncement about Hispanics in the US: 'The persistent inflow of Hispanic immigrants threatens to divide the United States into two peoples, two cultures, and two languages. Unlike past immigrant groups, Mexicans and other Latinos have not assimilated into mainstream US culture, forming instead their own political and linguistic enclaves – from Los Angeles to Miami – and rejecting the Anglo-Protestant values that built the American dream. The United States ignores this challenge at its peril.'[18] The question of Muslims in Western Europe seems to forecast the same set of problems. But, of course, exactly the same things were said (with correction for national self-image) about the Jews for two hundred years. This chapter sets out to explore how Jews (however defined or self-defined) were able to deal with their integration into a secular state as Jews, what negotiations and compromises occurred, and what radical responses from Zionism to neo-Orthodox fundamentalism answer them. While not producing a map for future action – historians unlike political scientists such as Huntington abjure prediction – I hope to sketch a set of debates that are now or soon will be present within Europe's sense of the future of Islam in Western Europe and the new EU – with or without the predominantly secular Muslim states of Turkey and Albania.

Central to our contemporary understanding of the role that Islam may and does play in the New Europe is the concept of multiculturalism that seems to provide a new model for understanding ethnicity and religion today. The multicultural can be understood, according to contemporary self-defined multicultural thinkers such as the late Gloria Anzaldúa, as the space where 'this mixture of races, rather than resulting in an inferior being, provides hybrid progeny, a mutable, more malleable species with a rich gene pool'.[19] Contemporary multicultural theory provides a further rehabilitation of notions of hybridity, of continually crossing categories of ethnicity, race and culture. The Canadian film maker Christine Welsh effects a similar, necessary rehabilitation of the anxiety about being *Métis*, of mixed race: the *Métis* becomes a type of one on the Canadian frontier.[20] By positing the 'cosmic race' as 'healing the split at the foundation of our lives', she removes the stigmata of 'illness' from those at the borderlands. Here one must note that the very meaning of the 'multicultural' is very different when one looks north and south of the US border. Mexico, at least since the 1910 Revolution, has represented the hybrid as encompassing the wide range of native peoples as well as Spain but not necessarily other immigrant groups. Canada for a very long time focused on the Anglophone–Francophone divide but now sees itself as a broadly multicultural nation encompassing the widest range of immigrants, many of whom are also present in Mexico. American academics such as Edward Said could state simply years ago that 'every cultural form is radically, quintessentially hybrid'.[21] And yet the multicultural is also the antithesis of hybridity, just as 'cultural diversity' countered the 'melting pot'.

It can just as frequently be the reification and commodification of ethnic identity. The advocacy and attacks on Afro-centric culture over the last thirty years stress the autonomy of cultural entities often described as 'races'. Thus Martin Bernal's important study of the denial of the African roots of Greece, in the first volume of his *Black Athena* (1987) gave way to an attempt to 'prove' the African (loosely defined) roots of Greek culture.[22] The argument was not one of hybridity but of the authenticity of the African roots. Its project is to stress the boundaries and borders between ethnic, cultural, religious or class groups. If the *Méti* is hybrid, then hip-hop is multicultural. (And 'world music' can be both!) While multiculturalism can allow for, and indeed celebrate, the merging of cultures so as to eliminate boundaries, one of its strongest claims (in the new global culture that is both hybrid and multicultural) is its insistence that each of us has a 'culture' in a reified, ethnic or class sense, and that the products of these cultures can be displayed, sold, consumed and exchanged across borders. More importantly, central to both models of multiculturalism is that 'culture' is the basis for our identities. 'Biological' difference, the difference of the older and some of the present views of 'race', is displaced on to a symbolic, cultural level. But at the same moment this cultural heritage is commodified and thus made available for all consumers.

Indeed it is the very concepts of multiculturalism, as hybrid or autonomous, parallel culture, that were shaped around the conflicts that arose in the late nineteenth century over the status of the Jews in High Culture. This debate continues the debate about how the experience of the Jews in Western European cultures shapes the discourses that now impact on Islam. Pierre Bourdieu and Loic Wacquant dismissed 'multiculturalism' in 2000, in an essay in *Le Monde Diplomatique*, as:

> recently imported into Europe to describe cultural pluralism in the civic sphere, whereas in the United States it refers, in the very movement which obfuscates it, to the continued ostracization of Blacks and

> to the crisis of the national mythology of the 'American dream' of 'equal opportunity for all,' correlative of the bankruptcy of public education at the very time when competition for cultural capital is intensifying and class inequalities are growing at a dizzying pace. The locution 'multicultural' conceals this crisis by artificially restricting it to the university microcosm and by expressing it on an ostensibly 'ethnic' register, when what is really at stake is not the incorporation of marginalized cultures in the academic canon but access to the instruments of (re)production of the middle and upper classes, chief among them the university, in the context of active and massive disengagement by the state. North American 'multiculturalism' is neither a concept nor a theory, nor a social or political movement – even though it claims to be all those things at the same time. It is a screen discourse, whose intellectual status is the product of a gigantic effect of national and international allodoxia, which deceives both those who are party to it and those who are not. It is also a North American discourse, even though it thinks of itself and presents itself as a universal discourse, to the extent that it expresses the contradictions specific to the predicament of US academics. Cut off from the public sphere and subjected to a high degree of competitive differentiation in their professional milieu, US professors have nowhere to invest their political libido but in campus squabbles dressed up as conceptual battles royal.[23]

Whatever the truth about this comment on the academic world of North America, this view of multiculturalism (defined here as an American discourse of victimization) retains one strong element inherent to the general sense of the multicultural: that of the multicultural as the invention of theorists arguing their own case. This would apply equally well to the theory debates of the early twentieth century, within the academy and beyond it, that created the very concept in its formulation of the ability or inability of the Jews to enter into or be isolated from modern High Culture. Indeed, inherent in the very history of multiculturalism, as Bourdieu and Wacquant see it, is a clear rejection of it as incomplete, limited, compromised and predictable. This was a hallmark of the debates in the early 1990s about the limits of the multicultural; but it was also a sign of the meanings associated with the multicultural almost a century prior. When the Chicago Cultural Studies Group tabulates 'a variety of means for the idea of multicultural: the corporate multiculturalism of global capital; the interdisciplinary cultural criticism that conjoins different publics around discourse, identities, and difference; the international comparativism that crosses boundaries to produce new knowledge and new challenges to the means of knowledge; as well as countless local impulses that appear to derive from pluralism, nationalism, or insurgent subcultural formations and alliances', they are reflecting the complex origin of the multicultural in the image of the Jew as well as its 'post-modern' history.[24] Today in the polemics surrounding the integration of Islam into Western culture, or, according to her, the modernization of Islam, the Canadian Islamic activist Irshad Manji dismisses the multicultural (read now as radical cultural pluralism) as a sop to the inhumanity of Islam: 'As Westerners bow down before multiculturalism, we often act as if anything goes. We see our readiness to accommodate as a strength – even a form of cultural superiority (though few of us will admit that). But foundamenalists [*sic*] see our inclusive instincts as a weakness that makes us soft, lardy, rudderless.'[25] Yet multiculturalism in the twenty-first century is still seen as a goal for the transformation of the separatism of Diaspora groups into members of a cultural community through the production of High Culture. Indeed, Irshad Manji over and over again evokes even the hybridity of contemporary Israeli society as an example of such productive multi-culturalism. The origin of both models of the multicultural, as we shall see, lies not in North America but in Europe; its adaptation and inflection vary from national culture to national culture. It seems inescapable. Even such pessimistic accounts of the afterlife of the multicultural articulated as Paul Gilroy's *After Empire: Melancholia or Convivial Culture?* postulated a new variant on the hybrid multicultural, the 'feral beauty of postcolonial culture'.[26]

The variant meanings of 'culture' (the discourses that define according to participant and/or observer a network) and 'Culture' (the production of aesthetic objects) are linked in the modern period by the central notion that both seemed to be defined by fixed ideas of 'nationhood'. Yet as Norbert Elias observed decades ago, 'the German concept of *Kultur* places special stress on national differences and the particular identity of groups; primarily by virtue of this it has acquired in such fields as ethnological and anthropological research a significance far beyond the German linguistic area and the situation in which the concept originated. But that situation is the situation of a people, which by any Western standards arrived at political unification and consolidation very late and from whose boundaries, for centuries and even down to the present, territories have again and again crumbled away or threaten to crumble away.'[27] It is the very indeterminacy and porosity of the concepts of 'culture' and 'Culture' that make the reading of cultural objects a means of understanding the strategies and rhetoric of the multicultural and the importance of multicultural objects, such as novels, poetry, art, theatre, film, in both presenting and constituting multiculturalism.

We can take one salient example from contemporary German–Turkish (Turko–German) writing. It is clear that some contemporary writers, at least, recognize the parallels between Jewish and Muslim experience. Here too the Jewish experience is that of the past, the Shoah, rather than that of the present. What is striking about the debates in Europe today is that they not only echo the debates, reforms and reactions of the nineteenth century, but that they also impact on Jews and Muslims in Europe today. As with the Jewish writing of the eighteenth century in German, French and Latin, it reflected by definition 'liberal' attempts to engage the 'enlightened' Europe. Today, as Olivier Roy notes, 'neofundamentalists ... are not interested in creating or asserting a "Muslim" culture. They reject the concept, even if they sometimes use the term to find a common language with Western societies, where the language of multiculturalism is the main idiom through which we deal with otherness. Conspicuous by their absence are neofundamentalist novelists, poets, musicians, film-makers or comedians.'[28] Thus the Muslims (now understood as 'ethnicity' rather than 'religion') engaged in the creation of High Culture are by definition those engaged in a process of acculturation, even if they deeply mistrust this process. One needs only to note that it is in the process of acculturation that the attack against Salman Rushdie's 'heretical' novel *The Satanic Verses*, initiated by the Bradford Council of Mosques in 1989, was launched.[29] In the Muslim Diaspora in the UK, High Culture, defined as the space of the multicultural, is and remains a place of contestation.

Zafer Senoçak's 'Dangerous Relations' (*Gefährliche Verwandtschaft*, 1998) sees the Shoah forming the background of the novel.[30] Senoçak provides the reader with a novel about Germany after the Shoah that is also an account of the tribulations of modern Turks in that Germany. Senoçak, while born in Ankara in 1961, has lived in Germany since he was nine years old. He writes in German (needless to say) from a self-consciously and ironic multicultural perspective. To do so he evokes the 'Jewish' experience as 'historical' while the 'Turkish' (but not necessarily Muslim) experience is contemporary.[31] As Olivier Roy has argued, one of the processes that happen is the creation of a virtual *ummah* by believers that is deterritorialized. This is a form of empowerment that transcends national limits and ethnic identity and can take on 'secular' form. For secular writers this process is the hyper-awareness of an 'ethnic' identity merged with an assumption that such a multicultural identity is simultaneously that of the victim. The problem that this evokes in the denial of the contemporary experience of Jews in Germany does raise further questions, but for the moment let us focus on his claims.

Senoçak's novel recounts the adventures of Sascha Muchteschem, the son of a German-Jewish mother and a Turkish, middle-class father. After the death of his parents he inherits a box with the notebooks of his Turkish grandfather, which he cannot read as they are written in Arabic and Cyrillic script. These unreadable texts place him on the search for his roots just as he begins to write his first novel. Central to this novel are both of his grandfathers, the German-Jewish Orientalist and the Turkish adventurer. Both are radically secular, but what 'secular' comes to mean in the context of a German 'secular' Diaspora is shaped by German expectations, not necessarily Turkish ones.

Senoçak presents a self-designated 'hybrid' author who in his own estimation is therefore the exemplary cosmopolitan German: 'I don't have an identity. People in my world have more and more problems with this. It is as if the fall of The Wall, the collapse of the old order, did not only have a liberating function. Without The Wall one no longer feels oneself protected. Identity is a substitute concept for being protected' (p. 47). He is, however, seen in the Berlin Republic as a Turkish writer. 'Are you a foreigner? I am asked when I spell my name. Earlier I spelled it without being asked. Indeed, according to the passport I am German' (p. 128). He is 'seen' as Turkish, nevertheless: 'Do you write in Turkish? I offer many contradictory answers to this question if only to confuse those who are already confused. Who could know that I hardly speak a word of Turkish...? Colleagues of mine, who are more evidently foreigners than I, who are dark skinned or speak German with an accent, seem to have little problem with their reception as "Foreign Writers"' (p. 130). Thus it is visibility (skin colour) and language that define difference. He is seen as different and the assumption is that his language must also be different. He, however, does not see himself as appearing different because of his 'Jewish' background. For him this appears 'white' but not for the Germans.

Sascha Muchteschem is very dismissive of 'Germanness'. 'Am I a German? This question never interested me. It seems to interest no one. The question about a German identity was an old fashioned question, a theme heavy with clichés and stereotypes, a type of heretical question, that any intelligent person would dismiss with a gesture that indicated that it was unimportant' (p. 127). Yet it is of course the history of the German Jews who saw themselves as Germans that haunts his own family: 'In the family of my mother there were no survivors. One didn't speak about this. My mother crossly answered the questions that I asked about the photos I found in the drawers in the library. She took the photos away and, as I later learned, called aunts and cousins merely strangers or friends of grandfather' (p. 59). That this vanished family wanted to be German did not mean that they wanted to become Christian. 'My grandfather was one of those German Jews, for whom Judaism was nothing more than the belief of their fathers. My maternal family felt itself for generations indebted to the Enlightenment … it would have never occurred to him to convert to Christianity, because this religion was just as passé as Judaism' (p. 57). Could one be a German who just happened to be a Jew, just as the narrator desires to be a German with Turkish and Jewish ancestry? The historical answer is clearly 'No'. And what has happened to the ethnic or religious in each case? Is the Turk not a Muslim and the Jew not a German? The answer is a historical one: after the Young Turks, Turkish identity is consciously distanced from Muslim identity and after the Shoah the idea of a German Jew in the older model of a cultural symbiosis is unthinkable.

Certainly, the narrator sees his 'Jewish' grandfather as a German. He reads his way through the library that his grandfather had built up in the 1920s and that survived the Nazis. It is filled with authors such as Thomas Mann (p. 59). He shares the cultural prejudices of the Germans towards other peoples, especially the Turks. His mother accepted his father, who was upper middle class and well educated only after a five-year courtship. 'The arrogance and disdain for the poor and primitive Turks that the German Jews expressed was a sign of their assimilation … Many Orientalists were German Jews. They attributed to the Orient eternal tyranny, fatalism, immutability, and difference. Who would have thought that their grandchildren would become Orientals like their ancestors?' (p. 92). The irony is double-edged. For the 'Orientals' (that is, the Turks) are simultaneously becoming Germans as the Jews are becoming Israelis. They are becoming Israelis because the project of their becoming Germans failed so horribly.

Belonging to the German cultural sphere is not sufficient to define 'Germanness'. There is the double problem, as Gershom Scholem noted about the 'German Jewish symbiosis', that the Jews never really belonged to it in the eyes of the Germans and that the Jews fantasized that they were included. And it is in the realm of High Culture that Scholem sees the fantasy having failed the Jews most egregiously:

> I deny that there has ever been such a German-Jewish dialogue in any genuine sense whatsoever, i.e., as a historical phenomenon. It takes two to have a dialogue … Nothing can be more misleading than to

> apply such a concept to the discussions between Germans and Jews during the last 200 years . . . To be sure, the Jews attempted a dialogue with the Germans, starting from all possible points of view and situations, demandingly, imploringly, and entreatingly, servile and defiant . . . and today, when the symphony is over, the time may be ripe for studying their motifs and for attempting a critique of their tones.[32]

Will the Turks simply replicate this error? 'One day a woman said to me, who lived in a very elegant and very well kept house in Dahlem, that today's Turks are much worse than the Jews of the past. The Jews would have masked themselves in Germanness. They acted as if they were Germans. One didn't believe them. But that was their problem' (p. 66). The 'mask' is what is central to the German Jews in Senoçak's image of history. It is a mask as seen by the Germans, but it was the only face that the German Jews, such as the narrator's grandfather, actually had.

To understand the distinction between appearance and reality of Jew and Turk is the key to the novel. The narrator enters into an exchange with his friend Heinrich, who is an expert on nineteenth-century German Jewish history, as to what defines a human being:

> 'The body is the only home that a human being has,' Heinrich claimed categorically.
>
> I contradicted him. 'Language is essentially more important. Only in language can you be at home.'
>
> 'Language alienates man from himself,' he argued. 'Man is a being without name.' (p. 82)

It is in the body that the essence of 'Jewishness' lies for the Germans. Language, the utopian space of the writer, is secondary. One thinks of Stefan Zweig's claim, shortly before his suicide in Brazilian exile, that language is the only home of the writer. It is a body that betrays even as it changes:

> Many generations of German Jews have concerned themselves with the question, when and how a Jew can overcome his Jewishness in order to become a total German. Lightening the skin and the hair, Germanizing language and belief did not free the Jews from the Jewish illness that they brought from Germany. The Jews took over these tortuous questions from the German society in order to belong to that society. They made them more sophisticated and asked them

> again. And they became the same questions in return. And so on. This reciprocal process continued until the question was reformulated in: 'When will Germany be free of its Jews'. (p. 89)

Historically this is quite accurate, if teleological in its argument that nineteenth-century anti-Semitism leads directly to the Shoah. By the latter half of the nineteenth century, Western European Jews had become indistinguishable from other Western Europeans in matters of language, dress, occupation, location of their dwellings and the cut of their hair. Indeed, if Rudolf Virchow's extensive study of over 10 000 German school children published in 1886 was accurate, they were also indistinguishable in terms of skin, hair and eye colour from the greater masses of those who lived in Germany. Virchow's statistics sought to show that wherever a greater percentage of the overall population had lighter skin or bluer eyes or blonder hair there a greater percentage of Jews also had lighter skin or bluer eyes or blonder hair.[33] But although Virchow attempted to provide a rationale for the sense of Jewish acculturation, he still assumed that Jews were a separate and distinct racial category. George Mosse has commented, 'the separateness of Jewish schoolchildren, approved by Virchow, says something about the course of Jewish emancipation in Germany. However, rationalized, the survey must have made Jewish schoolchildren conscious of their minority status and their supposedly different origins.'[34] Nonetheless, even though they were labelled as different, Jews came to parallel the scale of types found elsewhere in European society. They 'became' German in their very bodies, but these bodies were distrusted by the culture in which they found themselves.

At the close of the twentieth century it is the turn of the Turks. Can Turks, even hybrids like the narrator, really become Germans? Heinrich claims that 'The Germans have learned nothing from history ... now they have brought the Turks here. And they never came to terms even with the Jews' (p. 82). Physical assimilation through surgery or intermarriage seems to be no prophylaxis in Senoçak's world. Hybridity, such as that of the protagonist, means only that one is exposed to a double risk. One is at the end an Oriental, no matter what one's identity or language. Being hybrid only reinforces this. The protagonist's desire is not to be cosmopolitan but to be 'simply' German. This is denied to him by his Turkish identity and his Jewish ancestry reinforces this in his own estimation. Indeed the search for someone to 'translate' his Turkish grandfather's notebooks from the Arabic (presumably Turkish) and Cyrillic (presumably Russian) fails when it becomes clear that what is written is disguised in a personal code, not in a national language. This rather pessimistic view can only work if a specific idea of a Jewish history that ends in the catastrophe of the Shoah in Europe dominates. If modern Judaism as a series of cultural negotiations is taken as a whole, a wider range of possibilities exists.

The study of the history and the culture of the Jews of Germany has been formed for good or for ill on the notion of the 'reconstruction of a lost tradition'. Whether following the ideology of the 'Wissenschaft der Juden' (Science of the Jews) in the nineteenth century or the post-Holocaust fascination with the 'lost world' of the *Ostjuden*, Eastern Jews, or the 'Beitrag' (contribution) of Jews to German culture until 1933, little thought has been given to the questions of whether and how the model of the Jewish experiences in Germany (and Western Europe) may provide some hint of options and pitfalls for Muslims in today's Europe. The question of whether or not the experiences of the Jews in Diaspora Europe could provide some indicators for the world of European Muslims today may provide a new focus for German Jewish studies and a bridge to collaborative work with Muslim scholars in Germany today. As such it could have a political as well as cultural function in addition to its indubitable role in illuminating the ever-changing nature of Diaspora identities.

Notes

1. For background see Jonathan M. Hess (2002), *Germans, Jews, and the Claims of Modernity*, New Haven: Yale University Press.
2. Quoted in Elaine Sciolino (2004), 'Ban on Head Scarves Takes Effect in a United France', *The New York Times*, 3 September, p. A9.
3. 'A Tragic Twist of the Scarf', in *The Economist*, 4 September 2004, p. 40.
4. Olivier Roy (2004), *Globalised Islam: the Search for the New Ummah*, London: Hurst & Co., p. 24.
5. Quoted in Tom Hundley (2004), '"No Strikes, no Sit-ins" over France's Scarf Ban', *The Chicago Tribune*, 8 September, p. 6.
6. Here I reflect the debates about 'secularization' that have dominated much of the past half-century from Carl Becker to Hannah Arendt, from M. H. Abrams and Peter Berger to Hans Blumenberg's *The Legitimacy of the Modern Age* and beyond. See Elizabeth Brient (2000), 'Hans Blumenberg and Hannah Arendt on the "Unworldly Worldliness" of the Modern Age', *Journal of the History of Ideas*, 61, pp. 513–30.
7. Adam Sutcliffe (2003), *Judaism and Enlightenment*, Cambridge: Cambridge University Press.
8. Susannah Heschel (1998), *Abraham Geiger and the Jewish Jesus*, Chicago: University of Chicago Press.

9. Alexander Scheiber (ed.) (1978), *Ignaz Goldziher: Tagebuch*, Leiden: Brill, p. 59.
10. See, for example, David Biale (1997), *Eros and the Jews*, Berkeley: University of California Press.
11. Alan Dundes (1991), *The Blood Libel Legend*, Madison: University of Wisconsin Press.
12. See Michael Mack (2003), *German Idealism and the Jew*, Chicago: University of Chicago Press.
13. Two polemical but informative books shape their argument about contemporary Islamic identity primarily around the rhetoric of the Israeli-Palestinian conflict rather than this being seen as part of the struggle about the modernization of Islam both within and beyond Europe: Jack Goody (2004), *Islam in Europe*, London: Polity; and Gilles Kepel (2004), *The War for Muslim Minds: Islam and the West* (Pascale Ghazaleh, trans.) Cambridge, MA: Belknap Press/Harvard University Press.
14. Pierre Nora (ed.) (1993), *Les Lieux de mémoire*, vol. 1: *Les France: Conflits et partages*, Paris: Gallimard.
15. Zion Zohar (2004), 'Oriental Jewry Confronts Modernity: the Case of Rabbi Ovadiah Yosef', *Modern Judaism*, 24, pp. 132–3.
16. See Bassam Tibi (1995), *Krieg der Zivilisationen*, Hamburg: Hoffmann & Campe. His work is available in English: *The Challenge of Fundamentalism*, Berkeley: University of California Press, 2002; and *Islam Between Culture and Politics*, New York: Palgrave Macmillan, 2002.
17. Tariq Ramadan (2003), *Western Muslims and the Future of Islam*, New York: Oxford University Press; Feisal Abdul Rauf (2004), *What's Right with Islam: a New Vision for Muslims and the West*, San Francisco: Harper.
18. Samuel P. Huntington (2004), 'The Hispanic Challenge', *Foreign Policy*, March/April, pp. 1–16; later included in his *Who Are We: the Challenges to America's National Identity*, New York: Simon & Schuster, 2004.
19. Gloria Anzaldúa (1987), *Borderlands/La Frontera: the New Mestiza*, San Francisco: Spinsters/Aunt Lute, pp. 79–81.
20. Christine Welsh (1993), 'Women in the Shadows: Reclaiming a Metis Heritage', *Descant*, 24, pp. 89–103.
21. Edward W. Said (1993), *Culture and Imperialism*, New York: Alfred A. Knopf, p. 58.
22. Martin Bernal (1987), *Black Athena: the Afroasiatic Roots of Classical Civilization. I: The Fabrication of Ancient Greece 1785–1985*, New Brunswick: Rutgers University Press; see also David A. Hollinger (1987), *Postethnic America: Beyond Multiculturalism*, New York: Basic Books, pp. 126–7.
23. Translated by David Macey and available in March 2005 at: http://www.radicalphilosophy.com/print.asp?editorial_id=9956
24. See 'Critical Multiculturalism' by the Chicago Cultural Studies Group reprinted in David Theo Goldberg (ed.) (1994), *Multiculturalism: a Critical Reader*, Oxford: Blackwell, p. 135.
25. Irshad Manji (2003), *The Trouble with Islam Today*, New York: St. Martin's Griffin, p. 199.
26. Paul Gilroy (2004), *After Empire: Melancholia or Convivial Culture?* London: Routledge.
27. Norbert Elias (1978), *The Civilizing Process*: vol. I: *The History of Manners* (Edmund Jephcott, trans.), New York: Pantheon, p. 5.
28. Roy, *Globalised Islam*, pp. 264–5.

29. See Philip Lewis (2002), *Islamic Britain: Religion, Politics and Identity among British Muslims*, London: I. B. Tauris, for the background and history of this incident.
30. All quotes are my translation and are taken from Zafer Senoçak (1998), *Gefährliche Verwandtschaft*, München: Babel. On Senoçak see Leslie A. Adelson (2002), 'Back to the Future: Turkish Remembrances of the GDR and Other Phantom Pasts', in Leslie A. Adelson (ed.), *The Cultural After-Life of East Germany: New Transnational Perspectives*, Washington, DC: American Institute for Contemporary German Studies (AICGS), pp. 93–109; Andreas Huyssen (2003), 'Diaspora and Nation: Migration into Other Pasts', *New German Critique*, 88, pp. 147–64; Katharina Gerstenberger (2002), 'Difficult Stories: Generation, Genealogy, Gender in Zafer Senoçak's *Gefährliche Verwandtschaft* and Monika Maron's *Pawels Briefe*', in Stuart Taberner and Frank Finlay (eds), *Recasting German Identity: Culture, Politics, and Literature in the Berlin Republic*, Woodbridge, England: Camden House, pp. 235–49; Sandra Hestermann (2003), 'The German-Turkish Diaspora and Multicultural German Identity: Hyphenated and Alternative Discourses of Identity in the Works of Zafer Senoçak and Feridun Zaimoglu', in Monika Fludernik (ed.), *Diaspora and Multiculturalism: Common Traditions and New Developments*, Amsterdam, Netherlands: Rodopi, pp. 235–49; Matthias Konzett (2003), 'Zafer Senoçak im Gesprach', *German Quarterly*, 76, pp. 131–9; Katharina Hall (2003), '"Bekanntlich sind Dreiecksbeziehungen am kompliziertesten": Turkish, Jewish and German Identity in Zafer Senoçak's *Gefährliche Verwandtschaft*', *German Life and Letters*, 56, pp. 72–88; Leslie A. Adelson (2002), 'The Turkish Turn in Contemporary German Literature and Memory Work', *Germanic Review*, 77, pp. 326–38.
31. For more observations on this point, see Bodemann and Yurdakul, Chapter 4 in this volume.
32. Gershom Scholem (1976), 'Against the Myth of the German-Jewish Dialogue', in Werner J. Dannhauser (ed.), *On Jews and Judaism in Crisis*, New York: Schocken, p. 61. See also Peter Schäfer and Gary Smith (eds) (1995), *Gershom Scholem. Zwischen den Disziplinen*, Frankfurt am Main: Suhrkamp.
33. Rudolf Virchow (1886), 'Gesamtbericht über die Farbe der Haut, der Haare und der Augen der Schulkinder in Deutschland', *Archiv für Anthropologie*, 16, pp. 275–475.
34. George L. Mosse (1975), *Toward the Final Solution: a History of European Racism*, New York: Howard Fertig, pp. 90–1.

4
Learning Diaspora: German Turks and the Jewish Narrative

Y. Michal Bodemann and Gökçe Yurdakul

Introduction

From the beginnings of sociology in North America, the literature on migration, ethnicity, citizenship and multiculturalism has looked at the ways in which migrant groups integrate: how they are being incorporated into particular nation-states, their economies and their social and class structures, the ways in which their opportunity structures are limited and how they assimilate over several generations. While the form of ethnic integration usually differs substantially from one country to the next, it has rarely if ever been asked how a nationally specific character of ethnos is shaped by the ethnic groups themselves – by their leaders and organizations – not merely in relation to the state and society at large, but in particular in relation to other minority or immigrant groups. Immigrant groups and minorities, often in close social proximity to one another, do not only orient their behaviour towards each other, but more recent immigrants take their predecessors' narrative as a model; sometimes, in turn, the older immigrant group makes claims in relation to the more recent immigrants. Perhaps the best known case of one group adopting – and identifying with – the narrative of another group is the involvement of American Jews with the National Association for the Advancement of Colored People (NAACP) and the Civil Rights Movement in the US.[1]

In this chapter[2] we will attempt to show how interethnic relations play themselves out between Turks and Jews in Germany. Specifically, we look at how the numerically largest and most recent immigrant group, the Turks, take the small – albeit historically and culturally pivotal – Jewish minority in Germany, pivotal as to its long history in Germany as well as to its recent catastrophic past, as a model for its own future incorporation into German society. Riva Kastoryano has stated it most succinctly: in Germany, Turkish immigrants 'take Jews as a concrete example of a minority, in terms of history and organisation' (Kastoryano, 2002: 131). The following three episodes are exemplary in this regard.

Case 1

In the latter part of 2004, with the discussion on Turkey's admission to the European Union as backdrop, a debate developed in Germany regarding the alleged unassimilability of the Turkish/Muslim minority in German society, and the evolution of a Turkish/Muslim 'parallel society'.[3] On the occasion of awarding former President Johannes Rau the annual *Preis für Verständigung und Toleranz* (Prize for Understanding and Tolerance), Chancellor Gerhard Schröder gave the valedictory speech. Pointedly, in a symbolism that could not be missed, Schröder appealed to the Turkish minority to integrate into German society; he made this appeal at the Jewish Museum in Berlin where the award was presented.[4]

Case 2

In its edition of 23 September 2004, the German magazine *Der stern* published a cartoon showing a heavily moustached Turkish man crawling through a cat hole of a door named 'European Union', trying to gain entry into Europe. On the top of the cat hole is imitation Arabic writing in the shape of a verse. While the German public took little note of this racially stereotyped cartoon, an uproar surged in the Turkish community. Vural Öger, a prominent German-Turkish businessman and parliamentarian, wrote an open letter to *Der stern* calling the caricature defamatory, obscene and welcome material in neo-Nazi propaganda. Öger closed his letter as follows:

> A young Turkish man with a German passport, not only born but also raised here had heard about Hitler's beginnings in history class and said that this drawing was just like the ones in (the Nazi paper) *Der Stürmer*. Except that the Jews would have received different noses. Here in the *stern*, the nose was replaced by the moustache. But everything else is the same racist garbage. (*Hürriyet*, 2 October 2004)

In short, this event highlights how both a German Turk and a German political leader use the German-Jewish trope as an instrument either antagonistically towards the Turkish minority – or as one against the German political and media establishment.

Case 3

On 22 November 2002, the *Türkischer Bund Berlin-Brandenburg* (Berlin-Brandenburg Turkish[5] Federation, hereafter TBB) organized a commemoration in Berlin for the tenth anniversary of the Mölln pogrom, one of several racially motivated fire bombings that have occurred in Germany since the fall of the Berlin Wall. On the night of 23 November 1992, Nazi skinheads firebombed a house in the northern German town of Mölln. In the fire, three members of a Turkish family were burned to death: a 51-year-old woman, her 10-year-old grandchild and her 14-year-old nephew. This attack and others in Solingen, Rostock and elsewhere brought about a broadly based movement of protest in Germany; it drew attention to the increasing number of racist attacks against immigrants. In 1993, Turkish shop owners in Berlin closed down their shops for one hour and hung banners in their windows that demanded safety and equal rights for immigrants in Germany.

The parallels to the commemoration of Crystal Night, the November pogroms against the Jews in 1938, were apparent.[6] The Mölln commemoration began with the laying of a bouquet of flowers at the *Mahnmal für die Opfer von Krieg und Gewaltherrschaft* (Memorial for the Victims of War and Tyranny), the central German national memorial on Unter den Linden in Berlin; this memorial commemorates an array of victims, ranging from fallen German soldiers and the civilian victims of Allied bombings, to the anti-Nazi resistance and the Jewish victims of genocide.

The ceremony then moved to Berlin's City Hall. Guests included the Minister of Health for the Land of Berlin, Dr Heidi Knake-Werner, and Leah Rosh, chair of the *Förderkreis zur Errichtung eines Denkmals für die ermordeten Juden Europas* (the Sponsoring Committee for the Establishment of a Memorial for the Murdered Jews of Europe), as well as the President of the Berlin Senate, the former mayor of Berlin, Walter Momper. Leaders of the Jewish community and the Jewish Cultural Association were in the front rows. As the spokesman of the TBB, Safter Çinar, began his speech, it was apparent that the presence of people from the Jewish community was not coincidental.

Çinar's speech employed the Jewish trope: he invoked the history of Jewish-German relations in order to assert that German Turks are Germans: Çinar compared the pogrom in Mölln to anti-Semitic events in Germany during Nazism. Reminding the audience of the Holocaust, he emphasized that German Turks, as residents of Germany, should be ready to shoulder this part of German history. Here, Çinar referred to former chancellor Helmut Kohl's much quoted statement, *Gnade der späten Geburt* (grace of late birth), that the new generation of Germans is not responsible for the anti-Semitic German past because they were not alive at the time. Çinar, associating himself with a left-liberal German position, emphasized that there is neither a grace of late birth nor is there a grace of foreign birthplace. According to him, if Turks want to be residents of Germany, they are responsible for German history and must therefore take German national memory upon themselves:

> As residents of this country, we must share responsibility for this past crime. I don't know how to define this share – maybe it doesn't need any definition – we must take on our share of responsibility. And we must be ready to carry this responsibility with us. Ladies and gentlemen, I would like to formulate it as follows: there can be no grace of late birth . . . and there can be no grace of another birthplace. (Speech of Safter Çinar, Spokesperson of the TBB, 23 November 2002, City Hall, Berlin)[7]

The three cases that we have summarized here each contain the Jewish narrative and tell us how that narrative is employed. By the 'Jewish narrative' we mean a repertoire of elements of the Jewish story, entailing the Jewish minority status and the history of Jews in Germany, particularly the Shoah. Here, with case 1, Chancellor Schröder appealed to Muslims/Turks – in Germany the vast majority of Muslims are Turkish – to integrate into German society, an appeal made against the backdrop of the Jewish Museum and on the occasion of awarding a prize for 'understanding and tolerance'; in Germany, these two terms invariably evoke the Jewish question and anti-Semitism; and indeed, former president Rau received the award primarily for his involvement with the Jewish community and Israel as well as for his fight against anti-Semitism.

The backdrop, then, is Jewish, and the first message to the Muslims/Turks is to take the historic Jewish integration into German society – albeit imagined and romanticized – as a model. The second message is: we Germans are doing our share as we have proven with our good deeds against anti-Semitism and racism. Now the ball is in your, the Turkish, court: you have to do your share. The association with the Jews and the Jewish narrative is therefore apparent.

Case 2 appears like an anticipated response to Schröder: the reaction to the anti-Turkish caricatures in *Der stern* demonstrates that German Turks are not only knowledgeable about the German-Jewish narrative, but that they have learned to use it effectively as well. Accusing Germans of anti-Turkish racism per se is only partly effective. Rhetorically far more effective is to associate Turkish concerns with those of the Jews, because Turkish intellectuals find that they are being listened to when parallels are drawn to the Jews because the German environment is sensitive to these comparisons. This case, then, also represents the fundamental use of the Jewish narrative by the Turkish leadership. Additionally, we also see how the Orientalism in this cartoon parallels Nazi propaganda against Jews: the 'Jewish vermin' creeping into German society.

With the third example, we see two partly contradictory elements. On the one hand, with the Mölln commemoration, Turkish leaders are creating a precise congruence, if not equation, with contemporary Jewry and the Jewish narrative. Yet at the same time, by assuming responsibility for German history and the Holocaust, Turks put themselves squarely into German shoes. There is no more forceful manner in which to manifest solidarity with Germans than to commemorate the Nazi crimes. By the same token, it underlines how important an element the Holocaust, and what we call the 'Jewish narrative', has become to German national identity. In short, case 1 demonstrates, as one of many examples, the ubiquity of the Jewish narrative in the German national self-definition – a self-definition which the political leadership also imposes on the new immigrants; case 2 and case 3 show how Turkish organizations have taken on the Jewish narrative as homologous to their own predicament, thus attempting to equate themselves with the Jewish minority; yet at the same time, the Turkish leadership may also use the Jewish narrative in order to buttress its status as 'normal' German citizens within German society.

Ideological labour: minority narratives

The idea of the narratives that are being articulated by minorities and, possibly, by immigrants refers back to the notion of ideological labour that minorities engage in (Bodemann, 1996a, 1996b). Most generally, the otherness of the other manifests itself in economic, cultural and social practices that establish difference: the difference between the other and the dominant group. Typically, the practices of the other are seen as inferior or refer to counter-values: the other has no proper language but a 'jargon' and engages in stigmatized or 'impure' activities, such as Jewish usury in the Middle Ages or (Jewish) leather tanning in India and, broadly, holds on to 'inferior' religious beliefs, such as those of the Yezidi, the 'devil worshippers' in Turkey.

All these practices run counter to those of the dominant group and, by doing so, affirm those of the dominant group; as such we describe them as ideological labour. Ideological labour, then, is a circumscribed activity that is being performed by a subaltern group. African-American cultural practices, for example, are constructed by dominant white surroundings as instinct-driven and slothful, in contrast to the puritanical culture of (white) American society at large. On the other hand, by their sheer presence in American society as well as through their struggles within it, African-Americans confirm a basic American tenet that 'all men are created equal' as a visible sign that slavery and inequality based upon race are a past that has been overcome in the US. Similarly, the ideological labour of Jews in German society today encompasses the role of 'guardians of memory', not merely on their own behalf but also on behalf of their German surroundings. The presence of Jews evokes the glorious German Jewish pre-1933 past; their presence in Germany today is 'proof' that Nazism has been overcome and that German society is now truly democratic and tolerant of outsiders.

Immigrants and minorities are different in this regard: as a rule, minorities may be bearers of national memory while immigrants, more recently settled in a new environment, are not (yet). The ideological labour of immigrants is less differentiated than that of minorities, most of all because they lack deeper roots and a history in common with the receiving country. We would argue that often, however, immigrants choose specific historical minorities as models in order to negotiate their incorporation within an existing politico-historical paradigm. It is therefore not sufficient to analyse macro structures, such as the political structure of the receiving country and majority–minority relations. Instead, we must develop a framework that distinguishes between different types of minorities and one that explores the range of immigrant and minority relations. This in turn allows us to identify strategies immigrants create in order to incorporate into mainstream society.

However, as we shall illustrate, the difference between immigrants and minorities is not always clear cut. For one thing, the various groups of immigrants do not necessarily incorporate into the host society in the same unilinear and developmental fashion; for example, ethnic Germans from the former Soviet Union are incorporated quite differently compared to the Russian Jews who enter the country as *Kontingentflüchtlinge* (quota refugees); middle-class immigrants behave differently from lower-class or peasant migrants. In some cases, second and third generation children of immigrants still consider themselves 'foreigners', as do migrants to European countries such as France, the Netherlands or

Germany (Pogge, 2003). Similarly, when immigrants find themselves ghettoized or where their religious background is distinct from the receiving society, their reconstruction as a minority is more likely. German Turks fit that case: the new immigrant group associates with an established minority and is claiming that how they are being treated by their surroundings parallels racism directed against an older minority in that country. At the same time, rivalries often develop between minorities and more recent immigrants (Lipset and Raab, 1970). All these differences and rivalries between minority and/or immigrant groups demonstrate a relationship that is normally overlooked in the literature. In order to bring these into discussion, we will briefly introduce the Jewish and Turkish communities in Germany.

German Jews versus German Turks

The Jews

Obtaining German citizenship, a difficult process for other immigrant groups, is not as complicated for many Jews.[8] German law facilitates the acquisition of citizenship for former German citizens (and their descendants), Jews mostly, who were persecuted during the Nazi period – irrespective of which other citizenships they may hold (*Grundgesetz* Article 116 para. 2). Moreover, on account of the Holocaust, special conditions have been set up to encourage Jewish immigration to Germany. These new Jewish immigrants are eligible to apply for expedited citizenship.

New Jewish immigrants in Germany, mostly from Russia, are redefining the meaning of Jewishness in Germany on account of their own traditions, beliefs, as well as social settings and popular culture (Kaminer, 2000; Bodemann, 2005). Being challenged by these new settlers, the pre-war German Jews who returned to Germany and the Polish Jews who settled in Germany after the war are questioning how 'Jewish' the Russian Jews really are. Many Russian Jews are suspected of having fake papers or being part of the Russian mafia (Kaminer, 2000), and racist narratives against Russian Jews are common among Germans and the settled Jews alike.[9]

Prior to the influx of Soviet Jewish migrants into Germany, many argued that Germany would be the last country in which Jews would want to live (Fleischmann, 1986). Over the past decades, for example, Germany has been turned into a land of Holocaust memorials. Among these, the aforementioned Memorial for the Murdered Jews of Europe in Berlin occupies a site the size of two football fields across from the Brandenburg Gate and is surely one of the most valuable pieces, symbolically and materially, of real estate in Germany. Another site of memory, the Jewish Museum in Berlin, opened to the public in 2001. The building, designed by Jewish architect Daniel Libeskind, is attached to what was to become the Berlin Museum, with passageways that symbolize that Jewish history is embedded in the history of Berlin (Young, 2004). The small population of Jews in Germany notwithstanding, the Jewish past exists primarily as museums and monuments in Germany today (Bodemann, 1996a, 1996b), albeit often under police protection and sometimes surrounded by barbed wire (Legge Jr., 2003).

Today, however, German Jews are no longer 'sitting on packed suitcases' and especially for Russian Jews, Germany has become an attractive country to live in. National Jewish organizations are thriving, such as the *Zentralrat der Juden* or the *Zentralwohlfahrtsstelle* (Jewish social services), local Jewish congregations (*Jüdische Gemeinden*), community organizations and cultural centres in Berlin and elsewhere (for example the *Jüdische Kulturverein*), newspapers (for example, *Jüdische Allgemeine*), bookstores, synagogues, restaurants, cemeteries and museums. Local congregations have the church tax collected by the state from Jewish community members in order to finance the communities. The *Zentralrat der Juden*, some rabbis and community leaders enjoy national political recognition, and the *Jüdische Kulturverein* in Berlin and other Jewish groups organize Jewish cultural events. Moreover, Jews are entitled to practise *shechita*, the religious slaughtering of animals, and have their own religious schools. As they maintain a certain level of institutional separateness, however, it is questionable how or whether they feel at home in Germany, and some of the discussions in Berlin's Jewish Cultural Association (*Jüdischer Kulturverein*) debate whether a Jew should also call him/herself a German.[10]

German Turks

Seventeen years after the Jews had been exterminated in the concentration camps, Turks[11] started to migrate to Germany. After the Second World War, when Germany needed a labour force to rebuild the country, the government decided to import labour from nearby countries like Turkey (Çağlar, 1994). Turkish migrant workers were usually unskilled or semi-skilled peasants who were running away from the lack of choice, scarcity of land, unemployment and limited social services at home (Berger, 1975). Some of them managed to reunite with their families after the family reunification law of 1972, while others decided to stay permanently in Germany, leaving their families behind in Turkey (Brouwer and Prister, 1983). By 1980, there were approximately 115 000 Turkish people living in Berlin alone (Greve, 2001: 30).

Since the introduction of a new citizenship law (*Staatsangehörigkeitsgesetz*) in 2000, the German state has partially discarded the idea of *ius sanguinis* (law based on ancestral origin), and has started naturalizing the migrant population (Joppke, 2003). According to the *Staatsangehörigkeitsgesetz*, immigrant children born in Germany after the year 2000 are granted German citizenship in addition to their parents' native citizenship. In order to be granted German citizenship, however, a child born in Germany has to give up the citizenship of his/her parents' native country between the ages of 16 and 23 (Schirmer, 2002; Joppke, 1998 and 2003; Beauftragte der Bundesregierung für Migration, Flüchtlinge und Integration, 2000). According to December 2002 estimates, 7.34 million migrants live in Germany, with the Turks representing the largest group at 1.998 million (Statistisches Bundesamt in TBB, 2003). According to the 2003 estimates, there were 565 766 Turks with German citizenship in Germany (Statistisches Bundesamt, and the TBB, 2003), approximately one quarter of the whole Turkish immigrant population.

With the collapse of the Berlin Wall, a chaotic social environment and cheap labour from East Germany led to mass unemployment among Turks in western parts of Berlin (Joppke, 2003). Thus, after 1989, many Turks who had come to Germany as workers in the 1960s and 1970s became increasingly dependent on welfare. Now, 18 per cent or more of Turks in Berlin are unemployed (Landesarbeitsamt, Statistisches Landesamt, 1997). In February 2000, the Federal Commissioner for Foreigners, Marieluise Beck, stated that 'the unemployment rate among migrants remains at almost 20 per cent, demonstrating that foreigners continue to be subject to unemployment twice as often as Germans' (European Forum for Migration Studies, 2000).

The problem of unemployment is exacerbated by discrimination against immigrant children in the education system. Second and third generation German citizens of Turkish background and Turkish immigrant children complain that they are not given equal opportunity in the education system (Am Orde, 2002): 'While only 8 per cent of German young people and adults remain without vocational training, the rate of unskilled Turkish young people is five times higher, at about 40 per cent' (The Federal Government's Commissioner for Foreigners' Issues, 2000).

Racism, anti-Semitism: the 9/11 fallout

As elsewhere in the Western world, the attack on the World Trade Center cast a dark shadow on all Muslims in Germany and at the same time, paradoxically perhaps, intensified anti-Semitism: interethnic relations in general, then, were affected. On the one hand, many Muslims, Turkish Muslims included, accused Jews of being responsible for 9/11. Just after the attack, many of them adopted a widely held conspiracy theory that the Jews working in the World Trade Center were informed beforehand about planes crashing into the towers, and therefore they did not show up for work on that day (Lerner, 2002). German Turks, like Turks back home, however, are a diverse group; many Western-oriented Turkish Muslims have been sympathetic to Jews whereas others have sided with Arabs against the Jews on account of Israeli policies against Palestinians. Therefore, the aftermath of 9/11 also increased solidarity between Turks and Jews in Germany, as many Turks distanced themselves from Arab immigrants.

While both Arabs and Turks are Muslim peoples, Turkey, on account of the Kemalist modernization, has always wanted to be considered as a part of the West. The policies of recent Turkish governments[12] have been cautiously pro-Israel and tendentiously anti-Arab. Turks have collaborated with Israel on many occasions, including the 1999 capture of the Kurdish leader Öcalan in Kenya (*Turkish Daily News*, 18 February 1999; Rubin, 2001).

Anti-Arab sentiments in Turkey were exacerbated by the 2003 synagogue bombings in Istanbul (*Hürriyet*, 15 November 2003). In order to protest against the bombings, a group of immigrants in Berlin on the anniversary of the Mölln pogrom on 22 November organized a *Migrantische Initiative gegen Antisemitismus* (Migrants' Initiative against Anti-Semitism). Emphasizing that the Jews were not alone in their struggle against anti-Semitism, the Migrants' Initiative organized a demonstration to show their solidarity with Jews in Germany (Migrantische Initiative gegen Antisemitismus, 2003). The spokesperson of the TBB, Safter Çinar, sent a note to *Jüdisches Berlin* (the monthly bulletin of the Jewish Community in Berlin), saying that Turks were in solidarity with the members of Berlin's Jewish community (TBB, 2003).

The next issue of the *Jüdisches Berlin* published interviews and articles by Turks and Turkish Jews, as well as photographs from a joint *Chanukah* party that was organized by the *Jüdischer Kulturverein* (Jüdischer Kulturverein, 2004). The articles and interviews refer to the days of the Ottoman Empire and its *millet* system in which the Turkish/Muslim majority coexisted peacefully with Jews and other ethnic and religious minorities (Tulgan, 2004). It further emphasized that Jews who fled Germany after 1933, and after 1492 from the Spanish Inquisition, found shelter as refugees in the Ottoman Empire and Turkey, respectively (Shaw, 1991). Thus, the *Jüdisches Berlin* condemned the synagogue bombings in Istanbul and provided public space for Turks to show their solidarity with Jews (Yilmaz, 2004).

The Jewish master narrative: the common ground against racism and anti-Semitism

The 9/11 fallout, then, posed a twofold challenge to the Turkish leadership in Germany: they had to avoid being painted with the anti-Arab/anti-Muslim brush, while at the same time they had to combat anti-Semitism in their own ranks which had assumed a new intensity among both Turkish immigrants and the radical Right. Among the Right, the increased anti-Semitism came along with increased racism against Muslims. Neo-Nazi graffiti such as 'What the Jews have behind them is what is still to come for the Turks' (Kastoryano, 2002: 132) virtually forced Turkish-German leaders into an alliance with Jews, according to the theorem, 'the enemies of my enemies are my friends'. Accordingly, a photo, taken during a street protest in Berlin, and displayed at the Jewish Museum in Berlin during a short-term exhibition on Jewish history in Germany, responds to this slogan: a group of Turkish immigrants carry a banner, which reads, 'We don't want to be the Jews of tomorrow'.[13] In other words, the neo-Nazis use the Jewish narrative negatively and the immigrants respond by employing the cultural repertoire[14] of German-Jewish relations positively and for their own objectives.

The TBB, as a Turkish secular and social-democratically oriented immigrant association, employs the Jewish narrative to show that racism in Germany today is an extension of anti-Semitic history. The parallel between Jewish and Turkish associations is marked in the aspirations of the TBB which aims to attract young German Turks to its membership. The TBB wants to challenge its organizational concept and rid itself of the image of an ethnic organization, thereby also trying to find common ground with Jewish groups. This common ground is the relationship between anti-Semitism and racism and being a minority in Germany. The spokesperson of the TBB, Safter Çinar, comments:

> Many young German Turks would like to be involved in German society, German political parties and institutions. We will lose these young people if we fall into the trap of organizing only as an ethnic association. This is because we think of ourselves as ethnic immigrants. But our situation would change if we would organize around a social problem. There is a social problem [that is, *racism*] and we organize around it. (Interview with Safter Çinar, Spokesperson of the TBB, 3 November 2002)

Including the younger, German-born Turks in Turkish immigrant associations is important because as Safter Çinar argues, it would help transform a current ethnic association into a non-governmental organization (NGO) that fights social problems such as racism. It would do away with the idea of a separatist Turkish community and strive towards an assimilated Turkish community involved in, and concerned with, Germany's problem of racism. Just as German Jews are united against anti-Semitism, German Turks would be united against racism towards Turks.

In various anti-Semitic incidents, the TBB has shown solidarity with the Jewish community in Berlin. One example of the collaboration between these two associations occurred during the 2002 federal elections, when the Free Democratic Party (FDP) politician, Jamal Karsli, compared Israel's tactics in the West Bank to 'Nazi methods'. The vice-president of the party, Jürgen Möllemann, went on to offend a leader of the *Zentralrat der Juden*, Michel Friedman, by stating that Friedman's behaviour inspires anti-Semitism. With these anti-Israel and anti-Semitic political tactics, Karsli and Möllemann clearly hoped that their party would gain right-wing German and Muslim votes in Germany (*The New York Times*, 7 June 2002). But in response, the TBB joined members of the Jewish community in front of the FDP's party centre to protest against the anti-Semitic election campaign (Cziesche and Schmidt, 2002). The European edition of a major Turkish newspaper severely condemned Möllemann's anti-Semitic campaign aimed at attracting Muslim votes (*Hürriyet* European Edition, 10 June 2002).

In return for a showing of solidarity, the TBB received a positive response from the Jewish community in Berlin. The aforementioned Mölln commemoration is an example of Jewish support being given to the Turkish community. Leading Jewish representatives, for example, attended the event and brought greetings on behalf of their organizations. Moreover, when the TBB established the *Antidiskriminierungsnetzwerk* (network against discrimination) to influence the preparation of the new anti-discrimination law and then organized a seminar to inform the public about this law, some members of the Jewish community were present. In this and other similar projects, the TBB has cooperated with the *Jüdische Gemeinde zu Berlin* against discrimination and racism (*Hürriyet* European Edition, 17 July 2001).

The Jewish model from immigrant to diaspora

While the TBB, as we have seen, attempts to form an alliance with the Jewish community and employs the Jewish narrative in its substance, the *Cemaat*, one of its religious counterparts, employs Jewishness as form: it focuses on, and emulates, the Jewish institutional structure in order to receive recognition for Muslim religious rights in Germany.[15] Accordingly, for the first time, (Turkish) Muslims see themselves as a Diaspora and are looking for models of diasporic life. The vice-chair of the Central Council of Muslims in Germany, for example, recently observed that Muslims are lacking a theology of integration. The old scriptures rarely if ever gave directions on how to behave in non-Muslim societies.[16]

Jewish institutional structures are used as models for religious Turkish associations in order to achieve the type of community solidarity and collective unity they believe to be present in the Jewish associations. Although Jewish organizations have different interests and are often in conflict, these conflicts are not readily apparent to the mass media or to outsiders. Unaware of possible contention within Jewish associations, the executive committee member of the *Cemaat*, Ahmet Yilmaz, not necessarily a friend of Jews, glorifies their imagined strong fellowship:

> I wish from Allah that no other nation would live the difficulties that the Jewish nation had experienced, but [I wish from Allah that he would] provide their solidarity to everyone. There is a Jewish community that speaks for all Jews. My heart wishes that all Turkish organizations will come together under the same roof, and keep equal distance to all [German political] parties. (Interview with Ahmet Yilmaz, Executive Committee Member of the *Türkische Gemeinde zu Berlin*, 8 May 2003)

Although Yilmaz's yearnings have not been realized, his organization, the *Cemaat*, has modelled its organizational structure on the Jewish community in Berlin, in both its hierarchy and its religious orientation. The original name of the *Cemaat*, *Türkische Gemeinde zu Berlin*, is also inspired by the Jewish community's official name, *Jüdische Gemeinde zu Berlin*.[17]

Some leaders of the *Cemaat* openly state that they demand religious rights similar to those of Jews. They argue that the German state authorities should recognize the religious and national differences of Sunnite Turkish immigrants.[18] The *Cemaat* and other religious Turkish associations demand permission for 'ritual slaughtering of animals, permission for the Islamic call to prayer in public, provisions for burial according to the Islamic rite'.[19] One important difference between the Jewish and Muslim associations is their fiscal status. While churches and synagogues – as *Körperschaften* in public law – receive *Kirchensteuer*, that is, taxes collected by the state on their behalf, the mosques do not have this privilege. This issue causes major resentment among Muslims in Germany (Laurence, 2001), in particular as their number far exceeds the number of Jews; they are, however, not unified enough to establish political lobbies and to demand status as KdöR (*Körperschaft des öffentlichen Rechts*).

The most striking examples of religious claims-making and the use of the Jewish narrative involve issues such as the disputes over religious education of Turkish Muslim children, the wearing of the headscarf in public places, and the struggle over the right to eat religiously processed meat (*halal*). The religious education of Turkish immigrant children in Germany has been a much-debated problem for years. While Quran reciting courses[20] for children are legally allowed as a community service in many Sunnite mosques, the *Cemaat* is also lobbying to have Islam classes in German schools.[21] Jews, however, are allowed to have their own religious education, including high schools in Germany.

Along with the problematic practice of teaching Islam courses in secondary schools, a controversial public debate erupted over whether Muslim women teachers could attend classes wearing the traditional headscarves (known as *başörtü* or *türban* in Turkish) in public services and schools.[22] A decision in the constitutional court of Germany in 2003 left it up to the individual *Länder* (federal states) to legally enact a ban on wearing the headscarf in schools. Most German *Länder* were in favour of the ban, particularly the states that are governed by the conservative CDU/CSU party such as Baden-Württemberg (*Deutsche Welle*, 25 September 2003).

Turkish immigrant organizations are divided on these two issues. On the one hand, during a public controversy about wearing the headscarf in schools in late 2003, the religious immigrant organizations, such as the *Cemaat*, played the multiculturalism card and argued that immigrants' religious and cultural differences should be regarded as political rights, and therefore Muslim women should not be prevented from practising their religion in the public sphere. Indeed, until recently, it would have been unthinkable to ask a Jewish man, for example, to remove his *kippa* in Germany. This double standard, tolerating Jewish practices while opposing Turkish ones, is another reason why Turks have first associated themselves with Jews, and asked for equal recognition in public. The secular immigrant organizations, such as the TBB, on the other hand, identifying with the Jacobin tenets of the Turkish constitution, supported the ban on all religious symbols in public.

Granting *halal*, the ritual slaughtering of animals, has been an important cultural struggle for Turkish immigrants in Germany. *Halal* slaughter requires cutting the animal's throat with a sharp knife and then draining the blood from the vessels. This contradicts the German regulation requiring the stunning of animals by electric shock before slaughter. Although Jews are allowed to practise similar slaughtering, known as *shechita*, the situation for Turks becomes controversial, especially before the Ramadan Feast that requires a mass sacrifice and ritual slaughtering of certain animals, such as sheep and cattle.

Recently, a Turkish butcher, Rüstem Altinküpe, struggled to provide *halal* meat to his clients during Ramadan (*Evrensel Daily Newspaper* in Turkish, European Edition, 16 January 2002). He was supported by various Turkish and Muslim associations and organizations, who claimed it was their right to practise their religion in Germany. After days of public campaigning in the media and bureaucratic struggles with German authorities, the butcher, through the Muslim community, gained the right to slaughter animals according to *halal*, although under very strict conditions.[23]

Obviously, this is not simply about slaughtering animals and eating meat; it is about practising the laws of one's religion, something that the churches and the Jews are free to do in Germany. While Jews and Muslims are often in opposition to each other, Turkish Muslims point to the parallel with German Jews to claim their religious rights from the German state. Mustafa Y., the head of the law office of Milli Görüş, finds it natural to work with the German Jewish community on this and similar subjects.[24] For example, he once participated in a public debate to defend the Muslims' rights to slaughter animals according to Islamic ritual in Nordrhein-Westfalen:

> I have talked to them [panellists] for hours. I gave them all rational arguments. They are arguing harshly against us. [They say] you have to integrate into this society. So for them, my arguments are invalid. Then the rabbi, sitting next to me, started to talk. He said 'you [Germans] have no right to speak. You have massacred my ancestors.' Then the Germans were quiet. They couldn't say anything. But this is his [the rabbi's] capital. They [Germans] killed six million people, they cannot dare to leave [while the rabbi is speaking]. It would be a scandal in the newspapers. [The Germans] listened to [the rabbi] until the end. When we left the meeting, I told him 'Thank you very much. This is how you do business. We don't know how to do it.' He said 'I know that these Germans have grudges against me. This is almost in

> their genes. The best thing that you can do is to stand close to us [Jews]. We can struggle [against Germans] together. Because our word is valid here, your word is not.' (Interview with Mustafa Y., of the law office in Milli Görüş, Cologne, 27 July 2004)

Turkish fragmentation and the myth of Jewish unity

It has been argued that if 'Turks had more unified central organisations lobbying local governments, they might benefit to the same extent as Jews from funding for religious and cultural activity' (Laurence, 1999: 6). In the German corporately oriented democracy, German state authorities would welcome a strong representation by Turkish immigrant organizations that could represent their common interest – and discipline the Turkish community; but Turkish immigrant organizations are far from unified. The controversy around the headscarf is one example: the TBB campaigns are strongly against the use of the headscarf in public; the *Cemaat* on the other hand supports it – not by holding public campaigns but by providing social services for women with headscarves or assisting them with employment. As a result of this Turkish fragmentation, German state authorities play down the role of immigrant organizations as their interlocutors (while at the same time ignoring the fragmentations in the Jewish community).

Some political leaders of the Turkish immigrant communities, such as the foreigner's commissioner of Tempelhof-Schöneberg borough in Berlin, Emine Demirbüken, resent the political disunity among Turkish immigrant associations. She draws parallels between the Jewish community and the young Turks and stresses that it is essential to demonstrate the economic and intellectual potential of Turks to German society:

> The Jewish community combines its members' economic power with their brain power. Turks also have economic power here. We have many people who are bilingual, who can speak perfect German and Turkish. Why can't we combine our economic power with our brain power? Why don't we show our power to the Germans? Why can't we force them to take us seriously? If we don't do this, then they will always stereotype us as members of a society who do not want to learn German, whose women are battered by their husbands, and whose daughters are locked up at home. (Emine Demirbüken, foreigner's commissioner of Tempelhof-Schöneberg Municipality in Berlin, 4 March 2003)

Demirbüken argues that a consolidation of its organizational structures would lead to a change in the Turkish guest-worker stereotype. Despite their economic achievements, many Turks in Germany still pursue traditional practices such as violence against women and conservative child rearing habits. Moreover, many Turkish immigrants, forcibly and voluntarily, are isolated from German society and do not speak German, a problem Germans today decry as the *Parallelgesellschaft*. However, younger Turks are better educated, have better language and social skills than their immigrant parents, and according to Demirbüken, Germans will take the Turkish community more seriously when they have to deal with young German Turks as their counterparts in the immigrant associations. Just as in the Jewish associations, she looks for economically and socially capable people to be in the Turkish frontline.

The Jewish-Turkish (mis-)match: a literary excursion

We have argued in this chapter that social scientists have rarely looked at the ways in which immigrant groups orient their behaviour towards those who arrived before them; both immigrants and minorities model themselves on other minority or immigrant groups; in fact it is one way in which societal structures are reproduced and which gives ethno-cultural communities, globalization notwithstanding, their own character within particular nation-states. As we have demonstrated, Turkish leaders certainly have taken note of Jewish communal behaviour, and Jewish leaders have done the same vis-à-vis the Turks.

The presence of prominent Jews at some Turkish commemorative events such as the Mölln commemoration described above, however, should be seen in perspective: the Jewish presence on such occasions is still minimal overall, and while Jews are an important reference point for German Turks, Turks play a minimal role in Jewish debates except by default, as fellow targets of neo-Nazism[25] and as a religious community with occasionally or potentially similar political and legal claims. This pertains especially to seeing the religious needs of the respective communities recognized by the German state.

Nevertheless, individual Jews and Jewish organizations are playing an important role in the fight against racism, neo-Nazism and in fostering closer relations with the Turkish and/or larger Muslim community. One of these organizations is the *Amadeu Antonio Stiftung*, a foundation started by Annetta Kahane in Berlin, following some racially motivated killings by neo-Nazi skinheads; the other, the *Jüdische Kulturverein*, founded by Irene Runge, caters mostly to Russian immigrants and East German Jews, also in Berlin. It is indicative, however, that – probably on account of their East German Jewish background – both women have remained marginal to the Jewish leadership in Berlin and the Jewish community in Germany at large. Culturally, and in terms of class, Turks and Jews inhabit different worlds: most Jews are solidly middle class, in many if not most cases with higher secondary and often some university education. A small but significant number of Jews are recognized public intellectuals in Germany.

Most Turks, on the other hand, arrived as guest workers and are proletarianized peasants with minimal education; as Navid Kermani has observed,[26] in contrast to Britain and France, virtually no Muslim elites have arrived in Germany and even among most German-born Turks and Muslims at large, class and education are still clearly distinct from that of the Jews. Nevertheless, a small but significant stratum of educated, middle-class Turks has evolved, very much at the level of their Jewish counterparts, even though they still inhabit different worlds and their encounters with Jews are few and far between.

Still, given the uneasy relations between Jews and Germans after the Holocaust, the Turks would be natural partners for the Jews, as the 'other others' in German society, without, however, the grave historical baggage of German Jewry. German Turks are also not the grandchildren of the perpetrators which therefore should make for a more easygoing relationship between the two minorities. The Jewish writer Maxim Biller has conjured up that solidarity between minorities and immigrants against German majority society (Biller, 2001: 86ff.). Navid Kermani, a German-born intellectual of Iranian background has occasionally delineated the path German-Turkish intellectuals might pursue in the future. In a recent essay on German literature, for example, Kermani sees the German cultural formation of Franz Kafka and the German writers in exile, mostly Jewish and at the margins, as his own – a home for his own writing (Kermani, 2006).

At present, from the Turkish side, the goal of being recognized by the German majority society is more important than being recognized by Jews, and alliances with Jews are fraught with ambiguity. For Anatolian 'oriental' Islamists, for example, Jews, on account of Israel, are the prime enemy of Islam and anti-Semitism is rampant there. European secular-oriented Turks as well as moderate modern religious ones on the other hand, recognize a certain affinity: as Kemalists in Turkey and as Zionists in Israel, both groups are seen as European outposts in an 'oriental' and mostly Arab world; and in Germany, the Jews provide a model of minority–majority relations. Turks are not always cognizant of the historically unusual role of the Jews.

On the Jewish side, two novels come to mind in which Turks play a significant role. The first novel is by Doron Rabinovici (1997), born in 1961 in Israel and living in Vienna. In his novel, *Suche nach M.*, a surrealistic mystery novel, Rabinovici focuses on the lives of two young Jewish men whose parents were Holocaust survivors from Eastern Europe. One central chapter in the novel describes one of the two Jewish protagonists' fleeting encounters with Gülgün. Gülgün was Dani Morgenthau's fellow student; presumably upper middle class from Istanbul, she attended the German School there. She then studied economics in an unnamed German-speaking country and never wanted to return to Turkey. Dani was attracted to her but too shy to make a move; at the time, she had a German lover who was a law student. Later, she married Yilmaz, a waiter and musician, obviously below her social class and whom 'she would never have taken note of ... in Istanbul'. Eventually, Yilmaz is accused of shooting a fellow Turk in a bar in the red light and gambling area of the city. At the trial, the judge, an insincere friend of minorities, both Turks and Jews, describes it as a 'Turkish story', a strategy of ghettoizing that the judge would otherwise employ in relation to the Jews. At the trial, years after meeting Yilmaz with Gülgün, Morgenthau, now a juror, meets Yilmaz again in court.

The Turkish and Jewish communities are associated in other ways as well: the red light and gambling milieu with Turks alludes to similar East European Jewish milieux after the Shoah in Germany; the non-Jewish environment is similarly prejudiced towards Turks as it is towards Jews; and both the Jew Dani and Yilmaz, the Turk and accused murderer, live in the harmonies and 'echoes of alien melodies'. Similar to Jews, as well, Gülgün wanted to be 'cosmopolitan' – but for others, she was only mundane, bereft of her own traditions. In this novel, then, Turks play a peripheral, yet often kindred role for the Jews; too distant, however, for a relationship such as that between Gülgün and Dani Morgenthau to materialize.

Maxim Biller's novel *Esra* follows a similar triadic form. It is the story of the narrator's unhappy love for a Turkish woman, daughter of a difficult, domineering and prominent mother. Esra is, or is imagined to be, a Dönme, of Jewish descent – a point which is of such great significance to the storyteller that to him, the future of the relationship may even depend on it. With Esra, the storyteller establishes an imagined pure Germany: both of them speak a classical German without the flat colloquialisms of their German surroundings, and it is important to both that they are different: 'It was clear to us that we ourselves were different – which is why we were also convinced that we would do much better in another country' (p. 88). Their relationship seems to function best outside Germany, and Esra's Turkish hometown reminds him of Israel. Nevertheless, probably afraid of more complications in an unsettled relationship and her questionable Jewish background, the storyteller does not want to risk getting Esra pregnant; and because he does not want to allow more chaos in his life, she remarks that 'sometimes, you are very German', which he counters by saying that 'you ... you are very oriental'. Their common position towards their German environment, then, is fragile and they fall back into seeing each other as the 'other'. In the end, Esra's distant relationship to her husband, a German by the name of Frido, proves to be more solid; they already have a daughter together, and she is expecting a second child with him. The storyteller, then, is relegated to being an outside observer: he was also the witness at Esra's and Frido's wedding.

The Turkish-Jewish-German rivalry and triangle is not an issue with German Jews alone; Turks as well clearly and explicitly articulate this triangle. In Yadé Kara's *Selam Berlin*, for example, we have the story of Hasan, a young Kreuzberg ghetto kid who eventually is discovered by a film company. In the course of his new career he meets Cora, the partner of Wolf, a film director filming a movie in Kreuzberg. Cora and Hasan begin a passionate relationship of short duration. Subsequently, much to the chagrin of Hasan, Cora starts a new affair, this time with Vladimir, a (Jewish) violinist from Riga. In a racist incident, Hasan's friend is beaten up and Hasan cannot help but notice that Turkishness and Kreuzberg are no longer fashionable. To add to his dismay, Cora is now preparing a film with Wolf about Vladimir, the violin virtuoso and his new life in the West. Wolf finds that Jewish music, Jewish culture, is so much more exciting than Turkish culture: 'The Jews determine the direction now', and the Turkish theme has been overdone, 'the Turks cannot be integrated'. Hasan's own closest German or German-Turkish friends find Jewish culture more exciting and they discover the pre-Nazi world of 'simple, poor Jews' and are singing 'a Yemenite song', *Imin Alu* by Ofra Haza. Hasan, on the other hand, is taken as a Jew in a lower-class German pub, and attacked. He rides the subway back and forth and is reminded of a (Jewish) 'woman he once read about' who, during Crystal Night, took the subway from one end of the city to the other, in order not to draw attention to herself. In all these instances, Jewish history, that is, the Jewish narrative, serves as a model for Turkish existence in Germany.

Unquestionably, no other German author has written as trenchantly on the Turkish-Jewish-German triangle than Zafer Senoçak. Senoçak's novel *Gefährliche Verwandtschaft* explicitly articulates a triadic conversation, but does it differently from the other writers discussed above. The narrator, Sascha Muhteshem,[27] is the grandson of a Turkish man, probably complicit as a soldier in the American genocide during the First World War, and a prominent member of Kemal Atatürk's circle: but Sascha is also the grandson of a liberal Jewish businessman who with his wife and daughter – Sascha's mother – had to leave Munich during Nazism for exile in Turkey. In Istanbul, Sascha's German-Jewish mother and Kemalist father had met through their families. Significantly, Sascha was conceived in Turkey and born in Germany in 1954. Sascha himself had no identity (p. 47), and upon his return to Berlin in the 1990s from a lectureship in the US, announced that he wanted to discover his origins and no longer wanted to be 'rootless' (p. 118); Turkishness was merely 'another window in his house' (p. 107). He could have been a Jew and would have been more 'interesting' that way (p. 127).

Sascha is undoubtedly concerned with his Turkish grandfather's bourgeois heritage, but that heritage is thoroughly European; his use of Ottoman-Arabic and Russian-Cyrillic writing turns him into a mediator between cultures. The major theme of the novel is what Senoçak describes as the 'trialogue' between Turkishness, the Jewish and the German/Christian elements; Sascha is somewhere within this triangle: there is the Ottoman and European-oriented grandfather on the Turkish side, and the liberal-Jewish, enlightened grandfather on the German side, with the Christmas tree *de rigueur*. There is also the close, centuries-old fraternity between Jews and Turks, both of whom are hated by the Christians; Jews and Turks together are expelled from Thessaloniki, Jews are given a second home in Turkey during Nazism, whereas in Germany today, Jews are met with love-hatred and the Turks with hatred, pure and simple (p. 65). Jews and Turks are marked by a special relationship in Germany (p. 92), but Turks and Germans resemble each other far more than they would want to admit. Boldly, Sascha (or Senoçak) declares:

> In the Germany of today Jews and Germans no longer stand and face each other alone. Rather, a situation has arisen that corresponds to my personal heritage and situation. In Germany a trialogue is now emerging between Germans, Jews and Turks, between Christians, Jews and Muslims. The dissolution of the German-Jewish dichotomy could release both parties, Germans and Jews, from their traumatic experiences. But for that they would have to take the Turks into their sphere. (p. 89)[28]

On the one hand, then, what is suggested here is that the Turks are endowed with a German national mission, eventually relieving Germans of their historical burden in relation to the Jews. At the same time, the narrator dismisses that idea as a fantasy, 'when I am in a good mood'. His fantasy here is the vision of an egalitarian trialogue in which the Turkish element is recognized as an equal partner with the other two, which includes a recognition of the full value of the Turkish-Ottoman past; his vision, then, transcends the idea of the Jewish discourse as a model for German Turks, yet at the same time confirms it because he conceptualizes Turkish culture as a minoritarian culture in Germany on par with the Jewish one.

Conclusion

We have argued here that immigrant groups through their leadership take previously established minorities as master narratives and as political models in order to define their relations with the receiving state. Those narratives are the ideological labour provided by minorities for the state and its society. We have tried to show that the relationship between immigrant communities is important for understanding the process of immigrant integration in the receiving country: immigrant associations refer to the older minorities as models in order to prepare their own struggle against discrimination and then make political claims.

As we have seen, Turkish immigrants in Germany use the special position of German Jews in order to establish their own associational ties, map out discourses and strategies against racism, including anti-Semitism, and to make claims against German authorities. We have found that the secular Turkish organizations model their discourse on the German Jewish narrative, whereas the religious organizations attempt to emulate Jewish institutional structures in Germany.

There is no doubt that the Jewish case in Germany is a historically determined and specific case. Therefore, in order to understand the immigrant incorporation process, it is not sufficient to analyse majority–minority relations. We also need to look at how immigrants perceive themselves in relation to other minority groups, and how they draw upon historical patterns in the receiving country, patterns developed by and with established minorities. Our analysis of some Turkish and Jewish literary writing supports these findings: Turks and Jews see themselves in a triadic relation together with Germans, and Turks as the newcomers tend to look up to and emulate German Jewry in its relation to German society.

In the long term, it will be interesting to see whether the German Turkish leadership's attempt to adopt a narrative emulating that of the Jews will be an effective strategy in developing their relationship with the German state. Furthermore, there is at least the strong possibility that by emulating the Jews, the numerically strongest minority group in Germany will develop an alliance with the historically and symbolically most important minority in Germany. Given the incomparably greater numbers and the increasing economic and political clout of Turks, this alliance will be of interest to the Jewish community as well. An alliance, to be sure, that will have to be conflictual at times and full of obstacles. Greater unity among Turks and their organizations, the rise of the extreme Right, of concern to both Jews and Turks, and the rise of racism and anti-Semitism as we experience them today, may well expedite that type of coalition of the minorities.

Notes

1. The Jewish involvement with the Civil Rights Movement took a different form, however, and was largely 'altruistically' oriented, seen as assistance to the Black community. Nevertheless, working for civil rights at the time was important to the Jewish social position as well, in light of persistent discriminatory practices against Jews even in the 1960s. See Ezra Mendelsohn (1993), *On Modern Jewish Politics*, New York: Oxford University Press, pp. 133ff.
2. The authors would like to thank Leslie Adelson, Christian Joppke and Riva Kastoryano for their helpful comments on an earlier version of this chapter.
3. Most notorious among these was a cover story in *Der Spiegel*, 15 November 2004, entitled, 'Allahs rechtlose Töchter. Muslimische Frauen in Deutschland'. More at random, other articles include Navid Kermani in *Die Zeit*, 18 November 2004; Dick Pels in *Die Tageszeitung*, 23 November 2004; Pascal Beucker in *Die Tageszeitung*, 22 November 2004; Jens Jessen in *Die Zeit*, 18 November 2004; Ulrich Beck and Michal Bodemann, both in *Süddeutsche Zeitung*, 20/21 November 2004; Zafer Senoçak in *Die Tageszeitung*, 22 November 2004; lead article, *Berliner Zeitung*, 15 November 2004; Annette Ramelsberger in *Süddeutsche Zeitung*, 17 November 2004; Neukölln mayor Heinz Buschkowsky in *Der Tagesspiegel*, 13 November 2004.
4. See http://www.bundesregierung.de/Reden-Interviews-,11635.748232/rede/Rede-von-Bundeskanzler-Schroed.htm
5. Unless otherwise indicated, 'Turkish' shall mean here persons originating from Turkey, regardless of ethnic origin.
6. For the history of commemoration of Crystal Night in Germany, see Michal Bodemann (1996), *Gedächtnistheater: Die Jüdische Gemeinschaft und ihre deutsche Erfindung*, Hamburg: Rotbuch Verlag.
7. Similarly, Zafer Senoçak, in his *Atlas des tropischen Deutschland* (1992), Berlin: Babel Verlag, has raised this theme as well.

8. For more on the citizenship issue, see Chapter 8 by Schoeps and Glöckner and Chapter 7 by Kessler in this volume.
9. For details, especially on the demographics, see the chapters on Russian Jews in this volume.
10. This is discussed in Michal Bodemann (2002), *In den Wogen der Erinnerung. Jüdische Existenz in Deutschland*, München: DTV, pp. 185ff. and passim. The boldest statement, most recently, is by Micha Brumlik (2004) who has spoken firmly of German Jewish patriotism, in an article entitled 'Dies ist mein Land' ('This is my country'), *Jüdische Allgemeine*, 23 December. The title alludes to Lea Fleischmann's book title, *Dies ist nicht mein Land* (1986), Munich: Wilhelm Heyne Verlag.
11. Immigration from Turkey to Germany includes not only Turks, but Kurds and other ethnic and religious minorities, such as Alevites and Yezidis.
12. It is important to note that the Turkish government's pro-Israeli attitude does not necessarily reflect the beliefs and values of Turkish people towards Israelis and Jews. Many Turks are neither supportive of Israeli policies nor sympathetic to Jews.
13. The banner by Turkish immigrants at a demonstration against racism in Germany is reproduced in Gerdien Jonker (2002), *Muslime in Berlin*, Berlin: Ausländerbeauftragte Berlin. The fact that it is presented in a Jewish museum is indicative of the affinity of both groups, on account of some semblance of shared experiences.
14. On the idea of the cultural repertoire, following Charles Tilly, see Ann Swidler (2002), 'Cultural Repertoires and Cultural Logics: Can They Be Reconciled?' *Comparative and Historical Sociology Newsletter*, 14, 1, pp. 2–6.
15. It is obvious that the binary religious/non-religious organizational structure of Turks in Germany reflects the situation back home, between a strictly secular state and a large religious population.
16. Mohammed Aman H. Hobohm, cited in *Die Welt*, 16 November 2004.
17. The preposition 'zu' is somewhat antiquated, and it is therefore remarkable that the *Cemaat* would adopt this form.
18. This part of the discussion deliberately excludes religious groups other than Sunnite Muslims who migrated from Turkey to Germany, such as Alevites, Yezidis and Assyrians.
19. See *Islamische Charta* by *Zentralrat der Muslime in Deutschland* (2002) for a full list of Muslim demands.
20. Reading and memorizing Quran verses in Arabic.
21. One such association is the *Islamische Föderation Berlin* (IFB) which has the privilege of teaching Islam courses in German secondary education, in German. Currently, over 1600 students, about half each boys and girls, are taking Islam as a religion course; 74 per cent are of Turkish nationality, and 21 per cent are of Arab descent (IFB, 2004).
22. At issue was the following: a German schoolteacher of Afghan origin, Feresteh Ludin, insisted on wearing the hijab in the school. She was dismissed from her teaching job and subsequently complained that she was being discriminated against on the grounds of her religious beliefs. When her case was brought before the *Bundesverfassungsgericht* (the constitutional court of Germany) it ruled that 'Germany's constitutional law did not explicitly

forbid the wearing of headscarves in the classroom in state-run schools' (*Deutsche Welle*, 25 September 2003).

23. Recently, Altinküpe's shop was firebombed; the perpetrators are unknown (IGMG, 26 November 2004).
24. Although Y. states that it is natural to work with the Jewish community in Germany, later in his talk he also admits that it is not possible for Milli Görüs to work with German Jewish associations, because of their support of Israeli actions in Palestine, which is unacceptable for this Muslim community.
25. Nevertheless, the anti-Turkish pogroms have resonated with Jews individually. Michal Bodemann (2005) reports such an incident where a young Jewish man was severely shaken by the Mölln pogrom in *A Jewish Family in Germany Today: an Intimate Portrait*, Durham: Duke University Press, p. 22.
26. See his article in *Die Zeit*, 'Distanzierungszwang und Opferrolle' (18 November 2004). With a note of caution: over the years, a significant number of Turkish engineers and economists had studied at German universities or had worked in German factories. Necmettin Erbakan, founder of Milli Görüs, is one of these. Many of them are considered technocrat-intellectuals in Turkey (Nilufer Göle (1986), *Mühendisler ve Ideoloji*, Istanbul: Iletisim). Moreover, many Turkish intellectuals came to Germany to escape the 1980s military coup in Turkey. What Germany lacked, in contrast to France and Britain, however, were elite schools in colonies whose students were trained in the colonizers' language and culture; many of these eventually ended up in France or England where they fit in fully, in terms of both language and culture.
27. *Muhteshem* means 'magnificent' in Turkish; one might speculate that it refers to an affirmation of the narrator's Turkish background, perhaps analogously to 'Black is beautiful'.
28. We have used the translation in Adelson (2000), p. 124. Adelson's essay is the pioneering work addressing the question of Turkish tropes in German discourses. Jeffrey Peck's early essay (1998), on the other hand, pointed out how Germans were using the Jewish trope in relation to Turks. The narrative of the Shoah (Crystal Night, pogroms, persecution of Jews) was superimposed onto Turks especially after the Solingen, Mölln, and other incidents of racist anti-Turkish violence. It is arguable that Turkish leaders might have picked up the Jewish narrative indirectly, from anti-racist German discourses. Only recently, Zafer Senoçak (2004) has pointed to how Germans are borrowing the pattern of the anti-Semitic discourse and are applying it to Muslims.

Part III

German-Jewish Liminalities

5

Jewish Studies or Gentile Studies? A Discipline in Search of its Subject*

Liliane Weissberg

'What Am I Doing Here? . . .'

(Joachim Schlör, Professor of Jewish Studies, Moses Mendelssohn Centre of European Studies in Potsdam, title of a paper delivered at the Annual Conference of the Association for Jewish Studies, December 2004)

I

On 24 July 2003 the German weekly *Die Zeit* published an article on Jewish culture in Germany, entitled in Yiddish 'Der auserwählte Folk' ('The Chosen People'). The article concerned itself with Klezmer music, here described as the celebratory music of Eastern European Jews:

> Another accordion – that would just be too much. Three can be heard already, in addition to five clarinets, and there are two violins as well. This crowd has more than a dozen players, and they jam quite loudly while drinking apple juice and beer, and once in a while, a violin or a trombone is heard, a player jumps into the middle of this group and produces a solo of his own. Another accordion, one deems, would result in a contrapuntal effect; another bass fiddle would destroy the musical framework. But then, a bass comes weaving into the room, and curiously enough, it works: the music continues. For each additional player added, the others do not even have to interrupt the piece.

Thomas Gross, the author of this essay, concludes that '[o]ne cannot accuse the people at this "Klezmer-*Stammtisch*" of lacking a sense of fundamental democracy, or a joy in playing.'[1] Among the disembodied instruments – some accordions, clarinets, violins, trombones, basses – the journalist finds players that would appreciate a sense of political democracy. This music, brought forth by a chaotic mix of instruments, a doubling and tripling of keys, and carried by much improvisation, may be the sign of a new Germany.

Berlin, the old and new German capital at the country's new eastern border, has become a capital of Klezmer music as well. While Poland had moved westwards in a territorial shift after the Second World War, Berlin, now located a mere half an hour by car from this Polish border, has found its place not so much in a Central Europe of the past, but in a new Eastern Europe, one that would celebrate its former, now vanished *shtetls* in the courtyards of a post-industrial German metropolis. At the same time, Berlin may not be quite unique – the Klezmer scene described may be distinctive, but ultimately not much different, perhaps, from the music played on the outskirts of Polish Krakow today.

The description of a thriving musical scene evokes haunting images from the past. The reader envisions a resurrected Jewish population, one which does not mourn the dead, but celebrates its presence. The music seems to evoke the memory of an idyllic, life-affirming past, one that none of these people have experienced. But these musicians are no threatening Jews, no members of any world conspiracy, simply members of a chaotic, but stable, and fundamentally democratic organization. We can rest assured: these are merely Jews at play.

A couple of paragraphs further into the article, however, the reader has to realize that her assumptions have been wrong. It is not Berlin's Jews who are celebrating their chosenness here, but young Germans who have become the new 'auserwählte Folk'. Musicians and Klezmer fans have names such as Carsten Schelp or Heiko Lehmann, and they are reviving tunes that have been unknown to Berli's Gentile population, until fairly recently at least.[2] Now, they are embraced with gusto, by the musicians and their audience alike. Klezmer seems to transcend the simple demands of fashion. Those young Germans performing in Berlin's Hackesche Höfe or its former Scheunenviertel, a section of town that was populated by poor Eastern European immigrants before the war, are not just playing music. They are playing Jews. This role play has become very successful, and gives apparent satisfaction to actors and listeners alike, many of them tourists to the German capital, who encounter this phenomenon for the first time and wonder what it is that they encounter here. And while Klezmer music had previously been alien to any German-Jewish experience, it has come to identify Jewish culture – indeed, much more so than the aspirations of assimilating German Jews.

With the Klezmer musicians, as well as with Berlin's kosher-style restaurants, theme-oriented city tours and much, much more we have encountered a peculiar paradox. Jewish culture, we must suppose, can exist without Jews, and once the question of 'authenticity' is suspended, we may suggest the same for Jewish Studies as well – not necessarily by denying it a Jewish subject, but the need for a Jewish agency. Indeed, if one were to look at the many Jewish Studies departments that have sprung up and received funding at various German universities in recent years, one would observe that a phenomenon has taken hold that is not totally unlike that of the Klezmer musicians. In Germany, Jewish Studies is largely conducted by non-Jewish scholars. Scholarly degrees are, in turn, obtained by non-Jewish students, who travel to Israel or the United States to learn Hebrew, to further their studies, or to visit archives. Many of these Jewish Studies departments and institutes flourish in towns like Duisburg or Trier that until very recently had no post-war Jewish communities at all. And even where both scholarly institutions and Jewish communities exist, the relationship between the two is tenuous, to say the least. In Germany, one could argue, Jewish Studies has in the past twenty years become a popular field for the exploration of one's own German identity, via the study of the Other (more recently, one can perhaps observe a similar trajectory regarding German programmes in Islamic Studies).

But more than the study of one or the acquisition of another identity is at stake here. Jewish Studies has completed a shift from a field that should be able to give answers as to *who one is* – thus defining a person's Jewish identity via historical reflection – to a study of *subject matter*, one that could then be made available to all (and even be made available for the purpose of a renewed, or virtual, identification).

II

Germany has had, of course, a different tradition of Jewish scholarship. For generations, Jews had regarded their very 'chosenness', their special relationship to God, and the truth of the Biblical text as a warranty against historical interpretation. But in the early nineteenth century, the new importance of historical thought had entered Jewish thought as well. Young men such as Eduard Gans or Heinrich Heine began to meet in 1819, to discuss their own Jewish identity and reflect on a Jewish past. These gatherings could be seen as emergency sessions of a sort. In Prussia, a Jewish emancipation had been in place de facto since 1812, but a mere seven years later, anti-Semitic Hep Hep riots raged in Southern Germany and in many university towns. Gans and other young Jews – most of them law students enrolled at universities – were eager to discuss philosophical, educational and political issues which were, above all, of concern to Jews. But during these meetings, Jewish studies as Jewish historiography was born, and named the 'Science of Judaism', or *Wissenschaft des Judentums*.[3] Immanuel Wolf, a founding member of the group, was eager to describe this concept of a new 'Science of Judaism':

> It is self-evident that the word 'Judaism' is here being taken in its comprehensive sense – as the essence of all the circumstances, characteristics, and achievements of the Jews in relation to religion, philosophy, history, law, literature in general, civil life and all the affairs of man – and not in the more limited sense in which it only means the religion of the Jews.[4]

Wolf's claim not only widened the field of inquiry. He insisted on studying Judaism over time, but also as a 'characteristic and independent whole' (p. 143). Wolf did not stake out a special claim for German Jews. He wanted Jews to declare themselves as a people and not just as believers in a different religion, and to claim a nationhood of sorts. This nationhood would be able to cross state boundaries, and survive ongoing discussions about religious practices, as Reform Judaism as well as Orthodoxy began to emerge. This 'Science of Judaism' was a product of the Enlightenment, and even permitted secularization. The orthodox Jew was the student of the Torah; the modern Jew was the student of Judaism.

Scholars like Leopold Zunz or Isaac Marcus Jost continued to elaborate on this claim, and the group's journal, the *Zeitschrift*, offered lively discussion, although it was published in one year only, 1822. The group soon disbanded. Most of its members converted to Protestantism, some out of conviction, most of them for pragmatic reasons, as they wanted to enter careers in law or in other academic fields that were barred to Jews. When the Science of Judaism was finally institutionalized in the second half of the nineteenth century, and an academy founded, the *Hochschule für die Wissenschaft des Judentums* with its own scholars and publications to promote its ideas, history would finally enter rabbinical thought as well. Moreover, the school produced a curriculum of sorts. Religious texts were not only studied and argued about, but dated. Scholars wrote about German rabbinical scholars or German Jewish communities, but the news about communities in Bavaria was reported alongside reflections on former communities in Spain, or the meaning of Aramaic words. Abraham Geiger, who taught at the new institution, followed the tripartite distinction of philological, historical and philosophical aspects of Jewish studies. By the time Heinrich Graetz penned his *History of the Jews*, which was published in eleven volumes between 1853 and 1876, history reigned not only as an instrument of analysis, but as the *sine qua non*. Graetz's history was the first comprehensive, multi-volume history of the Jews ever to be written – those by Simon Dubnow[5] and Salo Baron would follow in due course. 'Judaism can be understood only through its history',[6] Graetz would write, and historical study thus replaced in importance that of religion.

At that point, a separation had become obvious as well, between the Jewish academy on the one hand, and the German university on the other. Indeed, Hebrew had been taught at German universities for centuries, but as a discipline within a Christian universe. In the early modern universities, Hebrew studies were taught by and for Christian theologians, and especially by converted Jews. Catholic theologians, and later Christian theologians in general, were looking back to their own religion's roots and trying to discover a *Hebraica veritas*. The place for the study of Jews as pre-Christians was in the theological faculty or Divinity School, the place for more detailed linguistic studies was in the institutes of Oriental Studies.

By the early twentieth century, the study of Jewish history had found its occasional echo in history departments as well. The field of medieval history may serve as an example. Harry Bresslau, a Jewish scholar who was only able to obtain an extraordinary professorship in Berlin in 1877, was called to a chair at the University of Strasburg in 1890. There, he founded the *Historical Commission for Jews in Germany* (*Historische Kommission für die Geschichte der Juden in Deutschland*). He headed that commission from 1885 to 1902.[7] Under its auspices, the Berlin scholar Julius Aronius began to work on a register of royal and imperial documents concerning German Jewry from the Middle Ages to 1273, a work that seemed to establish the necessity of using non-Jewish sources for the periodization of German-Jewish history. Aronius's work, published in 1902, was followed by the project of the *Germanica Judaica*, 'an alphabetical catalogue intended to identify all places in the German Empire in which Jewish settlements existed, from the earliest times to the Treaties of Vienna, and to describe them on the basis of a scientific investigation based on sources'.[8] The research on this project ceased only in 1934. The stated goal of the *Germanica Judaica* was an integration of Jewish and general descriptive historical scholarship dealing with German territories.

If much of the scholarly research in Jewish studies was still done at the Berlin *Hochschule* or other Jewish *Lehranstalten* in Frankfurt or elsewhere, there was an increased attention to Jewish scholarship at the universities as well. At the same time, there were larger numbers of Jewish students enrolled in Germany's universities. The growth of this number can already be documented for the early nineteenth century. *Bildung*, which has served as a promise for true emancipation since the Enlightenment, turned many Jews into *Bildungsbürger* par excellence. But while the universities had opened their gates to Jewish students, they were still barring their Jewish graduates from teaching positions. Most of them were unable to obtain professorships until the early twentieth century, unless, of course, they chose to convert. German universities were defined as Christian institutions, populated by officers of a Christian state. Jewish scholars like Bresslau had to move to Strasburg to obtain a regular professorship. Only after the First World War did Jews in Germany obtain university positions in larger numbers, and the increase continued until 1933. Germany's Jewish population in 1933 was about 0.8 per cent, but the percentage of Jews in academic positions was nearly 6 per cent; 4 per cent of the student body was Jewish.

However, only very few of the newly minted Jewish professors were interested in Jewish studies. Jewish students who were entering the state institutions of higher learning were attracted to subjects like medicine or law. They offered economic security as well as social acculturation. The bifurcation of German universities and Jewish academies continued to exist.

III

After 1945, hardly any Jewish scholars returned to teach at German universities, and these universities had made no efforts to call emigrants back into their fold. Instead, most faculty members who taught during the Third Reich continued to teach or were reappointed. This did not result in further anti-Semitism in higher education, but in a silence concerning Jewish affairs, punctured by occasional philo-Semitic statements.

The Jewish communities in turn had more pressing problems than the establishment of university disciplines. Moreover, most of the Jews that settled in Germany after the war hailed from Eastern Europe; they remained in Germany after the dissolution of the displaced persons camps, or were more recent refugees. Hardly any of them had connection to, or knowledge of, German-Jewish history, or the traditions of a Berlin *Hochschule* or a Frankfurt *Lehrhaus*. There were no rabbinical seminaries, and the options for a Jewish education in post-war Germany were sparse. Rabbis in Germany hailed from abroad, and often they were able to speak neither German nor any of the other secular languages represented by the members of their own communities. If post-war Jews instilled a wish for learning in their children, it was not simply related to social betterment. It was viewed as an instrument for future emigration. Parents encouraged their children to live abroad, and a German university diploma was a passport as well.

Jews who lived outside Germany, as well as the historians at German universities, began to view German Jewry as a thing of the past. Over twenty-five years ago, in 1979, the German Jewish Central Council proceeded to found a new *Hochschule für Jüdische Studien*. Ironically, it was founded in Heidelberg, a university town that housed an institution that had quite early embraced Nazi policies during the Third Reich.[9] The *Hochschule*'s goal was to continue a tradition of higher Jewish learning, as commenced by the Jewish academies before the Second World War, and to train teachers of Jewish religion. Two years ago, the Council decided to train rabbis there as well. Other, independent rabbinical institutions have also been founded in Potsdam, Munich and Frankfurt. In earlier years, the Jewish community had offered stipends to members who wanted to become teachers of religion or rabbis and train in London. Now, the Jewish community offers stipends to students who want to remain in Germany and study in Heidelberg.

While the Jewish Central Council's decision to found a *Hochschule* reflects its wish to account for the present Jewish population and plan for a future of Jewish learning, it curiously paralleled attempts by a new generation of German professors and administrators to establish Jewish Studies departments or chairs at their own universities. The older field of *Judaistik*, evolving from Oriental Studies departments, was revitalized in places such as the F. U. Berlin or in Cologne. *Judaistik* centres on the study of Hebrew, the study of the Hebrew Bible and the rabbinical tradition. It combines philological with historical work and consideration of the religious tradition. Most programmes of *Judaistik* concentrate on the study of ancient and medieval Jewry, and *Judaistik*'s representatives grope their way only slowly to the study of Jewish life in modern times. In the 1980s, Jewish Studies as *Jüdische Studien* established itself as a field in German universities. *Jüdische Studien* views itself as a largely historical field, not necessarily wedded to Hebrew study, or to other Jewish languages like Yiddish or Ladino, or to the study of ancient texts. Instead, *Jüdische Studien* prefers to concentrate on Jewish culture, which would include the study of acculturated or assimilated Jews. Most programmes of *Jüdische Studien* are administrated by historians with a more general training in German history – such as at the Centre for European Jewish Studies in Potsdam – and they concentrate on Jewish life, history and literature since the emancipation period, that is, since the eighteenth century. Needless to say, a rivalry has ensued between the departments of *Judaistik* and *Jüdische Studien*, each denying the other the claim to serious scholarship, on the one hand, or the scholarly relevance of their work, on the other. For representatives of *Judaistik, Jüdische Studien* ignores the core of Jewish language and learning. For representatives of *Jüdische Studien*, *Judaistik* has lost touch with modern Jewry and contemporary political issues.

But while the silence of previous years has been broken, the research done in those departments still bears the tone of memorialization, of dealing with a lost past. The new *Germania Judaica* consists of the publication of tombstone inscriptions, or the statistics of, and guides to, pre-Second World War Jewish populations in various villages, towns and city quarters, and of posthumous local histories. Often, it has assumed a peculiar form of documentation, contemplating the ruins of what has been lost. Much of this scholarship of the 1980s not only offers lists of lost artefacts, but the scholarship itself has become a *Trauerarbeit*, a work of mourning for a part of German history that was and was not the researcher's own.

This work did not proceed without continuity. One could claim a relationship between the silence regarding Jewish matters in the immediate post-war years, and the new work, as both insisted on the absence of Jews. More uncannily, the terms of the Nazi persecution proved to be long-lived as well. Even today, Jewish Studies institutes in Duisburg or in Potsdam are sponsoring biographical studies of persons who were Christians or of no religion, or of those who did not view themselves ethnically or culturally as Jews. If they had a Jewish grandparent, or a parent who was born a Jew, their lives are a subject matter eligible for funding within the field of Jewish Studies. It is as if racial terms define Jewish subjects still, and racial descriptions like *Halbjude* (partial Jew) abound. But increasingly, social and intellectual histories have been added to this research, and studies abroad in Israel or the United States have further internationalized both research and approaches.

IV

In her study of Jews in post-1989 Europe, written with much enthusiasm soon after the fall of the Berlin Wall, Diana Pinto sketches an image of Jews voluntarily populating Jewish communities now in Germany and elsewhere, and of a new German-Jewish relationship:

> Unlike Israel, which is its own vast Jewish-Jewish space, or America where Jewish space is filled by Jews themselves, in what can be called a sociological and cultural triumph, Jews in Europe are only one part of this new space. This is particularly true in Germany where in the Jewish study programs at the universities, inside museums, in the realm of

> publishing, as well as in every other Jewish manifestation (except for religion), non-Jews constitute the majority of the 'users' and even implementers of this space.[10]

What Pinto has viewed here as a triumph, and the construction of a post-modern Jewish space, could also be seen as a proliferation of Jewish spaces that seem mutually exclusive. Jewish Studies at the universities is still suffering from a phantom wound – it is a traumatic field no less. But the *Hochschule*, too, has come to fulfil a task that was perhaps not expected by its founders.

The small *Hochschule* in Heidelberg aims to serve primarily Jewish students. Most of those enrolled on its courses have transferred from other institutions, however, and do not regard themselves as Jewish at all. Full-time students at the *Hochschule* can be largely divided into two groups. One consists of recent immigrants from the former Soviet Union, who are supported by community fellowships. Most of them have grown up without religion, without previous knowledge of Judaism, or were – according to Jewish law – not even Jews. The other group consists of students who have recently converted to Judaism or are thinking of conversion. Thus, the *Hochschule* not only offers courses in Jewish Studies, but fulfils an integrative task for the community itself. It may have wanted to produce scholars of Jewish Studies, but it is primarily producing Jews.

The university programmes in Berlin or Hamburg or Cologne in turn do not attract German Jewish students, and hardly any Jewish faculty. Recently, there were plans to close the *Judaistik* programme at the University of Frankfurt, a city that boasts a long Jewish tradition and currently German's second largest Jewish community. The plan was to move the programme to Marburg, to a university that was once Martin Heidegger's home, located in a small town with hardly any Jewish population. For the Hessian Secretary of Arts and Science, Udo Corts, the shift from Frankfurt to Marburg was simply a move 'to save' one of the 'small disciplines'.[11] But for the task of *Judaistik* or Jewish Studies, Jews are hardly needed, and for faculty and students the studied subject matter is foreign or a thing of the past. The Jewish identity that the *Hochschule* wants to achieve, and the Jewish identity that the universities study, hardly match.

Beyond the institutions of higher learning, moreover, German's Jews and Jewish Studies scholars occupy parallel worlds. As the Jewish population in Germany increases, however, the discipline of Jewish Studies will have to change as well. This is not due to the larger numbers of immigrants who are no longer just clustering in Germany's major cities, but also in smaller towns and even villages. And it is not even due to the fact that these new *Ostjuden*, Eastern Jews, differ fundamentally from their former, mostly orthodox, counterpart, as they are mostly non-religious. It is due to one simple fact: most of these immigrants and their families did not experience the Holocaust, a fact that facilitates their life in Germany. While they receive social aid, few have demands for reparation. They feel little anger or guilt towards their German surroundings. Germany, once again, proves for many to be a country that represents *Bildung*, and also an economic wonderland. The children of these immigrants, who are neither survivors nor heirs of a German-Jewish past, may change the face of Jewish Studies in Germany once again – and perhaps provide some of the Jewish space that Pinto had been dreaming of.

Notes

* My longer survey of the past, present and future of the field of German-Jewish Studies in general appeared as 'Reflecting on the Past, Envisioning the Future: Perspectives for German-Jewish Studies', *GHI Bulletin*, 35 (2004), pp. 11–32.

1. Thomas Gross (2003), 'Der Auserwählte Folk', *Die Zeit*, 31, 24 July, p. 35 (translation mine).
2. Literature in German on Klezmer.
3. See, for example, Julius Carlebach (ed.) (1992), *Wissenschaft des Judentums: Anfänge der Judaistik in Europa*, Darmstadt: Wissenschaftliche Buchgesellschaft.
4. Immanuel Wolf (1974), 'On the Concept of a Science of Judaism', in Michael A. Meyer (ed.), *Ideas of Jewish History*, New York: Behrman House, p. 143.
5. For more on Dubnow, see Chapter 2 by Dan Diner in this volume.
6. Heinrich Graetz (1974), 'Judaism Can Be Understood Only Through its History', in Meyer (ed.), *Ideas of Jewish History*, p. 219; See also Heinrich Graetz (1975), *The Structure of Jewish History and Other Essays* (Ismar Schorsch, trans.), New York: Jewish Theological Seminar of America.
7. Edward Peters (forthcoming), '"Settlement, Assimilation, Distinctive Identity": the Historiography of Medieval German Jewry, 1902/3–2002/3', review article of Alfred Haverkamp (ed.), *Geschichte der Juden im Mittelalter von der Nordsee bis zu den Südalpen. Kommentiertes Kartenwerk*, *Jewish Quarterly Review*.
8. Marcus Brann (1963), 'Foreword', *Germania Judaica*, I, Tübingen: J. C. B. Mohr, reprint, pp. ix–xv; cited in Peters (forthcoming), '"Settlement, Assimilation, Distinctive Identity"'.
9. See Steven P. Remy (2002), *The Heidelberg Myth: the Nazification and Denazification of a German University*, Cambridge, MA: Harvard University Press.
10. Diana Pinto (2002), 'The Jewish Challenges in the New Europe', in Daniel Levy and Yfaat Weiss (eds), *Challenging Ethnic Citizenship: German and Israeli Perspectives on Immigration*, New York: Berghahn Books, pp. 250–1. Pinto has since viewed these statements as too optimistic.
11. Udo Corts, Letter to David Ruderman (July 2005).

6

How Jewish is it? W. G. Sebald and the Question of 'Jewish' Writing in Germany Today

Leslie Morris

In 2002 the late German writer W. G. Sebald received a 'special award' among the annual 'Jewish' book prizes given by the American Koret Foundation, for his 2001 novel *Austerlitz*. Despite the fact that Sebald received this 'special award', and not the annual award for fiction, no conversation ensued about how, or if, Sebald might or should be considered a Jewish writer, *Austerlitz* a 'Jewish' novel or, even more significantly, any discussion about the slipperiness of the very category of 'Jewish writing'.[1]

I begin with Sebald's Koret award not to come to a judgement on the relative Jewishness (or Germanness) of Sebald's novel.[2] Rather, Sebald's 'special award' offers a way to examine the larger issue of Jewish writing in Germany and to pose the following set of questions: is German writing now, in the post-Holocaust age, shaped by ruin and the rubble of German (and German-Jewish) history, an age in which the trace of Jewishness is omnipresent, always 'Jewish'? Is German-Jewish writing now marked *not* by the hyphen between German and Jew (a diacritical mark that keeps intact the myth of a German-Jewish symbiosis), but rather by the interplay among texts that results from translation – translation, literally, between languages, but also the translation of Jewish culture in Germany today? Does the 'Jewishness' of Sebald's texts consist in the encounter (or rather, the missed encounter) between the presumably non-Jewish, largely autobiographical narrator and the various Jewish characters? Is Jewishness a figuration in Sebald's texts, a narrative condition staged as an encounter (between German narrator and Jewish interlocutor) in the context of travel, migration, exile, in which the Jewish figure is the cosmopolitan, the flâneur, the emigré (I am collapsing these terms intentionally) who traverses city and national spaces? Is it the diasporic quality of Sebald's writing, where language and place are no longer linked, that enables the text to be seen as 'Jewish'? What is the relationship between Jewish text and text as ruin that is evoked in Sebald's work, and that has emerged as a dominant trope of contemporary German Jewish culture? And, finally: what is the place of Jewishness within a transnational Europe that has emerged since the 1990s and which has, in part, sparked various cultural imaginations of community? Does the translation of Jewishness into these new figurations of imagined communities help to create an imagined transnational community?

In part, I pose this series of questions in order to move beyond the critical impasses into which German Jewish studies and post-Holocaust studies of German culture have led: the impasse of identity debates ('How German is it?' and 'How Jewish is it?') and of representation in art and atrocity (Sarah Kofman's axiomatic questions, 'How can it not be said? How can it be said?'); and, finally, the impasse of having exhausted ourselves in thinking about the parameters of grief, mourning, loss, the interplay between presence and absence, between German and Jew, the reappearance of the past in the present, the exhausted tropes of testimony, witnessing, belatedness, trauma, post-memory, and even that of ennui itself. Rather than exhausting memory yet again, I approach these questions first with a return to Roland Barthes' paradigmatic reflections on the text: 'that neutral, composite, oblique space where our subject slips away, the negative where all identity is lost'.[3] It is precisely in Barthes' 'oblique space where our subject slips away' that I situate translations of Jewishness in the post-Shoah world, exploring the space of the diacritical mark of the 'German-Jewish' as a possible 'oblique space where our subject slips away'. By thus returning to Barthes, I seek to open up and break the hyphen that keeps intact the referent of 'the German' and 'the Jewish', not in order to restore Rosenzweig's infamous 'and' linking German and Jew, but rather to contemplate German-Jewish writing in the age of authorial disintegration. In other words, I propose that we think about Sebald as 'Jewish' author while at the same time abandoning the category of 'the author'.

Sebald, whose texts place the vicissitudes of ruin – architectural, narrative, visual, epistemological – at their centre, has played a significant role in the past several years in reshaping the contours of the public debates in the US about Jewishness, Germanness, and cultural and historical memory; yet at the same time his work highlights some of the divides of these debates between Germany and the US. As countless critics have now made clear, a large part of the appeal of Sebald for the Anglo-American reading public is that he crafts a notion of the narrator/author as nomad, wandering, post-traumatically, in the rubble and ruin of critical reflections that have piled up, 'Trümmer auf Trümmer', in the aftermath of the Holocaust.[4] While many German critics see his texts as 'larmoyant', as antiquated reflections of a hopelessly neo-Romantic European nostalgia and sentimentality, the Anglo-American press has praised the allusive, elegiac, fragmentary, ruminative and diasporic qualities of his writing. Oddly, for the German-reading public Sebald is figured as 'altertümlich', antiquated, archaic, and in this regard, intensely German;[5] for the American reader, Sebald's rumination on the German past makes him somehow legibly 'Jewish'. Sebald is, for some American critics, a quintessentially German author steeped in the German modernist narrative tradition, writing novels that express a Hegelian dialectic between prose and poetry that defines the conceptual narrative framework of the nineteenth-century *European* novel.[6] With countless references to high Modernist authors such as Kafka, Proust, Rilke and Nabokov, Sebald expresses for some critics an affinity with the narrative forays of European modernism, embracing in particular the dominant strand of German modernism, remaining thus first and foremost a *German* author. Others challenge the post-modern quality of the nomadic, exilic narrative voice and structure, arguing for the fundamentally modernist relationship to place and text found within Sebald's work.[7]

Rather than entering into the inevitable critical impasse of our age's version of the battle between the ancients and the moderns (that is, modernism versus post-modernism), I propose to cast some of these questions in a slightly different form – with the aim of reconsidering the larger question of the role of text and authorship, in particular Jewish text and Jewish authorship, in the production of contemporary Jewish identity in Germany. The twin questions of 'How Jewish is it?' and its absent echo 'How German is it?' enable reflection not only on why Sebald has dominated the critical field in the past few years, but more significantly, why this interest stretches from Germany to the Anglophone world in a way that is unprecedented for a German author in the post-war period.[8] The appearance of Sebald's work in English has shifted the terms that have dominated discussions of post-1945 history, memory and narrative, shifted the very terrain of national literatures as it blurs, intentionally, the lines between German literature written abroad and literature written in German on 'English soil'. In the case of W. G. Sebald, the place of literary production – simultaneously the place of immigration – becomes the defining mark of the national, not the language in which the text is written.[9]

Yet does Sebald's writing presence in England enable the reading public to construct Sebald – or, more precisely, the translation of Jewish memory in his texts – as simultaneously both a German and a British writer? More significantly, does the blurring of national identity and space of literary production carry with it the marks of 'Jewishness' that create the slide from German to – surprisingly – Jew? Reading Sebald, not only in the wake of the Koret award, but more significantly, after the publication of Günter Grass's *Crab Walk* and Sebald's own *Airwar and Literature*, his work has become inseparable from the recent debates about German victimhood and suffering that were circulating in Germany and the US. Public debate about memory and history post-1945 has been, to a very large extent, shaped by public discourse in both Germany and the United States, creating a litany of discourse/events that usually begins with the 1980 airing of the mini-series *Holocaust* on West German television, and then moves to the fuller recitation: Bitburg; Historikerstreit; Jenninger affair; Wilkomirski, and so on. There is a certain estrangement in the sound of this recitation, as it is no longer the event that is recalled, but the now seemingly endless chain of associations. There is, as well, an acoustic memory that has been created – not of the event (rallies; loudspeakers; the sound of Hitler's voice), but of the recitation of the events, a litany that creates a metonymic slide from one event to the next, linking them in cultural memory, in which the discussion of memory becomes a stand-in for memory itself. Thus the memory in Germany of the Holocaust is a speech act that consecrates the order of public events that mark turning points in the discussion. The debate ignited by Grass and by the publication of Sebald's *Airwar and Literature* (and which intensified with the popular and critical acclaim of his work that came immediately after his untimely death in 2001) grows out of and is then absorbed into this litany.[10]

Post-Holocaust literary and aesthetic studies were marked in the 1980s and 1990s by intense inquiry into the nature of representation and text (Lang, La Capra, White, Young) and by work on trauma and loss (Caruth, La Capra); the critical discussion sparked by Sebald incorporates these strands of literary and critical inquiry, yet at the same time the circuitous narrative structure and the interplay between text and image in Sebald's work demand a rethinking of aesthetic and literary categories that have, to a certain extent, created critical impasses in post-Holocaust discourse. Sebald's work has generated considerable scholarly attention to the role of the visual in post-Holocaust literature. Rather than privileging analytical and interpretive models in visual studies over the literary, I propose reading Sebald's visual narratives in order to realign the visual with the literary, thus reconstructing sites of memory in these works as textualized spaces that reveal how the literary is, as Paul De Man famously observed, 'a moment inherent in all cultural forms'. In fact, I argue, Sebald's texts forbid the reader from creating legibility of the links between the literary and the visual, as he constantly disrupts the possibility of legibility, creating instead both correspondences and dissonances not only between image and text but also intertextually, among texts.

In this, Sebald is in the company of writers such as Umberto Eco, Italo Calvino, Fernando Pessoa and Jorge Luis Borges, whose texts exceed the category of the literary to become blueprints for literary theory and philosophy. In Sebald's work it is the figurations of ruin, which have become a central organizing principle of current German-Jewish discourse, in which the lines between history and narrative, between German and Jew, become blurred; in the rubble of this new narrative world, epistemological certainty and literary and cultural 'legibility' also lie in rubble. Sebald presents topographies of destruction, ruin, rubble, spaces the narrator and others move through and dwell in, actual ruin, 'fields of rubble', transformed buildings that exist in metonymic relationship to each other. Yet it is not only that there are ruins scattered throughout the texts, spaces where the encounter between narrator and (often) Jewish traveller are staged, but that Sebald conceptualizes and creates narrative ruin. Here he is, in many ways, at his most German, continuing the post-war German and Austrian literary rumination on Adorno's most famous dictum and suggesting the ruin of coherent or unified historiography,[11] and thus following in the footsteps of mostly non-Jewish writers such as Peter Handke, Ingeborg Bachmann, Max Frisch, Christa Wolf, Günter Grass, Uwe Timm and Peter Weiss, as he weaves the autobiographical with the historical, both repressing and uncovering the traces of atrocity, violence and trauma.

Yet even in the context of this very German reflection post-1945 (and post-1989) on the viability of representation and of historiography, Sebald's work moves in a new direction. Not only does he place ruin at the very centre, but also, more significantly, translation as act and as idea is embedded in the texts as a layer in this archaeology of narrative ruin. In this, not his fellow Germans but rather writers such as Calvino, Eco, Borges and Pessoa become significant, all of whom have explored the intimate ties between place and text and translation. With the 'turn to translation' of many late twentieth-century studies of culture and with much scholarly work that has been devoted to examining both the 'task' and the after-tasks of the translator in the post-Benjamin age, Sebald's preoccupation with ruin raises the question of what it means to 'translate' Jewish memory and to create Jewish text. To read Sebald now – in English, after his death, and in the wake of his 'special award' – is to be engaged with a process of translating Jewish memory from and back to Germany today, translating the memory of Jewishness to a present-day Germany marked by its absence.

Translation occupies a major place in Sebald's work: the significance of the translation of Sebald's texts between German and English, the fact that Sebald founded an institute for translation studies at the University of East Anglia, and even the extended encounter between the narrator and Michael Hamburger – the Celan translator – in the *Rings of Saturn*. Yet I conceive of translation not simply as the literary act of moving from one language to another or as the cultural transmission that results from moving among texts; translation is a 'carrying over' ('über/setzen') not only of meaning, but more importantly, of the continual accrual of meaning, metaphor and sound. 'Translation', as I am bringing it to bear on Sebald's work, is a consideration of the mediation between aesthetic form (that is, between text and image) and between German and American culture, identifying forms of art and literature that cross over between these two separate but linked cultural spheres, establishing a new critical voice that can mediate between German and Jewish-American culture. Thus to translate Jewish memory in Germany, or German-Jewish memory in the United States, is to think about, and listen to the constant circulation of memory, post-memory and text beyond the borders of either the German or the Jewish. The work of the non-Jewish German writer W. G. Sebald bears the abrasions, marks (Jewish stigmata) and echoes of 'the Jewish' that are always present as trace within German text. In this way, Jewishness is the sign that is always implicit, present in its absence, returning over and over again. The 'translation of Jewish memory' that Sebald's texts enact is thus one layer in the palimpsest of memory texts circulating between Germany and the US. In this way, it fundamentally rethinks the status of Jewish text, creating from the material a more diasporic notion of text that takes into consideration the way in which texts traverse spatial, historical and personal memory.

As part of the task of 'translating' the Jewish into Sebald and thus asserting the diasporic in his writing, I propose yet another experiment: reading this non-Jewish German-born writer, whose texts were written in German but who lived the majority of his adult life in England, *not* as a German writer (who nonetheless sparks a very German debate about the Allied bombings and the role of German victims), but rather as a British post-imperialist writer, one who takes his place as much among writers such as Hanif Kareishi, Kazuo Ishiguro and Pico Iyer as beside Günter Grass and Uwe Timm.[12] Perhaps at stake is not whether Sebald is to be characterized as a German or a British author, but instead whether the very category of 'British fiction' or any national literature (or, to push it further, Jewish writing) is itself in ruin in the post-imperial era. If Sebald's work can, in fact, be read as post-imperial British fiction, then what are the implications of this for German history, German culture and the ongoing debates about German and Jewish memory? Does the 'Jewishness' conferred upon Sebald (or his text) place him as a kind of ex-territorial? Does this make of Sebald's texts a sort of European pastiche, a pan-post-everything (post-colonial, post-imperial, post-modern, post-German)? Is it the diasporic quality of his writing, where language and place are no longer linked, that enables the text to be seen as 'Jewish'?

Sebald's preoccupation with travel, airplanes and airports, movement, railroad stations, suitcases and knapsacks suggests the narrators' encounter and mis-encounter with Jewish Germans rooted in literary tropes of the flâneur, the wanderer, the cosmopolitan, the ex-territorial – in other words, the Jew who inhabits multiple urban spaces, moving between them and between layers of historical and cultural memory. Sebald's preoccupation in *Rings of Saturn* (*Die Ringe des Saturn*, 1995; trans. 1998), for instance, is with travel, movement and memory. The novel opens with the narrator describing how he ends up in the hospital in Norwich 'in a state of almost total immobility', a year to the day after he completed a walking tour of the county of Suffolk – walking for hours in the day, confronted, as we learn in the opening paragraph, 'with the traces of destruction, reaching far back into the past, that were evident even in that remote place'. It is in the confinement of his hospital room, where he experiences – like Gregor Samsa, to whom he compares himself – a bewildering relationship between the enclosure of the room and the once-familiar spaces beyond it, that the narrator begins to write what follows (or rather, to conceive of it: 'It was then that I began in my thoughts to write these pages').[13] (After another year, he assembles the notes written in the hospital and writes the text.) The illness – 'a state of almost total immobility', of stasis, of ceasing to move through space and time – signals the end to the narrator traversing the eastern coast of Britain and with that, British history and memory. Writing as illness; writing as sign of trauma and its belatedness, as the narrator writes the account one year to the day; writing that carries with it the belatedness of other texts, that is, Kafka; reflection as pathology of modernity; traces of destruction highlighting the acute subjectivity of the author: all of these, I want to argue, place Sebald as much in the German tradition (post-Kafka) as it does in the domain of British post-imperial writing.

The narrator's flight from Amsterdam to Norwich highlights this question of movement and travel, and suggests Sebald's affinity with global networks of travel that have been at the centre of British post-imperial writing. Sebald's description of Schiphol airport in Amsterdam echoes, for instance, the work of the Indian British writer Pico Iyer. Sebald starts the passage on Schiphol by noting the 'strangely muted' atmosphere of the airport, making it seem as if one were 'already a good way beyond this world. As if they were under sedation or moving through time stretched and expanded, the passengers wandered the halls or, standing still on the escalators, were delivered to their various destinations on high or underground.'[14] Sebald continues, embedding a line from Hamlet's famous soliloquy on death: 'The airport, filled with a murmuring whisper, seemed to me that morning like an ante room of that undiscovered country from whose bourn no traveler returns.'[15] Pico Iyer, in fact, cites precisely this passage from Sebald (citing Hamlet) in *The Global Soul*, linking the 'bright and sterile spaces' of the airport, 'a terminal zone', to the hospital, where 'one by one people disappear as their names or departures are called out'.[16]

In *The Emigrants (Die Ausgewanderten*, 1992; trans. 1996) the narrator's identity – always murky, unclear – merges, as it does later in *Austerlitz* (2001), with the stories of the emigrants whose lives he uncovers, layer by layer, in England. While critics have argued that Sebald eclipses and elides the Holocaust in the *Emigrants*, speaking of it only obliquely and in code, it is there as frame, as spectral presence, as displaced and belated memory, and as a sort of 'origin' for these tales. It is also, at times, literally incorporated into the mouth of the narrator, who recounts the story of the four emigrants within the embedded story. In both *Austerlitz* and *The Emigrants* the narrative is punctuated with the repetition of 'said Austerlitz', or 'said Ferber', thus blurring the lines between interlocutors, between transmitted and narrated memory, between the present moment in England and the German past.

The acoustic effect of the repetition of 'said Austerlitz' and 'said Ferber' frames the structure of narrative and translation that is central to all of Sebald's texts; it links the act of translation to the acts of bearing witness, giving testimony and story-telling, and to the elegiac nature of translation as a process of loss and recovery. Furthermore, this key narrative technique demands a focus on the role of the acoustic in Sebald's work; this shift to the acoustic might suggest new ways of approaching Sebald's work beyond the extensive scholarship that focuses on the primacy of the visual in his novels.

The confusion and blurring of the narrator's recounting with the narrative told to him by the Jewish figure (Austerlitz, Ferber) suggests as well that Sebald is bringing back to life the figure of the storyteller that Benjamin, in his pivotal essay, 'The Storyteller', lamented had ceased to be a force in the twentieth century. Benjamin's scrutiny of the art of 'experience that is passed on from mouth to mouth' has a bearing on Sebald's narrative technique in both *Austerlitz* and *The Emigrants*.[17] Benjamin asserts, furthermore, that

> storytelling is always the art of repeating stories, and this art is lost when the stories are no longer retained. It is lost because there is no more weaving and spinning to go on while they are being listened to. The more self-forgetful the listener is, the more deeply what he listens to is imprinted upon his memory. When the rhythm of work has seized him, he listens to the tales in such a way that the gift of retelling them comes to him all by itself.[18]

By turning to Benjamin's own focus on the acts of listening and repetition of the sound of the story being told, I hope to add the acoustic to the process of translation that I claim Sebald's work embodies.

Yet translation is not only part of the narrative structure of repetition in the text; drawing on Carol Jacob's insight that Benjamin's essay on translation itself performs an act of translation, I claim that Sebald's texts can be similarly read as performances of translation, as they continually unsettle words and meanings from prior contexts.[19] The blurring between narrator and Jewish figure is analogous to Benjamin's insistence on the translation's great ability to defamiliarize the original language, rendering the familiar 'original' language foreign and unknown. In a late fragment found in the Benjamin Nachlaß, 'La Traduction – le Pour et le Contre', Benjamin evokes precisely this sense of the unfamiliar and the unknown ('Das Unerkannte'). The dialogue, possibly originally intended for radio broadcast in France, begins with the first speaker recounting how he found a French translation of a German philosophical text at the bookstalls on the Seine. Only identifying the text as one by Nietzsche later in the fragment, the speaker goes on to express his surprise that the passages that had most occupied him in the past, in this text, were not to be found in the French translation. When asked by the other speaker if this means he simply did not find the passages, the other speaker responds that he found them, but that he had the feeling that the passages were as unable to recognize ('erkennen') him as he was able to recognize them. Concurring with the other speaker that the Nietzsche translator was highly regarded, the first speaker explains that what was disorienting to him was not a deficiency in the translation, but rather 'something which may even have been its merit, that the horizon and the world around the translated text had itself been substituted, had become French'.[20]

This fragment serves to open up several interpretive lines for reading Sebald. First, it is significant that the speaker (not Benjamin, but certainly in this text a heteronymous stand-in for him), comes upon the translation by chance ('zufällig'). The encounter with the translated text is evoked as analogous to the face-to-face encounter, as the speaker describes the act of looking for the 'missing' passages as one in which he peers into the face ('als ich ihnen ins Gesicht sah') of the passages, discovering their mutual illegibility (of face, of text).[21] The fragment, itself a found object, bears the mark of this illegibility. Similarly, Sebald's texts comprise a narrator's recreation of a transmitted conversation and, often, testimony, thus repeatedly highlighting that the text we are reading has been collected, often by chance, reconstructed from the ruins of memory and forgetting.[22]

Yet not only is it the presence of the narrator, but behind that, W. G. Sebald the author, that generates this testimony and witnessing. While critics have generally read the encounter (or mis-encounter) between the narrator and his various Jewish figures as one that probes the relationship between the German-Jewish past and the present in a landscape of ruin, I want to call attention to Sebald's own presence in the text – as well as in the translation of the text – as author and, at the same time, as translator, poet, collector, storyteller, émigré and, finally, as 'Jew'. The tendency in the scholarship on Sebald to read an autobiographical presence hovering behind the narrator, and the narrator's ramblings then as a pseudonymous screen for Sebald himself, has led to charges that Sebald 'appropriates' Jewishness. I propose abandoning the assumption of authenticity of experience and identity that underlies this charge of the 'appropriation' of Jewishness, and to focus, in the wake of Foucault's and Barthes' axiomatic reflections on the status of the author, on the more significant question of authorship.

Thus instead of approaching the narrator as a thinly veiled W. G. Sebald, and the narrative as the German-born writer's journey to recapture a lost Germanness that includes the loss of the Jewish, I claim instead that Sebald's texts create heteronyms that are reminiscent of the work of the Portuguese modernist writer Fernando Pessoa. Pessoa's best-known work, *The Book of Disquiet*, situates the author Fernando Pessoa behind what he terms the 'semi-heteronym' Bernardo Soares, whom Pessoa called 'a mutilation of my own personality'. Pessoa's *Book of Disquiet*, his collection of poems, and his collected writings have been famously referred to as 'a trunk full of people', texts that express what Agamben has termed a radical de-subjectification, in which the text is comprised of meditations by a heteronymous author that is not a stand-in for Pessoa. As Chris Daniels explains, 'A heteronym is a fictional writer that may or may not reflect or refract some aspect of the personality and desires of the inventing writer, who isn't trying very hard, if at all, to hide the fact that the heteronym is fictive.'[23]

Pessoa's heteronyms offer a new way of reading Sebald that can, potentially, eclipse the problem of 'authenticity' and authorship that plagues not only much critical work on Jewish culture in Germany, but more generally, discussions of art after Auschwitz. Heteronymity as literary practice and ethos provides, too, a way out of the circular debates about the ethics of authorship sparked by recent literary and memoir scandals such as Wilkomirski, Demidenko and Yasusada. As Bill Friend explains in his article on the Yasusada controversy, 'heteronymity offers a means of both acknowledging the continued desire of many readers for the presence of an author behind a work of literature while simultaneously calling attention to the fictive status of that presence. Rather than serving to limit or control the text, the heteronymic author instead becomes part of it and thus can be read and interpreted.'[24] In the debates following the Wilkomirski affair and the newly translated poems by Yasusada that were revealed as fakes, it became apparent that public and critical discourse about the 'authentic' writing subject are being enacted in the critical vacuum after Foucault's and Barthes' pivotal texts on the author. It is to these two key texts that I would like to return, for they offer a substantive framework for the turn to heteronymity that I propose as a new way of reading Sebald and, with that, a new way of thinking about German-Jewish subjectivity today.

Roland Barthes, for instance, prefaces his *Roland Barthes by Roland Barthes* with the following command about autobiography, placing the following just underneath the title on the frontispiece: 'It must all be considered as if spoken by a character in a novel.' Later in the text, he goes on to explain, 'I do not say: "I am going to describe myself" but: "I am writing a text, and I call it R.B. "'.[25] The desire for a nostalgic conception of the writing subject pre-Foucault and Barthes also sidesteps the debates in public art about the status of the referent. Perhaps more productive than the moral outcries following the revelations of Wilkomirski or Yasusada would be Pessoa's fragment about translation, written in English, in which he muses on the trilogy that remains to be written: a History of Translation, a History of Plagiarisms, and a History of Parodies: 'A translation is only a plagiarism in the author's name ... translation is a serious parody in an other language.'[26] In a more serious vein, Marjorie Perloff reflects on Foucault's importance in contemplating the impact of these literary hoaxes: 'Foucault's central position, which has come to be de rigueur in the academy, is that it is the culture that constructs or writes the author, not vice-versa.'[27]

To turn to Foucault and Barthes means, of necessity, entering into the debate about the ethical dimensions of writing; yet my turn to the heteronym is an attempt to pose a set of questions regarding what it might mean to create and disassemble narrative voices that are distinct from that of the author. One of Pessoa's heteronyms, for instance, writes, 'Strictly speaking, Fernando Pessoa does not exist.'[28] Outdoing even Barthes, Pessoa here proclaims the death of the author by the author's own alter ego. In writing about the genesis of his seventy-two heteronyms, Pessoa explains his desire to create a 'fictitious world, to surround myself with friends and acquaintances that never existed'.[29] In a letter to one of his heteronyms, Adolfo Casais Monteiro, he goes on to explain his penchant for heteronymity as his tendency towards 'depersonalization': 'Today I have no personality: I've divided all my humanness among the various authors whom I've served as literary executor. Today I'm the meeting-place of a small humanity that belongs only to me.'[30]

Pessoa's reflections in his *Book of Disquiet* wander and meander, with a common thread of the presence of art, the question of text and authorship, and, indirectly, the aesthetic question of translation. Throughout these reflections, however, Pessoa returns, again and again, to a stance of anti-subjectivity or what he termed extreme depersonalization, producing reflections in which the narrative standpoint is consistently obliterated, erased. For instance, he writes in one passage of the

> vagabond words that desert me as soon as they're written, wandering on their own over slopes and meadows of images, along avenues of concepts, down footpaths of confusion ... these pages are the scribbles of my intellectual self-unawareness. I trace them in a stupor of feeling whatever I feel, like a cat in the sun, and I sometimes reread them with a vague, belated astonishment, as when I remember something I forgot ages ago.[31]

Later in this passage, Pessoa, or rather his 'semi heteronym' Soares, claims with a characteristic crypticness that is itself a play with encryption: 'I sphinxly discern myself.'[32] In other words, the writing subject – in this case, not Pessoa but his beloved heteronym Bernardo Soares – is engaged in the Sisyphean task not of revealing or unravelling identity, thought, feeling, but rather the impossible, and always failed ('sphinxly') attempt to discern the self.

Pessoa's reflections on art, authorship and translation find resonance in the narrative structure of Sebald's works. Sebald creates a series of narrative subjects that in many ways function like Pessoa's famed heteronyms; through what Agamben has called, in reference to Pessoa, 'three different subjectifications/desubjectifications' that ultimately enact a 'radical desubjectification' of the primary narrative presences in the texts. The mystery of the narrator, a figure always loosely based on W. G. Sebald himself, but not purely autobiographical, becomes part of the mystery of the narrative he recounts and attempts to reconstruct; ultimately, this mystery returns to the puzzle of how to read Sebald as writer: German? British? Jewish?

This is particularly acute in the final section of *The Emigrants*, when the Jewish figure – Max Aurach in the original German, Max Ferber in the English translation – tells the narrator that he has not left Manchester for twenty-two years.[33] The first line of the story provides the echo for this, creating a doubling effect between the two figures: 'Until my twenty-second year I had never been further away from home than a five- or six-hour train journey.'[34] Like the painter Ferber, who continually undoes the images on his canvasses, the narrator, at the end of the story (now winter 1990/91) 'not infrequently' unravels what he has written to date about the account of Max Ferber, as he is cast into a crisis not only about the act of writing about Ferber, but more generally 'about the whole questionable business of writing'.[35] The text he has been working on – presumably, but not necessarily, the one we have been reading to this point – consists of hundreds of pages of scribble, 'in pencil and ballpoint. By far the greater part had been crossed out, discarded, or obliterated by additions. Even what I had ultimately salvaged as a "final" version seemed to me a thing of shreds and patches, utterly botched.'[36] By reading *The Emigrants* as a text comprised of heteronyms, we can read the narrator's expression of literary impotence at the end of the Max Ferber chapter not as (*pace* Adorno) an exploration of the limits of and failure of writing to capture the experience of the Shoah, but rather as Sebald's acknowledgement of his role as storyteller and collector (of the photographs and images that are found in the text).

This written version that is a condensed and 'botched' translation/transmission of Aurach's 'life story', again mirroring Aurach's 'botched' paintings, is also a translation/transcription from the English conversations between the narrator and Aurach and the German in which it is written down. When the narrator tracks down Aurach and spends 'three days and nights' in conversation (a conversation 'in which many more things were said than I shall be able to write down here'), we learn, for the first time, that Ferber has not spoken German since his departure from Munich in 1939 and has in fact lost his native tongue, thus suggesting traumatic loss as the basis of Ferber's loss of the German language[37]: 'It survives in me as no more than an echo, a muted and incomprehensible murmur. It may have something to do with this loss of language, this oblivion, Ferber went on, that my memories reach no further back than my ninth or eighth year, and that I recall little of the Munich years after 1933 other than processions, marches, and parades.'[38] The German text for the phrase 'the loss of language, this oblivion' ('diese Einbuße oder Verschüttung der Sprache') evokes language as entrapped – as in a bombed-out building – not spoken, banned from its natural environment, impoverished, language amid the rubble and in a process of decay. Drawing on this notion of decay, English phrases and expressions are scattered throughout the German original; like the photographs and images that interrupt the narrative, the eruption of English within the German text creates a layer of textual abrasion that sometimes interrupts, sometimes simply recasts the narrative. In this way, the presumed 'English' that Ferber and the narrator speak, in the German original text, always calls the Germanness and the idea of the 'original' of the text into question, suggesting instead that the German text is itself a translation of the transmitted, putatively English dialogue between Ferber and the German-born narrator.

While the English translation absorbs and erases the 'foreign' English of the German text, what we do not hear, however, in the German version, are the accents of Ferber and the narrator, the inflections that would be present in the English they speak. Thus we are reminded of the near-impossibility of the translation of sound and of the acoustic layers of speech, perhaps the aura of speech. The auratic 'sound' of Ferber's (Aurach's) lost, muted German that no doubt finds its echo in his accent in English is as much a layer of ruin as the photographs that punctuate the text. Finally, one has to ask whether the images in the English edition are also 'translated', or whether they stand as echo and trace of the original? As trace of the original, are the images the auratic in the text, the authentic original that cannot be translated?

The figure in the original German of *The Emigrants*, Max Aurach, is generally taken to be based on the British painter Frank Auerbach. The migration of sound and meaning of the name Auerbach to Aurach, and then to Ferber in the English translation, suggests a number of readings. First, the collapse of the name Auerbach to Aurach suggests the trace and spectral presence of the iconic name Auerbach, laden with traces of German cultural and intellectual history and also British art.[39] But the English translation of *Die Ausgewanderten* migrates even further, replacing the already-'translated' and collapsed name Aurach with the name Ferber, itself a pun on the vocation of the figure Max Aurach/Ferber, a painter who obsessively paints over ('übermalen') and thus erases, Penelope-like, his own canvases.

The puzzling switch from Aurach to Ferber in the English translation has been explained, in an article in *The Guardian* shortly before Sebald's death, as a result of Auerbach's refusal to allow his paintings to appear in the English edition. Aurach's name carries the echo of Benjamin's notion of the aura, while Aurach himself, as painter, continually fails to produce the original work of art, producing instead repetitions that are erased. Aurach, whose name suggests the trace and the aura of the German émigré and with that, a spectral presence of German Bildung, a figure whose life story is 'botched' by a narrator we never 'know', inhabits a Manchester that is an 'immigrant city',[40] a city of industrial ruin, and a place of British, German and Jewish memory. Recounting how he has never returned to Germany, Aurach tells the narrator: 'To me, you see, Germany is a country frozen in the past, destroyed, a curiously extraterritorial place, inhabited by people whose faces are both lovely and dreadful.'[41]

Returning to his room in the Midland Hotel in Manchester, after having visited Aurach/Ferber, who is in the hospital for pulmonary emphysema (and who now finds it 'next to impossible to use his voice'), the narrator wanders back through the streets of Manchester to the Midland, a once-glorious nineteenth-century hotel that is 'now on the brink of ruin', where one 'rarely encounters either a hotel guest or one of the chambermaids or waiters who prowl about like sleepwalkers'.[42] The narrator suddenly feels as if he were in a hotel 'somewhere in Poland', in a hotel room described as sepulchral ('the old-fashioned interior put me curiously in mind of a faded wine-red velvet lining, the inside of a jewellery box or violin case') and, in this state that evokes death, enters into a reverie sparked by the sound of a concert (which it is not clear he is really hearing – 'the sound came from so far away') that triggers the memory of seeing, 'one by one', the photographs from an exhibition in Frankfurt he had seen the year before of the 'Litzmanstadt ghetto'. Here the most significant linguistic displacement in *The Emigrants* is found, the one that most clearly situates the entire story as one that hinges on translation and the echo. Using the Germanized 'Litzmanstadt' for Lodz, the narrator remarks that Lodz was once known as the 'polski Manchester', which makes Manchester, then, the English Lodz/ Litzmanstadt. Translating the industrial city of Manchester to a Polish, and Holocaust-era equivalent, the narrator weaves together the Jewish spaces of Poland with the industrial spaces of England, recasting British history to include the ruined spaces of Europe. As we move, at the end of *The Emigrants*, from Manchester to Lodz, the 'polski Manchester', we are left in Poland, with the narrator, a Poland of historical photograph, a

Poland of memory, in particular Jewish memory, a Poland in the imaginary space of a narrator who remains unexplained and unexplored, and a Poland in which the name of a place is forever in ruin, forever fractured: Lodz/Litzmanstadt, hovering, always, between its original Polish name and its translated, Germanized name, between the 'polski Manchester', as it might have been known, and how it is known today, as the Lodz ghetto. We, the readers of this text, are at the end turned ourselves into émigrés, transported ('übersetzt') and dwelling, always, among languages, from Manchester to Lodz/Litzmanstadt, and back from Lodz to Manchester. In this way, Sebald suggests a new way of reading and writing German and Jewish memory, perhaps, even, a new way of being Jewish in England, Germany and beyond.

Notes

1. To be sure, some of the issues I raise about Sebald would apply to any writer on the Holocaust or on Jewish themes, in any language, who was not Jewish, but I will be trying to make the case that it is the interplay between German and Jew that makes Sebald's case particularly interesting.
2. The first part of my title, 'How Jewish is it?', echoes the 1980 novel by Walter Abish, 'How German is it?' Abish's novel, which won the 1981 PEN/Faulkner award for best fiction, is an interesting point of comparison to many of Sebald's texts, as it raises the question of a fundamental 'Germanness' (and Jewishness). As a Viennese-born Jew who emigrated to the United States after the war, Abish as author is also an interesting counterpart to Sebald.
3. Roland Barthes (2001), 'The Death of the Author', *Norton Anthology of Theory and Criticism*, New York: Norton, p. 1466.
4. My reference to Benjamin's angel of history underscores the ways in which German-Jewish discourse on history, landscape and memory grew out of critical encounters with Benjamin's notions of ruin in Baroque allegory (in the *Ursprung des deutschen Trauerspiels*), his concept of language as 'Bruchstücke' comprising original and translation, and his reflections on the materiality of memory. For a discussion of the links between Benjamin's insistence on memory as medium, see Karen Remmler's (2005) article 'On the Natural History of Destruction and Cultural Memory: W. G. Sebald'. For a reading of *The Emigrants* as a text about traumatic loss, see Katja Garloff (2004), 'The Emigrant as Witness: W. G. Sebald's *Die Ausgewanderten*', *German Quarterly*, 77, 1, pp. 76–94. There are, of course, other contemporary novels, such as Peter Nadas' (1997) *A Book of Memories* (New York: Farar, Straus & Giroux) that are even more complex, that create narrative ruin and theorize memory in an even more elusive manner. Sebald's work, similar and yet markedly different in its US reception from Nadas, Kertesz, Manea and other major contemporary voices grappling with (a largely Eastern) European past, can be read as a mediation between Germany and other geographical spaces through his foregrounding of the transmission of language.

5. See Rüdiger Görner (2003), 'Im Allgäu, Grafschaft Norfolk. Über W.G. Sebald in England', *Text + Kritik*, IV, p. 27.
6. See Martin Swales (2004), 'Theoretical Reflections on the Work of W. G. Sebald', in J. J. Long and Anne Whitehead (eds), *W. G. Sebald: a Critical Companion*, Seattle: University of Washington Press, pp. 23–8.
7. John Zilcosky (2004), 'Sebald's Uncanny Travels: the Impossibility of Getting Lost', in Long and Whitehead (eds), *W. G. Sebald: a Critical Companion*, pp. 102–20.
8. Thomas Mann and, in a different medium, Bertolt Brecht, might be the earlier analogous figures whose work had an impact on the Anglo-American world.
9. In thinking about intentional lacunae between language and place, a pivotal case is Marc Shell's encyclopaedic project of redefining American literature as work produced *in* America, regardless of the original language of the text. See Marc Shell and Werner Sollors (eds) (2000), *Multilingual Anthology of American Literature: a Reader of Original Texts with English Translations*, New York: New York University Press.
10. One small point that bears mention: the German edition of Grass's *Krebsgang* calls it a novella; by the time it appeared in English, it was super-sized to a novel. We can speculate about this, of course, and while the reason undoubtedly has to do with marketing, it is also clear that the weight of the novel swells, with the accumulated debate, by the time it appears in English. Similarly, Sebald's texts have increased in significance, through public debate and in particular through translation.
11. For an incisive discussion of tropes of rubble and translated language as Derridean trace in Bachmann's short story 'Simultan', see Siobhan Craig (2000), 'The Collapse of Language and the Trace of History in Ingeborg Bachmann's "Simultan"', *Women in German Yearbook*, 16, pp. 39–60.
12. I am grateful to Taryn L. Okuma for her insights on Sebald on post-Imperial British memory, delivered at a conference I organized in 2004. '"People nowadays hardly have any idea": Post-Imperial British Memory and W. G. Sebald's *The Rings of Saturn*' (Center for German and European Studies Symposium, University of Wisconsin–Madison, 29 April 2004).
13. W. G. Sebald (1998), *The Rings of Saturn* (Michael Hulse, trans.), New York: New Directions, pp. 3–4.
14. Ibid., p. 89.
15. Ibid.
16. See Pico Iyer (2000), *The Global Soul*, New York: Vintage, p. 67.
17. Walter Benjamin (2002), 'The Storyteller', in Howard Eiland and Michael W. Jennings (eds), *Walter Benjamin: Selected Writings Volume 3, 1935–1938*, Cambridge: Belknap Press of Harvard University Press, p. 145.
18. Ibid., p. 149.
19. Carol Jacobs (1993), 'The Monstrosity of Translation: Walter Benjamin's "The Task of the Translator"', *Telling Time*, Baltimore: Johns Hopkins University Press, p. 129.
20. Benjamin (2002), *Selected Writings*, p. 249. In the notes to the German edition, the editors stress the uncertain origin of this fragment that was found in the Benjamin Nachlaß. In 1935 or 1936 Benjamin and Günther Anders held a conversation, intended for radio broadcast, about philosophical problems of translation. It is possible, although not certain, that the fragment reprinted in the collected works is the same as the one Anders refers to.

21. Walter Benjamin (1985), *Gesammelte Schriften VI* (Rolf Tiedemann and Hermann Schweppenhäuser, eds), Frankfurt: Suhrkamp, p. 158.
22. Sebald's concern with transmission and translation of conversations recalls as well the pivotal relationship between testimony and memory for Jewish writing after the Shoah. It also calls to mind Giorgio Agamben's reworking of Primo Levi's turn to Coleridge's *Rime of the Ancient Mariner*, where Agamben's (re)citation of the Coleridge poem, through Levi's evocation of it, serves to remind us of the urgency of narration.
23. See interview with Chris Daniels in *Jacket*: http://jacketmagazine.com/29/kent-iv-daniels.html. Daniels goes on to explain that in addition to the 72 heteronyms in Pessoa's work, there is also the 'orthonym', a fictional writer named Fernando Pessoa who is not actually Fernando Pessoa, but an invented writer with the author's name. Often enough, it is impossible to know exactly which is the 'real' Fernando Pessoa. But overall, it is quite simple. The confusion does not come from Pessoa, really, but from his readers.
24. Bill Friend (2004), 'Deferral of the Author: Impossible Witness and the Yasusada Poems', *Poetics Today*, 25, 1, p. 139.
25. *Roland Barthes by Roland Barthes* (1977) (Richard Howard, trans.), New York: Hill and Wang, p. 56.
26. Richard Zenith (ed. and trans.) (2001), *The Selected Prose of Fernando Pessoa*, New York: Grove Press, p. 222.
27. http://www.epc.buffalo.edu/authors/perloff/boston.html
28. Fernando Pessoa (2003), *The Book of Disquiet* (Richard Zenith, trans.), New York: Penguin.
29. Zenith (ed. and trans.), *Selected Prose of Pessoa*, p. 254.
30. Ibid., p. 262.
31. Pessoa, *Book of Disquiet*, p. 286.
32. Ibid.
33. While I will use the name Ferber, from the English translation, I want to stress that the English is not a replacement for the name 'Aurach' from the original German, but rather carries the traces of that name.
34. W. G. Sebald (1996), *The Emigrants* (Michael Hulse, trans.), New York: New Directions, p. 149.
35. Ibid., p. 230.
36. Ibid., pp. 230–1.
37. For an excellent discussion of the link between trauma and language in Sebald, see Garloff, 'The Emigrant as Witness'.
38. Sebald, *Emigrants*, p. 182.
39. It also evokes Benjamin's notion of the aura. The name 'Aurach' is a homophone, interestingly, for the aurochs, a primitive race of cattle and the ancestor of all the bovidae, that survived until the Bronze Age in Britain and then in Europe. The last Auroch died in 1627 in a Polish park, but two German zoologists in the 1920s worked to recreate the species: Ur-ox, the primeval cow, cow as ruin, extinct in Britain but recreated through German science and wandering the Scottish highlands, an example, perhaps, of Sebald's ironic twist on his own natural history of destruction.
40. Sebald, *Emigrants*, p. 181.
41. Ibid.
42. Ibid., p. 233.

Part IV

Russian-Speaking Jews and Transnationalism

7

Homo Sovieticus in Disneyland: the Jewish Communities in Germany Today

Judith Kessler

The idea of a 'new German Jewry' is not a straightforward or obvious concept. This is particularly because I doubt whether a 'new German Jewry' in fact exists, whether the title is not simply wishful thinking, considering that only a tiny remnant of the pre-war community survives and is just barely able to maintain some key positions such as elected representatives and functionaries. While there is certainly a future for the Jewish community in Germany, I doubt it will have very much to do with what has traditionally been considered 'German' Judaism.

This chapter substantiates this claim by describing the reality of Jewish community life in Germany today. The immigration of almost 200 000 people from the former Soviet states (half of whom were non-Jewish relatives) since 1989 when the Berlin Wall fell, arguably saved Jewish communities throughout Germany from dying out; at the same time, this influx of migration has turned these communities upside down. From a population of 28 000 Jews prior to 1989, the numbers suddenly rose to approximately 102 000 people. About 8 per cent of the Jews currently living in Germany have emigrated from the former Soviet Union; in many communities they now comprise 100 per cent of total community membership.[1] The German-Polish majority that dominated prior to 1989 has become an ever decreasing minority; the influx of Israeli and American Jews, however, does represent a slight counterbalance to the Soviet Jewish migration.

Structural and demographic problems: education and employment

Every major long-term study confirms that after fifteen years of Jewish immigration, the Jewish communities in Germany have reached their limits. Furthermore, studies conclude that the integration of the majority of the Russian Jews has largely failed; the affinity of this population to Judaism or to German society at large is marginal at best.[2] More than 70 per cent of these immigrants are unemployed and up to 85 per cent are long-term welfare dependants.[3] Such statistics prove that the initial euphoria experienced in the aftermath of the fall of the Berlin Wall has now given way to disillusionment. Today, discussions abound about limiting Jewish immigration altogether. Jewish communities are thus placing their hopes on the next generation.

How did this state of affairs come about? Apart from the poor economic situation of the Soviet Jewish population, it is also important to consider its demographic and social structure: Soviet Jewish immigration to Germany is interconnected in the sense that entire families and communities have immigrated to Germany.[4] These groups encompass a disproportionately high percentage of elderly people. This is part of the explanation for the high unemployment rates of Jewish Soviet migrants now living in Germany. Unlike the classical working immigrants, the *Gastarbeiter*, who arrived in Germany mainly until the 1970s, only 15 per cent of the current group are under the age of twenty, while 34 per cent are older than sixty. The ratio between births and deaths within the Jewish communities is currently one to six. Most significant is the fact that the majority of these immigrants do not have any chance on the job market. Rather than employment agencies or day-care centres, Jewish communities in Germany today are most in need of nursing homes.

While almost 70 per cent of Soviet Jewish immigrants hold a university degree, the German professional and educational structure represents yet another obstacle to integration.[5] Back in the Soviet Union, most of these immigrants had careers in the industrial and technical sectors: 20 per cent of all immigrants (men and women alike) worked as engineers; followed by teachers, doctors and economists. However, many professionals cannot find work in Germany today. For instance, it is difficult to translate the skills of a Siberian botanist or a lecturer of Marxism-Leninism into a viable German employment. Immigrants also encounter language proficiency obstacles and competition with younger candidates and/or German employees (who have first priority for any job). Additionally, many certificates held by immigrants are not recognized in Germany (teaching certificates, for instance) and there are hardly any retraining courses available; the German state also imposes a 'residence requirement' that stipulates that immigrants have to reside wherever the state sends them.

As a result of these and other obstacles, three-quarters of all Russian Jewish immigrants remain unemployed. Another problem is one of unrealistic expectations on the part of the immigrants themselves. In their country of origin, most Soviet Jews had good positions and a relatively high social status with concurrent material benefits. Once in Germany, they are thus not willing to accept just 'any' job. Ironically, they do not have to accept 'any' job because they have the option of living on welfare. Sometimes this is in fact the most comfortable option. While these facts may sound anecdotal, they are based on my ten years of experience working in the welfare department of the Jewish community of Berlin.

The situation for the younger immigrants is somewhat different. Most of them speak German, are enrolled in a German university, and have contact with non-Russians. However, as discussed, there are a very limited number of young Jews currently living in Germany. Additionally, many of these Jewish youth are prone to distancing themselves from active Jewish life once they have come of age or have started a career. They are doing this partly to distance themselves from the prevailing post-Soviet structures in community life developed by their parents, and partly because they have developed relatively few connections with Judaism as such.

Reasons for migrating to Germany and 'religious' orientation

The character of Jewish Soviet migration of the past decade is thus quite different from previous waves of migration that were otherwise directed mainly to Israel. Earlier waves of immigrants from the 1970s and early 1980s were orientated towards religion or Zionism; they had an ideological message and many struggled for years to get out of their countries of origin. Immigration today is no longer as ideologically driven. Instead, the motivation to immigrate is based primarily on pragmatic considerations: it is a response to logistic or financial problems such as an uncertain economic situation (Belarus); an unreliable legal system (Yukos); poor prospects for children (military service in Chechnya); and, above all, the departure of close friends. As such, the typical Jewish Soviet immigrant of the 1990s is apolitical, secularized and Western-oriented, very strongly defined by the Soviet system and has a high percentage of non-Jewish family members.

One important question that follows is: why have so many Soviet Jews decided to immigrate to Germany? When the German government decided to admit Soviet Jews in 1990, many potential migrants were convinced that the Germans had learned their lesson from the past.

Only a few of those who decided to go to Germany were directly affected by the Shoah, and anti-Semitism was often considered a specific Soviet matter. Also, because the US, the 'paradise' most Russians dreamt of, had restricted its immigration quota and Israel was considered too dangerous and too 'foreign', Germany seemed to be the most viable option: 'the land of poets and thinkers', economically stable, cosmopolitan and theoretically at least as worldly as the US.[6] 2002 was the year when more Jews immigrated to Germany than to Israel; this is a trend that continues today. Now admission for Jewish Russian emigrants is to be restricted again. It should additionally be noted that while 200 000 Russian Jews immigrated to Germany, two and a half million Russians with German ancestry were taken in as well.[7]

Soviet Jews have also been prone to immigrate to Germany because of its geographic proximity, and climatic and cultural similarity. More than 90 per cent of the immigrants come from the European part of the former USSR, from large cities such as Moscow, Odessa, Kiev, St Petersburg and Dnepropetrovsk. But only 32 per cent of the 'Russian' Jews are from Russia proper. Nearly 50 per cent come from the Ukraine, and many others are from former neighbouring Soviet republics, such as Moldavia, or the Baltic states. While these immigrants come from different social and cultural backgrounds, they retain much in common, such as the Russian language and the continued influence of 'Sovietization'.[8]

The similarities between the Soviet groups do not end there, however; largely cut off from Judaism during more than seventy years of Soviet rule, their Jewish identities persisted only as a result of having a passport entry that read 'Nationality: Jewish'. As a result, most Soviet Jews today have minimal cultural and religious knowledge about or internal affiliation to Judaism (this is based on the small number of Soviet Jews who have had a *Brit Mila, Bar/Bat Mitzvah*, married under the *Chuppa*, or speak Yiddish or Hebrew). According to a 2002 survey of the Berlin Jewish congregation, most of the immigrants did not mention 'religion' as one of the reasons for joining the congregation. Instead, most indicated that they chose to join the Jewish community because they were hoping to receive assistance once in Germany, and representation of their interests and security more generally. Those who did indicate some form of religious orientation defined themselves mainly as 'liberal Jews'; only very few respondents identified themselves as orthodox. More than 50 per cent however, declared that they would not or could not decide about a religious identification, and 16 per cent claimed to be 'atheist'.[9]

Despite this apparent secularization, almost 80 per cent of Soviet Jews living in Germany consider it important to be buried in a Jewish cemetery;

and more than two-thirds(!) hope that their children will marry a Jew. Most of them do identify themselves at least in this way with their Judaism. On the other hand, nearly 50 per cent of the immigrants refuse circumcision; and over two-thirds do not want a *Bar-* or *Bat Mitzvah.*[10] The situation does look slightly better for those children who go through Jewish kindergartens, elementary schools and youth centres. Often, these children end up playing the role of 'cultural intermediary' for their parents.

The situation is particularly complicated for children with Jewish fathers but non-Jewish mothers (and thus, not considered Jewish according to *Halakha* law) and other non-Jewish family members. More than half of the Soviet Jewish immigrants are not in fact Jewish according to *Halakha* law, and are thus rejected by the Orthodox Jewish community. If these individuals were allowed to join Jewish communities – provided they wanted to do so – the 'Russification' of Jewish life in Germany would develop even more dramatically. To date, however, there are still more immigrants outside than inside the Jewish communities: only 83 000 of 200 000 immigrants have (officially) become members of a Jewish community in Germany.[11]

Because of the presence of many non-Jewish relatives and the growing influence of the church in the former Soviet Union, 'Jewish identity' is at risk of disappearing in Jewish circles in Germany. For example, throughout Germany – particularly in places where the congregation is unable to offer social services – various missionary sects manage to proselytize Jewish immigrants. We know that in places without a native Jewish congregation 'Jewish basic knowledge' is provided to Jewish migrants by members of the Catholic or Evangelical Church who take care of their integration, but who obviously have their own objectives. It is thus not surprising to find a new member of the Berlin Jewish community, for example, walking along one of the main avenues selling the *Watch Tower*, the Jehovah's Witness magazine.

'Sovietization' persists: transnational ties and Soviet networks in Germany

Another difference between the current and the former mass emigration of Soviet Jews to Germany relates to the overtly transnational character of this current wave.[12] In times past you left for good, losing your previous citizenship and, in many cases, any contact with your home country. Immigrants adopted the language and customs of their new country, and thus, there was virtually no turning back. Since the fall of the Iron Curtain, Jewish immigrants from the former Soviet Union may possess dual citizenship; they can keep their former Russian passports and apartments and thus move seamlessly between the two worlds. Most of them have friends and family all over the world, and they keep in touch with each other by mail, phone and e-mail. The Russian exile-newspapers are filling pages with advertisements of cross-border transports, marriage bureaus, satellite dishes, fax machines, plane tickets, exit visas and journeys to the 'old' country.

Together with the opening of the East, a new communications technology has evolved. You no longer have to wait twenty years to see an uncle again, and you can stay in touch with your own language and culture, never mind the ease with which you can cross geographic distances. And if you're living in Berlin, as my Lithuanian friends do, you can travel to Vilnius by air for 50 euros once a month on one of the many no-frills airlines, bringing back everything your heart desires – from salami to bread – paid for by the rent you continue to receive for your apartment in Vilnius. Even those who do not travel are likely to be 'networked' on a transnational scale. Moscow television advertises products available only in Israel; Russian authors located in the US have their texts printed cheaply in Russia and distribute them throughout the Russian Diaspora; you can get Berlin's Russian newspapers in Tel Aviv. These papers are important opinion-makers, and their influence in Jewish communities (for example during elections) is already bigger than that of the German Jewish press.

As the Russian Jewish population grows (in Berlin alone there are 200 000 former Soviet Jewish citizens) a kind of Chinatown-like infrastructure has developed, that, by now, can satisfy most of the needs of the Soviet immigrants: internal job markets, concert artists' agencies, brokerage offices. Nobody *has* to defer to the German or Jewish society or the new language. Although this may be a comfortable set-up and can help immigrants to overcome nostalgia for the home left behind, I argue that such infrastructure will yield negative effects in the long run. Elsewhere, I have referred to such immigrants as *origin-oriented* (in contrast to the mostly young *dually oriented* immigrants).[13] These origin-oriented immigrants hardly know anything about German political and social structures and participate only as consumers in their new society. As a result, it is unlikely that they will develop any loyalty and commitment to any larger group or society in their country of settlement.

Compared with the earlier waves of Soviet Jewish migrants to Germany, today's immigrants are more affected by their experience under the Soviet system; a high percentage of today's immigrants were far more involved in the Soviet system as former organization members and holders of leading positions. Since the Soviet system was characterized by an economy of scarcity, egalitarianism and paternalism, as well as by an omnipotent bureaucracy, corruption and patronage, it is realistic to expect the present of specific Soviet-influenced attitudes, what I call the 'Homo Sovieticus'. This attitude can be characterized by dependence on authority, denial of responsibility, separation of person and society, general indifference to public affairs and reliance on informal networks. While not every immigrant behaves according to this typology, there is considerable evidence that having lived in such a society has long-term effects on an individual's character and attitude. Much of one's behaviour can, for example, best be understood by looking at the context of origin, for instance, when immigrants 'collect' official stamps, signatures and letters of recommendation, or when a former female pharmacy employee claims a higher status than a professor, or when members of the community try to further their aims by referring to their connections with members of the board, or when their letters read like solemn reports of a party convention.

However, as immigrants begin to take more part in decision-making bodies, old attitudes are likely to adapt and change. I refer to a few examples based on my experience as a Jewish community worker in Berlin to highlight this point. A community deputy went to the Berlin senate offering a bottle of vodka as a gift while attempting to 'chat' about money for a project. Another is openly boycotting Jewish memorial services because he believes that the German politicians, whose cultivation took years of effort, will only deliver senseless babble. When our congregation's youth group bought some cheap furniture, terms like 'shameless waste', 'dancing at a funeral' and 'grim enemies' were used. Another Russian official had the board's job offers inspected by private detectives. In communities with Russian majorities a quasi-socialist system has been established, complete with rituals of submission, official statements, one-year-plans and censorship... Insignificant as all this may sound, it does give an idea of today's atmosphere. Rather more alarming are those immigrant communities who refuse support by the Central Welfare Institute of Jews in Germany because they do not want the long-established German Jewish institutions to meddle in their affairs. Consequently there are Russian Jewish communities branching out into new and independent 'law-abiding' communities and fighting for state funds among themselves. The situation in Potsdam is one recent example of this.[14]

Concurrent with the persistence of old Soviet-influence attitudes, changes are taking place at the grass-roots level nonetheless. According to my own polls,[15] immigrants from the former Soviet Union when compared to members who grew up in Western countries have more conservative and traditional values, a more self-centred world-view, are less prepared to develop any initiative on their own, rate 'discipline and teachers' authority' higher than 'autonomy' or a 'well-founded social and sociopolitical education', and tend to shift blame to 'the system' or 'the community'. Paradoxically the immigrants are preserving thought-patterns which are considered outdated in their home countries in view of the huge upheavals that have taken place there. Therefore it is getting even more difficult to have progressive ideas accepted in Germany by the Soviet Jewish immigrants. Furthermore, the lack of any private initiative is a result of a systemic socialization (the same goes for the German Jews after decades of being subsidized and courted); an individual had little influence under socialism, for example. The state provided and made all the decisions. Little wonder, then, that the immigrants crave a 'guiding hand' in their new country too.[16]

Another typical example: during a meeting community officials explained for hours that the communities were unable to change laws, could not provide jobs, and could only help people to help themselves. The immigrants were implored to lower their expectations (never mind their fine diplomas), to study German and to accept jobs that were 'beneath them', and become active themselves. The speeches were hardly finished when the first immigrant complained: 'I do want to integrate, but the community is doing nothing for me! Why isn't the community giving me a job?' The man had been an engineer in Berlin for three years, and he could barely understand when asked for his name in German! But the story continues: after the meeting the community started a job centre and persuaded Jewish employers to provide jobs and places of apprenticeship, which required a lot of energy and convincing arguments. And then what happened? Nobody answered the advertisements. And when job applicants could finally be found, they quit their jobs after just a couple of days because the work was too hard or the pay too low.

In the beginning, it was possible to explain this behaviour by the immigrants' lack of information. Most of them came to Germany with the naïve hope of a better and wealthier world, a sort of Jewish Disneyland that would be willing to make up for their earlier sufferings by allowing them a share of the country's wealth. Locals too – Germans and Jews – had wrong expectations, and assumed the Russian Jews would all be like their most eminent representatives, such as David Oistrach or Nathan Sharansky. These, they hoped, would fill up the communities and the synagogues. The average immigrant is different however; he/she is a civil engineer who expects the Jewish community to find them an apartment and a job. The Jewish infrastructure in the bigger German cities is enviable compared to that of other minorities: available to immigrants are advice centres, kindergartens, schools, community centres, retirement homes, social clubs, courses, theatres and so on. And many new Jewish organizations could only develop because of the immigration. Yet all this was not and is not enough.

The small communities are improvising to this very day, because they are not as financially prosperous, and the big communities and their expensive institutions are about to collapse, despite state aid. In Berlin – whose Jewish community is considered to be one of the 'rich' ones – only 2000 out of 12 000 members are paying Jewish community taxes.[17] And the communities have not managed to convey realistic moderation and the necessity of voluntarism to the new members. In Berlin, for example, the Jews coming from the Caucasus are demanding their own Sephardic synagogue and a salary for the rabbi, and so on. This, even though they have problems getting a *Minyan* – a group of ten Jewish men needed for prayer – together, and even though in other small (Ashkenazi) communities the rabbis are working without pay, and everybody knows that the community is burdened with debts to the sum of millions.

The immigrants' expectations complement the utopian structures, the 'Disneyland' of the old post-war community chiefs who built structures which do not fit today's circumstances anymore; in other words, today's realities are not met by the communities built on the values and possibilities of 1945. Theirs was a fragile dream which they built together with non-Jewish Germans, a world where everybody knew, understood and observed unwritten, but well-established rules. Yet these structures are not very clear and partly responsible for the immigrants' fear of not getting their fair share. Many communities are run – still or again – like tiny *Shtetls* by non-professionals with the right connections. But meanwhile they are as big as medium-sized companies and in dire need of professional management. Up to ten years ago they could somehow muddle along. But now, with tens of thousands of new members and a new 'elite' without sufficient knowledge of either the German language or the German law, we have a serious problem.

Explaining the difference

To elaborate on the unwritten rules mentioned before: it is, for example, unimaginable that a club of Shoah-survivors would want to meet former German Wehrmacht soldiers; but the former Jewish Red Army soldiers want to do just that. This is a difficult situation. Meanwhile there are 'Clubs of the Veterans of the Great Patriotic War' in nearly every Jewish community. And since the German or Polish survivors of the Holocaust are by now outnumbered, they do not set the tone for community events as they once used to. Now the 'war veterans' run the show, sing patriotic songs, wear decorations, and tell each other how they liberated Berlin or Budapest. Both groups find their identity in the Second World War, but every side can only feel its own sorrow – 'What do *you* want? You were just in central Asia. I was in a concentration camp!' – and ignores the other's story. And they are two totally different stories indeed. The Russian Jews were fighting against Hitler-fascism as Soviet citizens, not as Jews. The German Jews can think only of the horrors of the concentration camps in which they were not 'heroes', but victims. The 'heroes', on the other hand, members of the former victorious world power, privileged and respected in the past, are becoming dependent outsiders in their new country, about whom nobody cares, often not even their own children. These older people, and most of them are in their seventies and eighties, are suffering acutely from a lack of respect and from the loss of their former status. They followed their children because they did not want to be alone, but the family groups that had held together for generations are breaking up. A lot of them are embittered, they feel futile and humiliated. As they do not have any rights to a German pension, they have turned into welfare recipients, although they worked their entire lives. They are forced to remain in a marginalized position and often lead lonely lives, independent of the fact that some would want to master German culture and to get in touch with other people.[18]

Of course there is a younger generation worth discussing as well. This group has a more dualistic orientation, that is, younger individuals are oriented both towards the culture of their country of origin and country of residence, acquiring the competence and cultural savvy to be successful within the new environment. They are the most likely members to be interested in Judaism and Jewish politics. Unfortunately they are a tiny group. Germany has about 80 million inhabitants and just about 15 000 Jews under the age of twenty. Only about 10 per cent of them are active in Jewish life.

A new Jewish cultural scene exists, even if it mostly caters to non-Jews,[19] and there are Jews in places which have been without Jews since the Second World War. The objective is thus to bring the Jews in Germany together. Because of the Russian take-over of language and culture it is now often the non-Russian Jews who feel excluded. They quit their community membership or – like the Israelis in Berlin – do not bother to join at all. The situation is complicated for everybody.[20]

Diana Pinto wrote recently that the Jewish immigration to Germany was like every other immigration where communities had to integrate new members.[21] By contrast, I consider the Jewish immigration to Germany to be a unique event. First, this is because people are immigrating to the former 'country of their murderers', where loyalty and identification – which Diana Pinto refers to as well – are much harder to establish than in countries like Canada or France. There are immigrants who often want to be neither 'Russian' nor 'German', and partially not even 'Jewish'. I am not talking about the usual complaining of a few new members, but about a fundamental change that has occurred in the Jewish communities across Germany. The former majority has become a minority all of a sudden, and can neither absorb the new majority nor call the shots any longer, even if not all of its members have yet fully realized this. The former majority can at best try to keep part of its autonomy and find a way to develop common interests with the Soviet Jews. So far, neither side has shown any interest in collaboration of this sort.

I will conclude with one final – and telling – example of the rift between the different Jewish groups now present in Germany. Every two years the established Jewish community in Munich hosts a Jewish culture congress where they reflect on their aims as a religious community, explore new issues beyond the Shoah and Israel, discuss the realities of modern Judaism, and the possibilities for turning towards the future with self-confidence, and so on. This is a marvellous and inspiring event that takes place in a castle in the mountains, much like a fairy-tale. The 400 participants are, however, anything but a representative cross-section of Germany's Jewish communities. The Russian majority is hardly represented, either as theme or as participants.

The German Jews have to face many new realities about their growing and diversifying population. Yet those Soviet immigrants who want to find a way to connect themselves to their lost Judaism need time, lots of time. They are – apart from a few exceptions – far from being 'assets' in the political and religious discourse, as Diana Pinto demands of the European Jews. In order to achieve this, they will have to consider their own personal positions as Jews and citizens. Perhaps the next generation, born in Germany, will be less burdened by the German or Soviet legacies, and once again capable of thinking and acting politically as Jews.

Notes

1. Judith Kessler (1989–2004), 'Mitgliederstatistik Zuwanderer, Berlin 1990–2004', Frankfurt/M: Zentralwohlfahrtsstelle der Juden in Deutschland, Mitgliederstatistik der Jüdischen Gemeinden.
2. Bundesamt für Migration und Flüchtlinge (BaMF)/Haug, Sonja (2005), *Jüdische Zuwanderer in Deutschland. Ein Überblick über den Stand der Forschung*, Working Papers, March; Yvonne Schütze (2003), 'Migrantennetzwerk im Zeitverlauf – Junge russische Juden in Berlin', *Berliner Journal für Soziologie*, 13; Karen Körber (2005), *Juden, Russen, Emigranten: Identitätskonflikte jüdischer Einwanderer in einer ostdeutschen Stadt*, Frankfurt: Campus; Karin Weiss (2004), 'Zuwanderung und Integration in den neuen Bundesländern – zwischen Transferexistenz und Bildungserfolg', in W. Woyke (ed.), *Integration und Einwanderung*, Schwalbach/Ts: Wochenschau Verlag; Barbara Dietz (2003), 'Jewish Immigrants from the Former Soviet Union in Germany', *East European Jewish Affairs*, 33, 2, pp. 7–19.
3. Michael Wuttke (2005), 'Deutschland: Diskussion um jüdische Zuwanderer', *Migration und Bevölkerung*, 1, 5, February. http://www.migration-info.de/migration_und_bevoelkerung/artikel/050101.htm; Marlies Emmerich (2004), 'Berlin statt Israel', *Berliner Zeitung*, 2 December.
4. Judith Kessler (1998), 'Jüdische Migration aus der früheren Sowjetunion seit 1990. Resümee einer Studie mit 4000 Zuwanderern aus der früheren Sowjetunion in Berlin', *Trumah*, 7, pp. 140–62.
5. Ibid.
6. Julius Schoeps, Willi Jasper and Bernhard Vogt (eds) (1999), *Ein neues Judentum in Deutschland, Fremd- und Eigenbilder der russisch-jüdischen Einwanderer*, Potsdam: Verlag Berlin-Brandenburg; Judith Kessler (1995/1997), *From Aizenberg to Zaidelman: Jewish Immigrants from East Europe and the Jewish Congregation Today*, Berlin: Die Ausländerbeauftragte des Senats.
7. Bundesverwaltungsamt Köln, Zuwandererstatistik 1991–2004.
8. Judith Kessler (2003) 'Jüdische Migration aus der früheren Sowjetunion seit 1990. Beispiel Berlin', *Hagalil Online*, 23 February. http://www.berlin-judentum.de/gemeinde/migration.htm
9. Judith Kessler (2002), 'The Cultural and Religious Self-image of Berlin Jews: Results of the First Congregational Survey', Berlin: Umfrage.
10. Ibid.
11. Zentralwohlfahrtsstelle der Juden in Deutschland, Mitgliederstatistik der Jüdischen Gemeinden, 1989–2004, Frankfurt/M.; Bundesverwaltungsamt Köln, Zuwandererstatistik, 1991–2005.
12. Julius H. Schoeps, Karl E. Grözinger and Gert Mattenklott (eds) (2005), *Menora: Jahrbuch für deutsch-jüdische Geschichte 15: Russische Juden und transnationale Diaspora*, Berlin/Wien: Philo Verlag; Andrei Dörre (2004), 'Transnationale soziale Lebenswelten jüdischer Zugewanderter aus den Nachfolgestaaten der UdSSR', unpublished Diploma Thesis, Berlin: Humboldt University.
13. Judith Kessler (2003) 'Jüdische Migration aus der früheren Sowjetunion seit 1990. Beispiel Berlin', *Hagalil Online*, 23 February. http://www.berlin-judentum.de/gemeinde/migration.htm
14. See 'Ungebetene Hilfe', *Jüdische Allgemeine* 1, 5, 6 January, 2005, p. 20.

15. Judith Kessler (2003) 'Jüdische Migration aus der früheren Sowjetunion seit 1990. Beispiel Berlin', *Hagalil Online*, 23 February. http://www.berlin-judentum.de/gemeinde/migration.htm; Kessler (2002), 'The Cultural and Religious Self-image of Berlin Jews'.
16. Judith Kessler (1999), 'The Search for Identity and Subculture: Experiences of Welfare Work in the Jewish Congregation', in Julius H. Schoeps (ed.), *Ein neues Judentum in Deutschland, Fremd- und Eigenbilder der russisch-jüdischen Einwanderer*, Potsdam: Veralg für Berlin-Brandenburg, pp. 87–100.
17. Protokolle der Repräsentantenversammlung der Jüdischen Gemeinde zu Berlin, 2004.
18. Judith Kessler (2004), 'Foreigners in Wonderland? A Critical View of the Expectations and Experiences among Jewish Immigrants from the Former Soviet Union in Berlin', paper presented at the conference Russian-Jewish Emigrants after the Cold War, Brandeis University.
19. This is a major point in Liliane Weissberg's chapter in this volume (Chapter 5).
20. Judith Kessler (2004), 'Klezmerfreie Zone oder Jewish Disneyland', in Wiltrud Apfeld (ed.), *Klezmer. Hejmisch und hip*, Essen: Klartext Verlag, pp. 100–4.
21. Diana Pinto (2004), 'Zukunft Europa. Wie die Juden sechs grundsätzliche Herausforderungen meistern können', *Jüdische Allgemeine*, 52, 4, 30 December.

8
Fifteen Years of Russian-Jewish Immigration to Germany: Successes and Setbacks

Julius H. Schoeps and Olaf Glöckner

In response to current changes in German immigration policy towards Russian Jews, it is necessary to summarize the successes and setbacks linked to the influx of this population over the last fifteen years. In 1991, the German government passed the so-called 'Contingency Refugee Act' for all Jewish inhabitants from the then crumbling Soviet Union. Since the implementation of this act, about 200 000 Russian Jews have migrated to Germany.[1] The impact of this new wave of migration into the country of Mozart, Goethe and Kant – but also of Hitler, Goebbels and Himmler – has been significant on a number of levels.

Indeed, only extreme optimists were hopeful that German Jewry could be revitalized after the tragedies of the twentieth century. But a revitalization is exactly what has happened thanks to the Russian-Jewish influx; from the mid-1990s until 2003 there were between 15 000 and 20 000 immigrants annually. Regardless of whatever else is written about them, it is undeniable that Russian Jews have saved the demographic stability of the Jewish communities in Germany, and generated, at least in part, a cultural and religious revival.

For the general public, it was more or less surprising when the Russian-Jewish immigration to Germany took shape at the beginning of the 1990s. It was also surprising that in the summer of 2006, modifications were passed in the conference of German Ministers of the Interior that seriously restrict Russian Jews' admission into Germany. From this point on, future Russian-Jewish immigrants have to pass a German language exam at their place of residence, will be assessed by a points system and are dependent on the agreement of a local Jewish community in Germany. In other words, each of the applicants has to prove that he/she will not be dependent on social welfare, and German politicians as well as Jewish leaders seek guarantees that he/she will be active within the

Jewish community. Why this change in policy now? Broadly conceived, these changes in migration policy reflect hardened social problems among the immigrants from the former Soviet Union, exhaustion in some of the receiving Jewish communities and the desire to win more Jews who are willing to be committed to the religious communities.

Fifteen years later

Before dealing with some of the current integration problems, it is useful to begin with a retrospective of the positive contributions that the Russian-Jewish influx has made to German-Jewish life. At the end of the 1980s, when the Iron Curtain still divided the Western world and the Eastern bloc, the German-Jewish communities faced an imminent demographic collapse. Most Jewish community members were quite elderly. In East Germany, still existing as the German Democratic Republic (GDR), the Jewish communities counted only a few hundred registered members in 1989. As a result, both German policy and Jewish communities welcomed those Russian Jews who were looking for the chance to 'break out', to leave the crumbling Soviet Union in the shadow of new threats of anti-Semitism. On the whole, these Russian Jews were increasingly opting to resettle in Central and Western Europe. They seemed to give little attention to the fact that although Germany was, for the time being, a safe haven, it was also the country of the former Nazi rule and the Holocaust. Whatever they themselves may have intended, the Russian Jews became the ones to fill the demographic gap that would ensure the continuation of Jewish life in Germany. Today there are more than 100 000 registered Jewish community members in Germany, with more than 80 per cent of Russian or East European origin.[2]

Berlin profited the most from this surprising Russian-Jewish influx. The Jewish community in Germany's capital boasts over 12 000 members today, compared to 6400 members in 1989.[3] Nearly ten synagogues are now open for services and other community events, and a vibrant Jewish cultural and educational life has also developed in the city. In smaller communities across Germany, there is now the possibility to recreate a full religious and cultural life; that alone marks a great success. New synagogues were built, for example, in Munich and Duisburg (Western Germany) as well as in Dresden and Chemnitz (Eastern Germany), and a considerable number of new communities – for instance in Emmendingen, Lörrach, Schwerin and Potsdam – were founded or refounded almost exclusively by Russian Jews. In cities like Berlin, Frankfurt and Munich, a Russian-Jewish cultural scene has begun to enrich the broader cultural landscape with people like singer Mark Aizikovitsch and young writers Wladimir Kaminer and Lena Gorelik. At the same time, the first Russian-Jewish scholars have been appointed to professorships at German universities.

Germany has suddenly climbed to third place in the ranking of the largest Jewish communities in contemporary Europe, after France and England. In the years 2002 and 2003, more Russian Jews settled in Germany than in Israel or in the United States. Already at the end of the 1990s, the social scientist Diana Pinto published a text in the German-Jewish yearbook *Menora* in which she referred to a 'newly developing Jewish Europe'.[4] Pinto suggested that a unified Germany had the potential to play a key role in 'Jewish Europe', primarily due to the mass immigration of Russian Jews since 1989. Some media have in fact promoted the idea of a 'Jewish Renaissance' in Germany. The intellectual discussions that followed asked whether Europe thus had the potential to become a third strong centre of contemporary Jewry, alongside Israel and the United States.

A damper on the euphoria

Such euphoric statements and discussions have, however, dwindled in recent years. Particularly in Germany, a muted discussion has emerged about significant setbacks regarding the Russian Jews' integration. Statistics from the late 1990s give evidence of a rapid increase in Jewish community membership. Those in Berlin and Munich almost doubled, and those in Cologne and Stuttgart tripled. The most extreme increases, however, were noted in Hanover, where there are now twelve times more community members. On the one hand, such an influx is very positive because it gives evidence for a real demographic stabilization of the Jewish communities. On the other hand, the influx has been so massive, that a German-Jewish minority is now challenged to integrate a Russian-Jewish majority. Costs were exploding for such tasks as social work and senior citizen welfare services, but also for the extension of the communities' infrastructure (new buildings for worship services, kindergartens, seniors' clubs). Some Jewish relief organizations, for example the Ronald S. Lauder Foundation, have provided much external assistance, materially as well as in personnel.

However, it soon became clear that substantial support was needed from the German government and German officials. In January 2003, a federal contract was signed between the German government and the Central Council of Jews in Germany confirming that there will be annual governmental funding of three million euros to be used primarily for the integration of Russian Jews. In addition, many state governments have signed federal state contracts with the state associations of Jewish communities.[5]

Ultimately, even the support by the German government and by state ministries cannot prevent some of the toughest integration issues outlined below. These problems are related to the two major challenges posed by the Russian-Jewish influx: first, the integration of the Russian Jews into German society, and second, their integration into the local Jewish communities. Below, we discuss a few problems which illustrate a stagnating integration process.

Extraordinary high unemployment

According to a survey by the Moses Mendelssohn Centre in Potsdam, about 50 per cent of the immigrants feel that their integration problems are far from being settled.[6] Indeed, about 40 per cent of them are unemployed,[7] and there has been no improvement since the beginning of the 1990s. As a result, the tax yield of the Jewish communities – which is linked to personal income levels – has remained at a very low level, thereby making it almost impossible to cover anything other than the pressing tasks such as integration, religious services and social work.

Disappointed community boards

The German Jewish community boards, or at least a part of them, have expressed disappointment that only a minority of the Russian Jews had really become active in community life. Several surveys confirmed that a majority of the Russian Jews are more or less secular, quite similar to those in Israel. According to several surveys, the interest in religious issues is lower than among the German Jews.[8]

Frustration in the Russian basis

The Jewish community basis, which consists of a Russian majority now, started to openly accuse the Central Council of Jews in Germany of ignoring their basic problems. According to the criticism expressed against the Russian Jews in the monthly *Jevrejskaja Gazeta*, for example, the Central Council was 'more concerned with the fight against anti-Semitism than with taking care of Russian-Jewish new arrivals'.[9]

Low identification with the host country

Finally, a current comparative study on Russian-Jewish migration to Germany, Israel and the US revealed that about 70 per cent of the immigrants in Israel and the United States identify with the host nation, compared to only 10 per cent identification with the host country for those in Germany.[10]

Such enormous differences in Russian Jews' identification with Israel and America on one side, and Germany on the other, highlight a wide range of unsolved problems and conflicts accompanying the Russian-Jewish immigrant experiences from Hamburg to Munich, Berlin to Düsseldorf. It is therefore necessary to take a closer look at the origins, characteristics and dimensions of these problems in order to gain insight into the current changes in German migration policy, as well as to better understand the criticisms and protests raised by the Russian- Jewish immigrants themselves.

Community conflicts

At the beginning of the 1990s, the German-Jewish leaders welcomed the Russian Jews as refugees and newcomers who could strengthen community life and hopefully revitalize every facet of Jewish life. However, it soon became clear that many Jews from the former Soviet Union arrived with very vague notions about their own Jewish identity. Many immigrants tended to use the communities as more of a general meeting and communication point, than as a place of religious activity. While Russian Jews tend to show a strong interest in aspects of Jewish history and culture, they are less concerned with religion, seeing their Jewishness primarily as an ethnic identification. In many cases, they do not understand why *halakhic* law prevents those immigrants who 'only' have a Jewish father from being allowed to become full community members; in other cases, they do not accept that their non-Jewish spouses are not eligible to receive community services. This is one of the biggest sources of contention, and as in Israel, there are similar conflicts between the Russian Jews and the Chief Rabbinate.

Russian-Jewish immigrants sometimes argue that the veteran members in the Jewish communities, the German-speaking members, are not really interested in their situation, and that they would prefer to maintain a cultural distance. This is one of the reasons why some immigrants tend to meet and organize among themselves, rather than inside the synagogue community. Thus, fifteen years after the beginning of the Russian-Jewish influx, a deep divide still exists between veterans and newcomers, and parts of the German media, well aware of theses problems, are quite keen on reporting such internal community conflicts.

It is no longer a secret that some Russian Jews sometimes prefer to act separately from the rest of the community, in order to establish

'Russian' literature, chess and music clubs inside the Jewish community. Others show a distinct interest in gaining power in the Jewish communities, and attempt to do so by using their growing majority in the representative platforms and organizational bodies. In many cases, this has led to feelings amongst the German-Jewish veterans that they are now a distinct minority whose own needs are being ignored. Nonetheless, in some of the Jewish communities where German Jews have retained the leading positions, the same asymmetrical relations can be noticed between the German-Jewish establishment at the top of the Jewish organizational bodies and an overwhelming Russian majority at the bottom.

The large Russian influx has also led to a structural differentiation inside organized German Jewry that is the source of some conflict. It is the first time since the Holocaust and the Second World War that the model of the Unified Jewish Community (*Einheitsgemeinde*)[11] is being questioned in regard to its usefulness. Several factions and religious groups, backed by a growing number of Eastern European immigrants, are seeking independence and official recognition by the German state. This makes it extremely difficult for the Central Council of Jews in Germany to continue uniting them under one roof. Among the most prominent new groups which have entered Jewish life in Germany since the 1990s are, for instance, the liberal communities of the Union of Progressive Jews in Germany (UPJ), several orthodox communities like Adass Jisroel in Berlin and the ultra-orthodox Chabad Lubawitsch movement. Chabad Lubawitsch has established a dozen community centres all over Germany and is providing a wide range of social and religious support to Jews, especially in underdeveloped areas in Germany, including a large number of Russian-speaking immigrants.

Russian Jews are not (yet) in key positions of the new flourishing Jewish groups and organizations, regardless of whether they are liberal or orthodox. This can partly be explained by tediously lengthy processes designed to reunite them with their Jewish roots, but also by their current social, economic and professional difficulties in Germany, which also hamper a greater commitment within the Jewish communities.

Failed social integration?

In general, Russian Jews do not belong to those immigrant groups and other minorities within Germany who face a constant fear of poverty or social decline. However, there has been an accumulation of social and economic problems among the Russian Jews in Germany. The high rate of unemployment among these immigrants marks another significant difference as compared to those Russian Jews who emigrated to Israel and the United States. Moreover, the unemployment rate of Russian Jews in Germany is significantly higher than the average unemployment rate among all foreigners in this country. In larger cities like Berlin, many Russian-Jewish immigrants seek a job in the Russian ethnic market. Admittedly, an increasing service sector with Russian shops, import–export, restaurants, bookstores, casinos and marriage agencies is likely to strengthen the Russian-speaking community itself, but it can hardly be a reasonable professional alternative for highly qualified scientists, doctors, engineers and artists.

To date there have been no studies conducted on the psychological problems among Russian Jews (although these abound for the Turkish minority in Germany). There are, however, confirmed indications from Jewish community employees and social workers that the number of Jewish immigrants suffering from serious depression has risen significantly over the last few years.[12] The Jewish communities are well aware of this problem, and try to provide practical and psychological support. Some of them, like the Jewish community in Berlin, have established their own job agencies, which provide jobs from Jewish employers for potential Jewish employees. Other communities have established telephone crisis lines for immigrants who are depressed or mentally ill.

The increased efforts of Jewish community workers to support Russian immigrants and to provide primarily practical help has caused a serious debate about the primary tasks expected of a modern Jewish community in Germany today. Some German-speaking veterans lament that religious concerns are neglected or even ignored today in favour of successful social and economic integration of the Russian Jews. Others argue that in a couple of years the 'Russians' will not only represent the demographic majority, but will also have taken over the leading positions in most of the Jewish communities. They also believe, however, that comprehensive support for the new members, even concerning job seeking, housing, occupational training and legal advice, is an important investment in the future of the synagogue community itself.

'Russian colonies'?

In regard to Central European immigration more broadly, the fact that Russian Jews represent only one group of the wider Russian-speaking community in Germany should also be taken into account. There are also a great number of ethnic German repatriates from the former Soviet

Union (*Aussiedler*), many of whom continue to speak Russian as their primary (and sometimes sole) language. Additionally, a considerable number of former Soviet dissidents, including former employees of the old Soviet military administration, have been granted permanent residency in Germany. Russian Jews are part of this greater migrant community, and at the very least share cultural interests with these other Russian speakers.

In Berlin, it is estimated that there are about 200 000 Russian-speaking people. It is obvious that some Russian Jews have intermingled with other non-Jewish Russian-speaking groups. Dense Russian neighbourhoods have emerged, for example, in the West Berlin neighbourhood Charlottenburg, to the extent that it is now popularly referred to as 'Charlotten*grad*'. Reviving an old immigrant tradition from the 1920s, Russian speakers with very different backgrounds are coming together here and establishing communication networks, theatres, cultural clubs and media concerns. At the moment, it is not yet clear whether the Russian Jews inside these neighbourhoods will dissolve inside the general Russian community, or whether they will play their own, unmistakable role as Jews with an Eastern European background. Their strong commitment inside the greater Russian community – some call it a 'Russian colony'[13] – indicates that these immigrants are searching for a new identity in a triangle between Russian, Jewish and German culture and tradition.

Not only Russian Jewish artists and scholars, but also journalists and publishers have been very active in their fields since the middle of the 1990s. However, several attempts to establish a Jewish magazine or monthly in the Russian language have for the most part failed. One exception is the monthly *Jevrejskaja Gazeta* ('Jewish Newspaper'), established in Berlin in the autumn of 2002, and now serving a Russian-Jewish readership across all of Germany. Consequently, the *Jevrejskaja Gazeta* reflects the integration problems experienced by its own readership. From time to time, for example, this monthly harshly criticizes the German-Jewish establishment as well as German immigration policy. The *Jevrejskaja Gazeta* periodically publishes the positions of secular Russian Jews, as well as immigrants who have joined German-Jewish communities, but who still do not feel respected by their respective leadership. The somewhat belligerent reports and comments of the *Jevrejskaja Gazeta*, which currently has a circulation of about 45 000 throughout Germany,[14] has led to much criticism of the Russian-Jewish population. Non-Russian Jews, for example, have claimed the last board election campaigns in the Berlin Jewish community were dominated by Russian weeklies and monthlies.[15] Some German-Jewish veterans are now not only complaining about a surge of Russian-Jewish separation, but also fear a 'Russification' of their communities.[16] Others hope that the current conflicts and the obvious cultural barriers between German Jews and Russian Jews will eventually disappear with future generations.

Lack of contact with native-born Germans

Since the late 1990s, there has been an ongoing discussion as to whether the 'Russian colonies' promote or hamper successful integration of the immigrants into German society. In fact, many Russian-speaking immigrants continue to maintain strong ties to their former home countries, enjoy Russian culture and arts, buy Russian products wherever possible, attend Russian clubs and do not forget to celebrate Russian anniversaries.[17] As experience in other countries has shown, cultural retention can coexist with immigrants' successful adaptation of elements of the host culture; thus it is possible to remain Russian while at the same time becoming involved in one's new surroundings.

However, a considerable number of the Russian immigrants in Germany are reporting great difficulties in gaining contact with the German population and culture. Most immigrants attribute this to an insufficient command of the German language, while others also refer to cultural differences and personal insecurities. Nonetheless more than 50 per cent say that they would like to have more contact with German natives.[18] This underlines the fact that the motivation is still high and that there are good possibilities for more interaction between the Russian immigrants and indigenous Germans in the future.

As of yet, there have been no studies conducted on the attitudes of the non-Jewish and non-Russian German population towards East European minorities, Russian-speaking immigrants and Russian-speaking Jews in particular. There is also a lack of research regarding the role of the German media in representing the integration of the Russian Jews into German society.[19] We do not know much about the interest or lack thereof of the host society to learn more about the Russian-Jewish minority. Interethnic contact and cross-cultural communication cannot be forced. The ongoing debate in the German public discussing the possibility that the model of a multicultural society has failed, reflects this lack of cross-cultural contact, and, as it seems, this is not a problem only between Russian Jews and the German host society. On the other hand, we assume that some deficits in current migration policy are partly responsible for the Russian Jews' limited success in integrating professionally, and also for their underdeveloped interaction with the German population.

One of the major obstacles in this process is the current distribution system for Russian Jewish arrivals' initial settlement. According to a special distribution key ('Königssteiner Schlüssel'), Russian Jews are proportionally assigned a place to live respective to the population size of the various federal states in Germany. In most of the federal states, there are no existing rules as to *where* the new arrivals should live. Cases are often reported wherein highly qualified experts and highly cultured, well-educated immigrants are 'landing' in rural areas, small towns or even villages. Although it is quite clear that immigrants with an academic occupation, strong cultural interests and the wish to join an established Jewish community are almost 'lost' in peripheral areas, migration policy has not yet drawn the conclusions to develop an agreement which gives Russian-Jewish arrivals the possibility of settling directly in urban areas. An appropriate agreement would, in our understanding, significantly increase the Russian-Jewish immigrants' chances of successful professional, social and cultural integration.

Conclusions

The ongoing Russian-Jewish influx to Germany, initiated by the collapse of the Soviet state and the opening of the borders in 1989/90, has greatly benefited Western and Central European Jewry. Without Russian-Jewish immigration to Germany, organized Jewish life would have died out over the coming decades. Now, however, more than sixty years after the Holocaust, we can witness a Jewish revival across the entirety of a reunified Germany. Apart from this enormous impact on the future of Jewish communities in Germany, the Russian-Jewish influx to Germany has experienced successes and setbacks during the last fifteen years.

The Russian-Jewish migration to Israel and the United States since the early 1990s provides excellent sources of comparison. There can be no doubt that Russian Jews are, in all three countries of destination, a highly motivated, flexible group of immigrants, willing to adapt to the host societies, but also wanting to preserve elements of culture and language adopted in the former Soviet Union and its successor states. The immigrants have to decide for themselves how important it is for them to be involved in Russian communities, in Jewish communities and in the host society. These aspects of identity shaping are not to be underestimated when trying to understand what roles Russian Jews play in these different environments, especially inside the Jewish communities in Germany, where they now form a large majority.

For the German-Jewish communities, the situation is also quite unusual. It is clear that a future German Jewry, already dominated by Russian speakers demographically, has almost nothing in common with the pre-war German Jewry of Einstein, Liebermann or Baeck. The new Jewry even seems to be in closer touch with the Russian transnational Diaspora than with German society.[20] Thus, it is also less surprising that the specific interests, attitudes and world views of the Russian Jews are in many aspects quite different from those of the established German-Jewish veterans. The cultural divides between veterans and new members in the Jewish communities are obvious, and often are the source of much misunderstanding and tension.[21]

In contrast to some euphoric reports made by Germans, foreign publicists and scholars, it remains obvious that a great number of Russian-Jewish immigrants have not yet found their way into German society. Despite their generally high level of qualifications and motivation to overcome the difficulties of the first stage of resettlement, a significant number have not yet succeed in entering the labour market or rising to the middle class. This also marks a significant difference to those groups of Russian Jews who have gone to Israel and to the United States since 1989.

Some Russian-Jewish writers, artists and scholars are already quite successful and well known to the German public, but they are hardly representative of the whole group. It is more or less alarming that fifteen years after the beginning of this wave of immigration, 40 per cent of Russian Jews are unemployed, and between 60 and 85 per cent continue to be dependent on social welfare.[22] We have reason to assume that these persistent problems of social and economic integration were the main cause of the 2006 policy decision to impose more restrictive conditions for future Russian-Jewish immigration to Germany. In all likelihood the newly imposed German language exam for future applicants, the points system designed to assess the likelihood of successful integration in Germany and the required agreement of local Jewish community support will lead to a significant decrease in the rate of immigration by Russian Jews to Germany.

Several German and Russian-Jewish groups and organizations have sharply criticized these new policies for Russian-Jewish immigration, while some German policy-makers argued that the influx has to be better controlled in order to prevent serious problems in the long run. In any case, German migration policy-makers will be forced to reconsider general support programmes for those Russian-Jewish immigrants who have already arrived in Germany. In many cases, it could be helpful to adopt immigrant-supporting measures similar to those carried out in Israel. For example, a stronger promotion of vocational retraining, an improved system for the recognition of professional degrees and, last but not least, a reduction in the time spent in Germany required before applying for German citizenship could substantially help solve many of the social and economic integration obstacles experienced by Russian-Jewish immigrants.[23] It will also be important to change the distribution system for Russian-Jewish arrivals, offering them a chance to settle in larger cities immediately upon arrival.

The immigrants' hardships described above are most common among the older and middle-aged generation (who constitute the majority of the immigrant population). Younger immigrants are reported to have fewer problems in gaining contacts within the host society and enjoying educational and professional success. It is very encouraging that a clear majority of Russian-Jewish adolescents, similar to their parents in the former Soviet Union, are attending secondary school and are highly motivated to start a university programme afterwards.[24]

In the long term, the younger generation of Russian-speaking Jews is expected to integrate into German society and culture to a greater extent than their parents' generation. But it will be of special interest to see to what extent and in what numbers they will then engage and take responsibility inside the Jewish communities as adults. It is the hope of the German-Jewish establishment of today – and the hope of some politicians as well – that the younger generation of Russian Jews will soon form a strong backbone of the Jewish communities. Since a dynamic process of structural and religious differentiation inside the present Germany Jewry has already begun, it is also possible that Russian Jews will take leading positions in liberal and orthodox groups, which act outside of established umbrella organizations.

Notes

1. Federal Office for Migration and Refugees (BAMF), Nuremberg. Annual Statistics: www.bamf.de
2. Central Welfare Board of the Jews in Germany (ZWSt).
3. Ibid.
4. J. H. Schoeps, K. E. Groezinger and G. Mattenklott (eds) (1999), *Menora: Jahrbuch für deusch-jüdische Geschichte* 10, Berlin/Wien: Philo Verlag.
5. These contracts are based on the same models as those which are signed between the state governments and the Catholic and Protestant churches in Germany.

6. J. H. Schoeps, W. Jasper and B. Vogt (eds) (1999), *Ein neues Judentum in Deutschland. Fremd-und Eigenbilder der russisch-jüdischen Einwanderer*, Potsdam: Verlag Berlin-Brandenburg.
7. Ibid. The unemployment rate of 40 per cent among Russian Jews in Germany was confirmed by S. Gruber and H. Rüßler (2002), *Hochqualifiziert und arbeitslos: Jüdische Kontingenflüchtlinge in Nordrhein Westfalen*, Opladen: Leske & Budrich, and by E. Ben Rafael et al. (2006), *Building a Diaspora: Russian Jews in Israel, Germany and the USA*, Leiden: Brill.
8. A. Silbermann (1997), 'Participation and Integration of Jewish Immigrants from the Former Soviet Union: a Case Study in the Synagogue Community of Cologne', unpublished manuscript (in German). See also J. Kessler (2002/3), 'Analysis of a Questionnaire in the Jewish Community of Berlin', *Jüdisches Berlin* (in German).
9. Ben Rafael et al. (2006), *Building a Diaspora*, pp. 104 and 256ff.
10. Ibid., p. 183.
11. The model of the Unified Jewish Community as a binding form of Jewish organization for all religious groups has been in place in Germany since the end of the Second World War. There have not been any serious attempts to question this model over the last decades, by orthodox, conservative or reform groups. The Jewish community had no resources and no power to undergo a process of religious differentiation until the 1990s.
12. In December 2003, the Central Welfare Board of the Jews in Germany (ZWSt) organized a national conference in Frankfurt/Main which exclusively dealt with psychological and psychosomatic problems among Russian-Jewish immigrants.
13. J. Kessler (1998), 'Jüdische Migration aus der früheren Sowjetunion seit 1990. Resümee einer Studie mit 4000 Zuwanderern aus der früheren Sowjetunion in Berlin', *Trumah*, 7, pp. 140–62.
14. Interestingly, this is already a larger circulation than that of the established German-Jewish weekly *Jüdische Allgemeine*.
15. Thanks to the continuous Russian influx to Berlin, several Russian language weeklies have been established in the last few years, among them *Russkij Berlin, Evropa Express* and *Berlinskaja Gazeta*. These weeklies target all Russian speakers in the German capital, including Russian Jews, ethnic repatriates, students and others.
16. Additional areas of conflict between German Jews and Russian Jews are whether community journals should be published in German or Russian, and whether it would be useful to employ Russian-speaking rabbis.
17. On the issue of transnationalism, see in particular Chapter 7 by Judith Kessler in this volume.
18. Schoeps, Jasper and Vogt (1999), *Ein neues Judentum in Deutschland*.
19. The German cultural anthropologist Franziska Becker (2001) conducted a special study to examine images, clichés and stereotypes about the Russian-Jewish migrants produced by established German print media (for example in the weekly magazines *Der Spiegel* and *Focus*). Becker's hypothesis is that the German media have a considerable impact on the hosts' attitudes towards the Russian-Jewish immigrants. Furthermore, Becker assumes that the immigrants themselves, when in contact with German natives and then necessarily confronted with such media-produced stereotypes as 'Homo Sovieticus', will

be influenced in their own self-image and identity. Becker's assessment of the German media reports on Russian Jews is, in general, very critical. According to her, German media tend to play a hampering role in the process of a successful integration of Russian Jews into German society. A critical dispute with Becker's methodology cannot take place in this chapter due to limitations of space. Franziska Becker (2001), *Ankommen in Deutschland: Einwanderungspolitik als biografische Erfahrung im Migrationsprozess russischer Juden*, Berlin: Reimer.

20. It is no coincidence that the World Congress of Russian Speaking Jews, an international organization which was founded in 2002 in Moscow and Jerusalem, now has its own office in Berlin.
21. Silbermann (1997), 'Participation and Integration of Jewish Immigrants'; Kessler (1998), 'Jüdische Migration'; Schoeps, Jasper and Vogt (1999), *Ein neues Judentum in Deutschland*; Rainer Hess and Jarden Kranz (2000), *Jüdische Existenz in Deutschland heute*, Berlin: Logos Verlag.
22. *Die Welt*, 20 January 2005, citing a German state secretary.
23. The situation of Russian-Jewish medical doctors in the eastern part of Germany is an absurd example of this. In rural areas of the former German Democratic Republic (GDR), private medical offices have closed down in such huge numbers that adequate medical coverage will become impossible in the next few years. Russian-Jewish doctors, however, are not only obliged to pass an 'equality exam' for foreign doctors, but also need German citizenship to be allowed to open a medical practice of their own. In general, Russian Jews can only apply for German citizenship after seven years of residence in Germany. A reduction in the time needed before applying for German citizenship could be helpful in two ways: it could improve the professional integration of the Russian-Jewish doctors, but at the same time release the overburdened system of medical coverage in eastern Germany.
24. There is as yet no empirical data to prove this tendency. We draw this conclusion from reports and interviews with Jewish community workers in several towns in eastern and western Germany.

9

In the Ethnic Twilight: the Paths of Russian Jews in Germany

Y. Michal Bodemann with Olena Bagno

The problem of numbers

Over the past fifteen years, an estimated 220 000 Jews, including their non-Jewish dependants, used the right of asylum to immigrate to Germany from the former Soviet Union.[1] After the demise of the USSR, Jews were given the right to immigrate as asylum seekers since as ethnic non-Germans they did not fit the *ius sanguinis* criterion of the German citizenship law. By February 2006, 197 195 Jews and their (non-Jewish) family members had arrived in Germany under these regulations. Another 8535 entered as tourists and were 'naturalized' once residing in Germany, as long as they could prove their Jewish background.

These immigrants are usually described as Russian Jews – but in fact at least 50 per cent are actually from Ukraine and many others from the Baltic states. According to information supplied by the *Zentralwohlfahrtsstelle der Juden in Deutschland* (hereafter ZWST),[2] Ukraine supplied 50 per cent of immigrants who had already arrived in Germany. Russia is in second place having supplied 35 per cent of immigrants; 10 per cent arrived from Lithuania, Latvia and Estonia, and the remaining 5 per cent are from Bukhara, Moldova, Kazakhstan and other parts of the FSU.

Overall, in the years from 1991 to 2005 German embassies on FSU territory accepted and processed 243 684 applications. Some of these applications were received after the new immigration law came into force (1 January 2006) and might therefore already be processed according to the new regulations.[3] Each *Land* (state) in Germany has its particular quota for accepting newcomers.[4] On the other hand, later movements of Jewish immigrants and their dependants are not regulated; they are free to move, according to their preferences, needs and their financial situation. Thus, relatively low ranked Berlin has turned into the largest Jewish community in Germany. Official *Gemeinde* (Jewish community) data indicate that it hosts around 12 000 Jews, while estimates suggest that about 40 000 Jewish migrants are living there, not including their non-Jewish dependants. The discrepancy is notable because it is indicative of a larger problem – the absence of reliable statistics on Jewish immigrants in Germany. This explains also why Kessler and Schoeps and Glöckner (Chapter 8) have arrived at figures different from ours. Indeed, more generally, figures on immigration according to ethnic background are notoriously unreliable.

There are several more reasons for these disparities: first, many Russian-Jewish immigrants were not recognized as Jews on grounds of *halacha*. Lena Gorelik, a young Russian-Jewish writer born in St Petersburg, aptly entitles one of her short stories, 'Herr Grinblum, sie sind kein Jude!' ('Mr Grinblum, you are nor Jewish'), because Herr Grinblum's mother is not Jewish and he cannot join the *Gemeinde*.[5] Many such immigrants, in fact, are facing problems with the Jewish *Gemeinden* when their spouses and children are not Jewish; and many feel they have not been made welcome and either leave the *Gemeinden* once they have exhausted all sorts of benefits, or they choose not to join from the start; or they leave the *Gemeinden* and join other Jewish or non-Jewish religious organizations such as the ultra-orthodox Chabad Lubavitch movement, cultural organizations or messianic (Christianizing) sects. Still, the massive influx has increased the number of Jews registered with congregations from under 30 000 in 1989 to a little over 100 000 today. This is a bewildering array of numbers, and therein lies part of the problem, as we shall see.

Despite its Nazi past, then, Germany ranks third after Israel and the United States in the number of Russian-speaking Jewish immigrants it has accepted. In 2004, for the first time since the collapse of the USSR, twice as many Jews from the CIS – or 20 000 individuals – have chosen to move to Germany instead of Israel, and this trend continued into the following year. Germany encouraged this immigration while barring other immigrants; however, it also took in about 2.5 million ethnic Germans from the former Soviet Union. Many Russian Jews decided to come to Germany on account of its superior health system and its social network, and one way or another they have made their peace with the German environment.

It is important to note that there are two distinctive waves of this Soviet Jewish migration. The first wave, before 1989, came to Germany from the Soviet Union, often via Israel, whereas the second wave came to Germany directly. The big difference is that the first wave, in part on account of its Israeli socialization, knowledge of Hebrew and so on is more 'Jewish'. It also means that members of this wave had prior Zionist and/or religious orientations before coming to Israel and Germany. Jewish immigrants of the second wave, on the other hand, are more transnationally (or rather bi-nationally) oriented, and with important repercussions. On the one hand, these recent immigrants were more likely to retain their pre-migration ties to back home. Indeed, their travel back and forth to their countries of origin has significantly reduced the psychological trauma related to immigration. On the other hand, it is doubtlessly true that, in many cases, they have found themselves between two worlds: while no longer part of the 'Russian' past, their close ties to the home country have often kept them from integrating into their new 'German' reality.

Adela Dzialowski,[6] for example, an immigrant from the first wave (1978) and a WIZO activist,[7] explicitly mentioned that ties to back home are partly responsible for the dual identity of most of the newcomers. She recalls that her family's immigration was 'similar to death': they left the USSR, their relatives and friends, never to return. Germany therefore was perceived as the second home to be built from the ground up and cherished. Marina's family members, another example, tried to find their way in the new society, also by being very open to new experiences and the German way of life. Only when they had found their way in Germany could they begin to newly elaborate Jewish values and their relationship to Israel.[8] However, while, typically, 'veteran' immigrants from the first wave, with advanced cultural and language skills, have taken leadership positions in numerous *Gemeinden*, it is the numerically much greater influx of the more recent immigration that has contributed to an increased sense of communal and ethnic awareness.

The reasons given for this impressive flow of Jewish immigrants to Germany are, from the German side, the notion that Germany can herewith repay a historic debt. This idea has even been voiced by the former foreign minister Joschka Fischer among others, who suggested that Germany should return to the pre-1933 numbers of 500 000 or 600 000 Jews. Jews, moreover, are thought to contribute both culturally and economically to a dynamic society, to the overall benefit of Germany. The reality is a bit different however, and a more careful look at the numbers is instructive.

For example, the Russian-Jewish migration is unusually over-aged, compared to the migration to Israel, the US and Canada. One study speaks of a median age of 54 years. In her essay in this volume, Judith Kessler has pointed out that 70 per cent of the immigrants are unemployed, 85 per cent are dependent on welfare and only 15 per cent are younger than 20 years of age. Almost 70 per cent are university graduates, many in technical domains and engineering, but most of these people cannot find jobs in their fields and few are prepared to accept lower qualified jobs.[9] We can therefore argue that while Russian Jews in their productive years have migrated to the US and Israel, Germany has become their nursing home – or their medical centre.

There is a particular twist to Judith Kessler's statistics, however. The studies regarding labour and social integration were conducted on the basis of data received via the official *Gemeinde* channels: questionnaires were distributed among registered members. Among the 106 000 registered *Gemeinde* members in Germany, the unemployment figures are indeed very high and their integration in German culture and society is relatively low. However, what can be said about the 111 000 migrants who are either not eligible or not interested in being registered in the community? We would speculate that in the latter group the rate of employment is much higher,[10] though most of them, especially in the middle-aged groups, are employed in what Germans, applied usually to Turkish immigrants, call *Parallelgesellschaft* – the ethnic economy of the 'Russian' sector; in services provided to fellow immigrants such as care for the elderly, or in business relations with the FSU countries, and the like. This group is virtually invisible in the studies conducted through Jewish communities and the ZWST.[11]

The proximity to Russia or Ukraine, also in terms of climate and culture but separate from health care and the social network, also plays a role in attracting Soviet Jews to Germany. The relatively high age of the immigrants means, however, that we have to expect a substantial decrease in that population once the older generation has died. Moreover, for the younger generation, Germany is not necessarily a great prospect: many of the younger Russian-speaking Jews, educated in part in Germany, appear to be moving on to the US and elsewhere in search of better opportunities. The Jewish situation, however, should be seen in perspective: the economic situation in Germany in recent years has also inspired many ethnic Germans to try their luck abroad. The percentage of younger Jewish students or professionals leaving the country should be compared to that of younger Germans undertaking the same dramatic shift in their careers.

The problem of ethnos

A warning is therefore in order about an overly optimistic interpretation of these immigration figures overall. In our own estimate, barring unforeseen further immigration to Germany, the Jewish community membership of roughly 100 000 today will have shrunk back to about 60 000 in twenty-five years. In all likelihood, the Russian-Jewish immigration to Germany catered to more assimilated Jews, not the more Zionist or religiously inclined ones who as a rule prefer Israel or the United States. On these grounds, it is at least possible that much of the immigration will blend into German society without leaving any visible trace in ethnic terms. While a smaller group of young Russian Jews is active in the *Gemeinden*, most others have turned their back on the established Jewish community and have cancelled their membership. At best, they have turned to the reform-oriented World Council for Progressive Judaism and have even established independent reform congregations, as in Hanover, for example. The attraction of the reform movement is that it recognizes patrilineality, that is, individuals with a Jewish father and a non-Jewish mother as Jews, and even welcomes their non-Jewish partners to take part in certain community activities.

The reasons for this turning away from organized Jewish life of the majority of immigrants are complex and controversial. Respondents who actually cancelled their membership suggest that their *Gemeinden* failed to treat them fairly along the standards of the old membership; younger respondents speak about discrimination and the hostility of *Gemeinde* officials; they also felt that youth clubs were 'boring' and, instead of helping them to integrate into their new environment and develop their talents, the leadership were preoccupied with imposing religious and dogmatic practices on them. Jewish functionaries, on the other hand, blame the newcomers for being too passive and only out for the benefits extended by the community. The truth is as usual somewhere in between, but it is clear that the communities face enormous challenges with immigrant absorption and cannot function adequately as centres that would consolidate the Jewish minority in Germany.

We may also need to distinguish between an ethno-religious and a purely ethnic identification. Judith Kessler, for example, reports from her survey that almost 80 per cent of the immigrants want to be buried in a Jewish cemetery and two-thirds hope their children will marry Jewish partners. On the other hand, about half of her respondents refuse circumcision and two-thirds are not interested in Bar or Bat Mitzvahs. For a possible Russian identity with a Jewish tinge, the following example from our interviews may illustrate this: it is the case of a family of musicians. The grandfather, father and son are all practising musicians, father and son without any palpable Jewish tradition whatsoever, the faintest knowledge, if any, of Jewish holidays for example, and vague memories that the grandfather still heard his own parents speak Yiddish. The 20-year-old son, of a Jewish father and a non-Jewish Russian mother, and with no Jewish schooling, has grown up in Germany where at present he attends a music college. Questioned as to whether he had many German friends, he responded, 'No, actually not. But as it turns out, at the college there is a group of us, of Russian background, and we hang out together a lot. We just have more in common.' It is apparent that his circle of friends is part of the Russian-Jewish migration, not of ethnic German immigrants.

As mentioned above, much like in the Israeli case, this migration has, in part at least, a distinctly transnational character. Russia, Ukraine and especially the Baltic states are close by, and the Jewish immigrants, where possible, prefer to have dual citizenship.[12] As Judith Kessler shows, many immigrants have kept their post-Soviet citizenships and their old flats and move easily between both worlds. Mail, phone, e-mail and Russian-language papers such as the *Evreya Gazeta* or Russian travel agencies enhance these transnational/bi-national ties.

Apart from the fact that these immigrants may generally be more assimilated, less 'Jewish', their habitus as well is markedly different from that of the old German and especially the so-called Polish Jews – those who normally came to Germany as displaced persons and got stranded there. An extraordinarily high proportion of them is highly educated and values education particularly highly, from engineering and the sciences to literature and the arts. Many younger to middle-aged immigrants have become small entrepreneurs, with a smaller number in the broader Russian milieu who have, willingly or not, become embroiled in Mafioso business structures. Of those between 20 and 35 years of age, most have gone on to higher education or hold a university degree already, with a technical or professional background such as computer science, law and medicine.

A few years ago, to the horror of the non-Russian-Jewish community, (Jewish) war veterans of the Great Patriotic War (the Second World War), and now residents of Berlin, decided to meet and reminisce with German veterans of the *Wehrmacht*. This anecdote points to three issues: first, while other Jews in Germany experience the Second World War and the Holocaust as the great trauma, this is not necessarily so for the Russian Jews; for them, present-day Russian anti-Semitism and earlier, the Gulag, have often been the greater traumatic experiences. Secondly, with their departure from Russia and Ukraine and elsewhere, and as former professors, doctors and engineers, they have become déclassés.

Their previous social status has crumbled and they are seeking recognition from outside, within their new environment.[13] Thirdly, their biography, their experience, their consciousness and their language diverge from that of the non-Russian Jews in Germany, which in turn is reflected in altogether different institutional structures: ever since they arrived, they have set up a large array of clubs and associations particularly in the cultural arena, from chess clubs and theatre, study circles, dance and sewing, to seniors' and young people's groups, in addition to a range of religiously oriented educational programmes organized by and for Russian immigrants. The wealth of organizational energy is puzzling at first, but we have to keep in mind that the large majority of these immigrants are pensioners or unemployed, with spare time and energy which they can devote to these activities. The rich institutional structure which they have developed in Germany will also disappear with the first generation of immigrants; at the same time, however, the overwhelmingly large majority of the new Russian-Jewish membership will lead to an almost total change of leadership in the communities. The recent putsch-like transfer of power in the Berlin community is only a case in point, and Jewish intellectuals will be ever more remote from the *Gemeinden*. The cultural gap is too great to overcome.

The Jewish community

Many Russian Jews have come to view the Jewish community as a fortress and as a generally inhospitable environment. In late 1990, for example, the Jewish community council in Berlin (*Repräsentantenversammlung*) debated whether or not Soviet Jews should be accommodated in Berlin.[14] A strong opinion at the time opposed giving them support. It was argued by one councillor in particular – a man who of all people left Israel to return to Germany after the war – that their place is in Israel, not Germany. A second issue relates to the fact that most communities are dominated by – at least in name – an orthodox establishment. That establishment enforces a rigorous policy of excluding from community affairs and *Gemeinde* benefits self-identified, yet non-halachic Jews and non-Jewish family of Jews; this includes especially also social, non-religious programming. In the Soviet Union, on the other hand, persons of Jewish ancestry were normally classified as Jews, irrespective of their halachic status. This leads to the bizarre situation where individuals with Jewish surnames, identifiable therefore as Jews, bore the brunt of anti-Semitism in the Soviet Union, and were often more reflexive of their Jewish heritage back home, yet in Germany, they are excluded by fellow

Jews from the community – and in the future, vetoed by the *Zentralrat*, they will not be allowed to come to Germany. Those, on the other hand, whose background was more easily concealed because they were Jewish on the mother's, not the father's side, who may have suffered less, have rightful access to the Jewish community and its services and facilities. Lena Gorelik's short story mentioned above addresses precisely this situation.

Russian Jews arriving in Germany, then, enter as ethnic Jews, based on their nationality status, and once in Germany, are being sorted by their own Jewish community into either religiously defined Jews or into non-Jews, irrespective of their cultural and religious experience back home; young Russian Jews, for example, who went to Hebrew school in Dnepropetrovsk now cannot even gain membership in a *Gemeinde* unless they agree to convert; it is an abrogation of status and identity that is often experienced as a trauma, and deeply resented. Russian-Jewish immigrants, then, are being polarized into Jews and non-Jews in Germany.

The story of the Mintz[15] family may be illustrative here. Upon their arrival to Germany in 1994, the father joined the (nominally orthodox) Jewish *Gemeinde*. Soon after, however, he was repelled by the arrogance and hostility of its functionaries. His daughter, at that time 13 years old, was ostracized from the youth club because she 'did not know the details of the Shabbat service and prayers'. Undoubtedly, her father's problems with the *Gemeinde* had played a role here. The 'veteran' members of the youth club looked down on her and were not discouraged from doing so by the rabbi, sent from Israel (and of Chernovitzi background). Like her father before her she decided to quit the club. On the other hand, she knows that she is Jewish, never hides the fact and her father hopes that one day she will become more involved in the Jewish world, though not in the orthodox *Gemeinde*.

On an altogether different plane that does not refer to any formal criteria, however, we find that even those immigrants not involved with the *Gemeinden* have elaborated a milieu that is neither 'Jewish' nor 'Russian' pure and simple. It is not what Homi Bhaba has described as hybridity either, rather a milieu sui generis. They have become what I would describe as 'Jewssians' – Russian-Germans with a Jewish tinge. Lena Gorelik has put it aptly when she describes herself and her friend as being Russian and German with a little Jewishness. The Russian-Jewish presence in Germany, and the deconstruction of the Jewish ethnos there, raises serious issues concerning the salience of the demographers' and the sociologists' clear-cut ethnic categories: where does Jewishness end, where does being Russian end, and where does being German begin? And how useful are ethnic categories in the first place?

A literary excursion

Being Jewssian, however, means primarily sharing a common background and a common culture that is conjugated by an ancestral Jewish past without being Jewish itself. Some of the points just made are vividly expressed in the writings of a number of younger Russian-Jewish (or Jewssian) writers in Germany. As we shall see, Wladimir Kaminer, born in 1967, a representative Jewssian and a post-modern writer to boot, addresses the question of the deconstruction of ethnos, thereby discounting and ironizising Jewishness; Vladimir Vertlib, born in 1961, addresses issues of the denial of Jewishness on the part of the *Gemeinden*, the theme of exclusion as well as the uneasiness of Jewish life in Germany; and Anna Sokhrina's work deals with the inquisitional abrogation of Jewishness on the part of the established Jewish community and the difficulties of reformulating an ethno-national conception of self, as in Russia, into a religiously defined one in Germany. Finally, the young writer Lena Gorelik has gone a step further. Born in 1981 in St Petersburg and living since 1992 in Germany, being Jewish is not insignificant – but inseparably intertwined with her Russian background and her being at home in Germany.

Wladimir Kaminer

Wladimir Kaminer was born in Moscow, received training as a sound engineer for theatre and radio, and later studied dramaturgy at the Moscow theatre institute. He is married to a non-Jewish woman, and in 1990 he emigrated to Berlin. He became known through his legendary evenings at the Kaffee Burger in Berlin and his stories appear in major German dailies. He even has his own radio show in Berlin and his first book, *Russendisko* (2000), turned into a resounding success, as did two later books, including his *Mein Deutsches Dschungelbuch* (2003, 'My German Jungle Book') – a positive to curious appraisal of small-town Germany.

Two questions should be asked in relation to Kaminer, who is clearly the most popular Russian-Jewish writer in Germany and indeed perhaps the most popular cultural figure of that immigrant group overall. First, do his writings give us any clues about that immigrant group, and second, why is Kaminer so immensely popular with a broad German readership? Let us look briefly at some of Kaminer's stories, typically located between the fantastic and the absurd.

The success of Kaminer's stories can be attributed to their controversial, hilarious language and witty plots, as well as to their sociological gaze. In *Russendisko*, K's figures arise from the immobilized Soviet past, then slip in and out of identities: a Moscow prostitute into a Roman countess; K in the clothes of a count; we see a virtual random mix of ethnicities, between Albanians and Africans in Rome, Vietnamese and Russians in Berlin, Jews and Russian Germans in Potsdam, elsewhere of Chinese, Africans, Yugoslav and Russian healers and patients, of Bulgarians pretending to be Turks at a Turkish fast food outlet, the Italians at the Italian restaurant turn out to be Greek and at the Greek restaurant, the employees are Arabs instead – and more: false Indians, Chinese or Africans. Their attachment to Germany is contingent or irrelevant, and K and his figures seem to float across nationalities or countries – as in the case of his mother, now roaming the New World beyond the fixities of the Soviet Union. Ethnic belonging as stick-on labels that can be changed at will.

What, then, about the Jewish theme and Kaminer's Jewish world? *Russendisko*, tellingly, starts out with a sketch of the historical background to the Russian emigration to Germany, and Honecker's accepting of Jews from the Soviet Union to East Germany. Here, in his first story, anti-Semitism as a motive for emigration is discounted and in a rather twisted explanation, Jewish emigration is attributed instead to stalled careers on account of the Jews' privileged position of being able to request exit visas for immigration to Israel. After 1989, Jews were allowed to leave the Soviet Union to anywhere in the world, he says, all they needed in order to receive visas was to demonstrate that they were really Jewish, and people who before did their best to have the world 'Jew' deleted from their passport, now did their best to produce Jewish papers instead. Regardless of whether they were Christians, Muslims or atheists, blond or red or black, a Jewish passport was enough.

Nevertheless, they were as likely to reproduce anti-Semitic stereotypes as non-Jews and had little knowledge about Jewish traditions; one Jewish woman in his stories, for example, claims that Jews bake matzo with the blood of children. K and his buddies at first enjoyed going to the Jewish community, evidently mostly for the food, and one of his friends had himself circumcised, but eventually decided to quit the business with Judaism. All of them were puzzled, K says, as to why Germans would be interested in letting them into their country. It is remarkable that Kaminer's only 'Jewish' story, and the longest one, appears at the beginning, and with a message that relativizes Jewishness completely, as a fleeting and superficial phenomenon. Here and there, Jews appear briefly as shrewd traders who try to take advantage of fellow Russian Jews by denouncing them to the authorities as false Jews.

The Jewish motif, where it appears, is entirely fortuitous. In one vignette, for example, K is asked by a newspaper editor to prepare an article about youth culture, and he starts preparing for it by watching MTV. After some time, he learns that the editor did not mean Youth Culture, *Jugendkultur*, but *Judenkultur*, Jewish Culture. The story ends with the words, 'A lost day.'

What, then, has made Kaminer such a resounding success in Germany? There are several reasons. The stories are humorous, with an erotic tinge, the language, uncommon in German literature today, is clear and simple, and he provides insight into the world of Eastern European immigrants. Most of all, however, his writings resonate with a young, post-modern urban culture that sees itself as mobile and transnational, supposedly without ethno-national attachments. But there is more to it than that. *Russendisko* opens, as I have mentioned, with a distinctly Jewish story, but it is the story of an outsider to the Jewish community or at least of one located at its periphery, and the entire message is that the Jewish community and with it Jewish practices and traditions are irrelevant – it is therefore manifestly a denial of Jewish culture and ethno-national solidarity, and the Russian culture is of far greater relevance. Similarly, his misunderstanding, mis-hearing 'Jewish culture' for 'youth culture', and his unwillingness, in fact, to write about Jewish culture instead, only underline that denial.

Yet throughout the book, signals of K as the Jewish other appear like brief flashes here and there, and indicate their underground existence. It is as if Kaminer wanted to let his readers faintly know that he is Jewish, but that for him Jewishness does not count, and that really all ethnic identities are fleeting, easily removable labels. What appears as a disabling of the Jewish theme, its depoliticization, makes it also unthreatening and in the end allows the German reader to follow this harmless stranger – Germans can be grateful both *for* K's Jewishness and for discounting the relevance of his Jewishness at the same time. It is easier to live with this kind of Jew.

This is how it may appear to his non-Jewish surroundings; but how, if at all, does his case tell us anything about this Jewish immigration to Germany? It is my contention that his self-presentation, regardless of how it is being read by his German surroundings, is also telling about second-generation Russian Jews in Germany.[16] It is foremost a Russian identity with a faint Jewish identity underground – what I have called 'Jewssian'. This identity, however, is difficult to define sociologically in conventional ethnic terms because ethnicity remains unarticulated in terms of the typical organizational structures. It is an ethnicity that expresses itself in terms of mentality and as such makes these immigrants form loose cultural environments and personal networks with each other.

Anna Sokhrina

The second author whom I shall briefly discuss is Anna Sokhrina. Born in the late 1950s in St Petersburg, she is a few years older than both Kaminer and Vertlib. She emigrated in the early 1990s from St Petersburg to Berlin. Her husband, who is in his early seventies, is a renowned art collector and writer, both have published extensively in Russian, and a volume of Sokhrina's short stories has now appeared in German. Like Kaminer, she is a non-observant Jew, and as with so many other emigrants, her emigration to Germany had forced her ethnic identity into sharper focus. In her story 'Frau Katz und Frau Vogel', which in part still sounds like Kaminer with its permutations of class and ethnicity, the Russian-Jewish narrator finds herself at the house of the German Frau Vogel as a cleaning woman; the husbands of both women have left them and they discover their commonalities. The narrator's daughter Olenka falls in love with a Moroccan Muslim, 'her great-grandfather, the rabbi, would turn over in his grave – but what the hell. We ourselves are in Germany now.'

Falling in love with a Muslim young man is not described as a tragedy, but rather as a case in point of cultural and ethnic mixture inspired by the vibrant German society. However, a real life may be harsher as follows from the records of one of our anonymous interviewees: approaching the age of 70 she regards her life as a complete failure. Being married to a Russian artist who cannot speak one word of German, she feels alienated regardless of her German citizenship. Her daughter, in turn, is married to an Arab man, and her grandchildren are unaware of their grandmother's Jewish roots. She has no relationship with her son-in-law. Unsurprisingly, in this situation she blames his ethnic origin rather than anything else. Being secular all her life, she has now bought a bible and tries to find her way to God. 'With all her soul' she feels she belongs to the Jewish people and regrets 'very much' that her parents were assimilated and had never given her a sense of being Jewish. If she had been able to change her life, she would have tried to get integrated into the Jewish community.

Back to Sokhrina, the ethnic permutations notwithstanding, it is, *against* Kaminer, an affirmation of Jewish memory and tradition; the variant, chaotic encounter with other Jewish immigrants to Germany as well does not allow Jewishness to be taken for granted. Anna's story, 'Ich arbeite als Jüdin' ('I am working as (a) Jew'), on the other hand, describes her less than positive encounter with the Jewish community in

Germany: the narrator finds that 'the shortest path to anti-Semitism is working in a Jewish organization'.

Her office reminds her of a Soviet house of culture, with a strong Jewish accent. Elderly immigrants in the literary club come to give her manuscripts to examine – engineers who are convinced that they have just written *War and Peace* and *Anna Karenina* together. Then the tragic comedy of living in Germany: giving military orders to unload matzo from a truck, or a woman who is asking for admission to the *Gemeinde*: 'What, you don't believe me? I swear by the Lord Jesus Christ that I am Jewish!'

Again and again, her Jewish identity that she had taken for granted in Russia is now thrown into disarray, is being redefined and given a sharp profile. In her short story, 'The Path to the Dead Sea', a Russian non-Jewish woman who marries a Jew subsequently converts and becomes orthodox; she lives in Israel with her husband and daughter. She now teaches the narrator, who lives in Germany and is on a visit to Israel, about the rules of kashrut and keeping shabbat. She concludes, 'what a strange life where Mascha's [the Russian convert's] blonde blue eyed children speak Hebrew and where my classical Semitic child with black hair speaks German'.

The post-emigration changes reach deeply into the narrator's family, especially where the younger generation redefines itself and creates a new form of Jewish identity. Her story 'Die Beschneidung' ('The Circumcision') is about the narrator's son's travails – he wants to get to his Jewish roots and get circumcised in the process: 'Why do you need a circumcision? Isn't the name Rabinowitsch enough?' ('Warum brauchst du das [die Beschneidung]? Reicht dir der Name Rabinowitsch nicht?') 'That this was an idea they gave you at the youth club of the *Gemeinde* ... Was it that I came to Germany for? That my son can get himself circumcised here?' With Anna Sokhrina, we have someone who confronts her Jewish heritage head on, torn between her Russian-Jewish past and her presence as a Jewish immigrant in Germany, having to come to grips with entirely different coordinates of ethno-national identity.

Vladimir Vertlib

Vladimir Vertlib is quite different in this regard. In contrast to Kaminer and Sokhrina, Russia, for Vertlib, is merely a distant, somewhat romanticized past; born in Leningrad in 1961, his parents moved with him to Vienna, Israel, Boston, and back to Vienna where he grew up, as portrayed in his book *Zwischenstationen* (1999). His world today is in Germany or Austria and antagonistically inside or outside the Jewish community there. In contrast then to Kaminer, for Vertlib, the Jewish community plays a central role. But, as for many Russian Jews, the encounter with the German-Jewish community is uninviting at best, and mostly traumatizing. In contrast to Kaminer, moreover, he is a virtual unknown – known almost exclusively in Jewish circles. Ironically, in much of his work, Russian Jews play a minor role and many of their problems are projected on to marginalized German Jews. A remarkable short story, entitled 'Der Zwanzigste April' – 'The Twentieth of April' (Hitler's birthday) – portrays just that type of environment, and a rather unfriendly portrayal of Polish Jews who had settled in Germany.

His story 'Der Zwanzigste April'[17] presents a variety of scenes from the *Jüdische Club* in Vienna: Daniel Weißberg, former chair of the club, moves to Israel with great aplomb and a pretentious departure speech, pointing especially to Austrian anti-Semitism, but within six months, Weißberg is back in Vienna. The storyteller, a Russian Jew, seeks admission to the club, and is questioned intensely: how do we know that he is a Jew, and then: 'not again a Russian'? The club is thus characterized by a morbid obsession with the past, a form of negative memory that the group feeds upon and that constitutes part of its existence.

Much of that is brought home in Vertlib's latest novel, *Letzter Wunsch* (*Last Wish*, 2003). It is once again the story of Jewish community exclusion and, I would argue, reflects the shock of many Jewish men and women from Russia who were forced to discover that they were not halachically Jewish and who are pushed away from the Jewish community or are being made unwelcome in some manner. Again, however, the experience of being excluded is projected from Russian Jews on to German Jews. It conveys a sentiment that Polish Jews have displaced the old pre-war German Jews.

This, in fact, is the story of Mr Salzinger in this novel about a father who had returned from Israel to his medium-sized home town in Germany, who had lived on a kibbutz and fought in the Israeli war of independence. Back in his town, at his place of work, he experiences anti-Semitism and he lives an isolated life, without Jewish contact. It appears that his father's generation after the Shoah faced mostly anti-Semitism, that it harboured deep resentment, whereas the younger generation has to contend with philo-Semitism. There is the scene of the Salzingers' home town remembering its 'silent heroes' – people who supposedly resisted Nazism or saved Jews, and then honouring Jews, among other things by providing kosher food which the honoured Jewish elderly woman rejects because she prefers to eat ham. When Salzinger junior returns from the city's event, his father asks how it was with the *Gutmenschen* und *Vergangenheitsbewältigern* (do-gooders and the professional rememberers). The narrator, nevertheless, is firmly embedded in a non-Jewish, German net of friends and acquaintances.

But to the main story in this book: Salzinger's father had asked to be buried together with his previously deceased wife, and at his death, all the preparations had been made, everything goes according to plan. On the day of the funeral, the coffin is lowered, the mourners spread earth onto the coffin below, the narrator recites the kaddish, with the *Gemeinde*'s cantor present. Suddenly, a functionary from the Jewish community arrives and orders the funeral to be stopped immediately because in the 1930s, the deceased's mother was converted by a liberal rabbi, that is, a heretic from the orthodox *Gemeinde*'s perspective. The conversion therefore was not valid and the deceased not Jewish according to halacha. The coffin therefore was ordered to be pulled back out of the grave and a meeting of the (Polish-Jewish) community executive recommends that Salzinger senior be buried outside the cemetery walls.

Salzinger junior resents even entering the *Gemeinde* office, a fortress-like institution, where his only means of admission is with a piece of identification. Mr Salzinger senior's body eventually, and in a clandestine action, is buried at sea. Vertlib, then, furnishes a scathing critique of the Polish-Jewish dominated community structure that rejects newcomers.

Lena Gorelik

Of all the authors discussed, Lena Gorelik is the youngest, in her mid-twenties, who arrived in Germany in her early teens from St Petersburg. But St Petersburg and her Russian past do not play any vivid role in her life or in her two novels. Gorelik went to school in Germany and the principal contacts in her stories are with non-Jewish Germans. Anja Buchmann, her authorial voice in *Hochzeit in Jerusalem* (2007), her recently published second novel, does not know what 'Heimat' is, and yet Germany is clearly her home which she seeks to defend against the nasty comments of her relatives in New York. The storyteller sees herself as a 'russisch-jüdische Deutsche' who celebrates 'Weihnukkivester' – a German, Jewish and, with *Sylvester* (New Year's), Russian mid-winter holiday.

She detests German philo-Semitic 'Gutmenschen', or benefactors who force themselves into her family with huge menorahs as gifts and try to bring Jewish culture to Russian Jews while celebrating Christmas Eve with the Jewish family, but she is just as turned off by an oppressive orthodox Jewish environment that takes a dim view of her non-Jewish life and non-Jewish environment. In contrast, Israel is an environment whose secularism and cultural variety, including the Arab element, is a comfortable Jewish haven that she can describe with great wit and irony. Paradoxically, however, it is the German environment that is forcing her to confront Jewishness: Anja Buchmann's friend Julian, who has grown up as a non-Jewish German, but then discovers that his father was of Jewish origin, drags her to rabbis, synagogues and to Israel.

At the core of this and of her previous novel, *Meine weissen Nächte* (2004), however, is her family as a complex and conflictual anchor whose Jewishness is expressed in Russian terms – or is it that their Russianness is expressed in Jewish terms? Gorelik's dedication at the beginning of *Hochzeit in Jerusalem* sums it all up: dedicated to her 'very best' Jewish girlfriend, dedicated to her friends who make Germany her home, and dedicated to her family, 'of such wonderful Russian warmth' – she herself, however, simply wants to be herself.

Both her Russian and her Jewish identities, then, are resolutely private, at great distance from any institutional Jewish life. On these grounds, it would be unrealistic to expect much in terms of Jewish communal revival – unless the German Judeophile environment, or as the case may be, its subtle anti-Semitism, would force unattached persons of Jewish background to return to organized Jewish life – an unlikely prospect in most cases.

Conclusion

Anna Sokhrina's world is Russian, her Jewish memories, family memories, are juxtaposed to the German-Jewish reality from which she remains excluded. Her imaginary world is still that of St Petersburg – and there is still her real audience. Vladimir Vertlib, on the other hand, finds himself in a contradictory location. He is antagonistically tied/oriented towards the Jewish community, there is the trauma of being excluded, and he faces an unpleasant German environment that produces his unease – but his social network, more often than not, is non-Jewish German nevertheless. Lena Gorelik's location is similar in this respect, but the Jewish community is absent and Jewishness/Russianness is being withdrawn into the family. Wladimir Kaminer's world, finally, is located on the far periphery of the Jewish community, an aporetic space, and if anything, far more 'Russian' than 'Jewish'.

Ironically, Russian Jews were brought to Germany to boost the Jewish numbers and help perform the ideological labour of German multicultural openness and recognition of German responsibility for

Nazism. But the history of these immigrants is different from the pre-existing Jewish community, their mentality and interests are different, and their transformation of German Jewry, with their different concerns, subverts the very reason why they seemed to be useful to Germany in the first place. Given the spare time on the hands of mostly the older, unemployed immigrants, and their overwhelming numbers, it is only a matter of time until they take control of the *Gemeinden*. The next question is, will this lead to a downright Russian/non-Russian split of the *Einheitsgemeinden*, or some other transition that would subvert the present socio-political role of German Jewry and its ideological role as witnesses of memory?

The sociological lessons we can draw are that ethnicity is never homogeneous, people are linked to ethnic – here, Jewish – institutions in a great variety of ways, and lastly, that statistics such as '150 000 or 190,000 Jews in Germany today' hide far more than they reveal.

Notes

1. In Germany, the right of asylum anchored in the 1951 Geneva Convention on Refugees is enshrined in the constitution as a fundamental right (Article 16a of the *Grundgesetz* – Basic Law). Demographically speaking, Jewish immigration to Germany is, however, only a minor element in a larger process experienced by this country in the post-war period. Traditionally, German citizenship was granted on the *ius sanguinis* basis. Reality, though, appears to be much more complex. In 1950, there were only about 500 000 foreigners living in the Federal Republic of Germany, or about 1 per cent of the total population. Since then, the situation has changed significantly: the Central Aliens Register currently lists about 6.8 million foreigners originally from about 200 different countries, or about 8 per cent of Germany's total population of approximately 82.45 million (FRG Ministry of the Interior, official statistics). Of the approximately 6.8 million immigrants in Germany (as of 31 December 2005), about 2.1 million are citizens of one of the other twenty-four European Union member states (31.7 per cent of all foreigners). The largest groups of immigrants are made up of Turkish citizens (1.8 million, or 26.1 per cent of all foreigners), Italians (approx. 500 000 or 8 per cent), citizens of Serbia and Montenegro (approx. 500 000 or 7.3 per cent), Poles (300 000 or 4.8 per cent) and Greeks (300 000 or 4.6 per cent). The above figures suggest that Jewish immigration to Germany is not as massive as the immigration from other countries. The unwillingness of German authorities to keep careful statistical records of this immigration may therefore be explained not only by the historical sensitivity involved in this issue, but also by the relative insignificance of its scale.
2. Interviews with Anatoli Purnik, statistician with ZWST, conducted in February 2006 and January 2007.
3. Starting in January 2006 only FSU Jews who have some background knowledge of the German language will be eligible to immigrate. See Krieger

Hilary Leila (2004), 'Germany to Limit Immigration of FSU Jews', *The Jerusalem Post*, 19 December. Note: recent negotiations of the Jewish Council with German authorities resulted in abolition of the above requirement. For more data see http://vorota.de/Thread.AxCMS?ThreadID=498083

4. This quota is calculated according to each state's (*Land*) particular financial indicators. Accordingly, Berlin for example received 2.3 per cent of Russian-Jewish immigrants, whereas Lower Saxony and North Rhine Westphalia received 9.3 per cent and 22.4 per cent respectively. The actual Russian-Jewish membership in the Berlin *Gemeinde* of well over 6000 individuals, however, far exceeds that quota and demonstrates the movement to the larger cities. What we do know, furthermore, is that around 90 000 new Russian-Jewish immigrants registered with the *Gemeinden* after 1991. There are no official statistics regarding the fate of 111 730 immigrants who are not registered in *Gemeinden*.
5. Lena Gorelik (2005), 'Herr Grinblum, sie sind kein Jude!', *Aufbau*, 71, 1, January, pp. 20–1.
6. Pseudonym.
7. Women's International Zionist Organization.
8. Interview, August 2006.
9. The ZWST data suggest that 75 per cent of immigrants to Germany have higher education. The five most popular occupations are (in descending order): mechanical engineer, electrical engineer, construction engineer, economist/accountant, teacher/artist/musician.
10. The survey 'Democratic Values, 2006' should shed some light on this problem, though it is too soon to make stronger suggestions because the data are yet to be processed.
11. To provide evidence for our speculation we built a cross-sectional representative sample based on the Microcensus 2004, although the available instruments were restricted. The sample does not allow tracing Jewish CIS migrants that either already have only a German passport or double citizenship. However, the most restricted sample created on the basis of Microcensus 2004 gives us 732 respondents who have no German citizenship. Even among this group the full-time employment rate reaches 37.6 per cent. It is reasonable to suggest that among those who already received citizenship this rate is substantially higher. See on this point, Olena Bagno's forthcoming '"The Destination Does Matter": a Life-Long Openness Model of Political Socialisation Applied to the Study of FSU Jewish Immigrants in Germany'. Discussion paper prepared for the Graduate Conference, Haifa, Israel, 26 December, 2006. Manuscript available at: http://gradcon.hevra.haifa.ac.il/19.pdf
12. For example, Russia and Lithuania allow their citizens to have dual citizenship, while Ukrainian or Latvian Jews do not have this opportunity in accordance with the Ukrainian and Latvian constitutions respectively.
13. In contrast, members of the 'Russian' Jewish community of Hameln protested last year against the annual meeting of *Wehrmacht* veterans in their city. The above stories only re-emphasize the heterogeneity of the community where a lot, if not everything, depends on the personalities at the local level.
14. According to Article 83 of the Basic Law, the German federal states (*Länder*) are solely responsible for carrying out the law concerning foreigners. For this

reason, the local foreigners' authority, as a state government agency, is responsible for deciding on residence law issues in accordance with the law. Therefore, local communities have the right to reject the newcomers and the local authorities have to support them should that indeed become the case.

15. Pseudonym.
16. By 'second generation' we refer here to that group of immigrants who received at least some of their schooling in Germany. Kaminer is at the far end of this continuum.
17. Published in *Golem*, No. 1 (1999).

Afterword

Jeffrey M. Peck

This volume is notable not only for the prominence of its contributors, but also for the timeliness of the essays. The subject of the collection, 'The New German Jewry and the European Context', illustrates that the vexed question of a Jewish life in Germany has moved beyond reproaches condemning its existence to an acceptance of the community's new status in a changing Europe, especially since its sharp population growth post-1990. In this regard the authors are all far ahead of a more slowly changing North American Jewish public that still remains burdened with stereotypes and clichés about Germany. This less-informed Jewish population is, however, coming to recognize what major Jewish institutional elites and academic experts have long acknowledged, namely, that the Jewish community in Germany, like Germany itself, has a central role to play in European and global Jewish matters. What that precise role will be, however, still remains to be seen.

Acknowledging the new status of a Jewish life in Germany is, of course, only one side of the equation for understanding the complexity of new domestic actions, policies or statements that resonate beyond Germany's borders. New European agendas, particularly in the wake of the eastward expansion of the European Union to include countries with Jewish populations or international conflicts in the Middle East with global consequences, also affect Germany's Jewish population. Nevertheless, whatever emerges from these new relationships, Jewish life in what was so long considered 'the land of the perpetrators' is assuming a new place. These essays contribute to a more differentiated and informed perspective on this topic, particularly in a European and global context.

Precisely since Germany has Europe's, and in the case of the Jews, the world's attention, so what happens there often takes on symbolic significance far beyond the still small – even at 110 000 – number of Jews in the German population. The towering golden cupola of the reconstructed Oranienburger synagogue and the Star of David atop that shapes the Berlin skyline has become both a symbol of Jewish life in the nation's new capital and an icon of the new Berlin that brings Jewish and German life together in a dramatic and prominent image. Jews from Europe, North America and Israel visit Berlin in increasing numbers and charting 'Jewish Berlin' has become a growing tourist business. Conversely, the domestic Jewish population, or at least some individuals in and out of the community, are also joining other Jewish voices worldwide to form a chorus that is not always in tune with its internal co-religionists or world Jewry in general, particularly when it comes to the Israeli–Palestinian conflict and Jewish responses to it. Such diversity of opinion on multiple fronts testifies to what I see as the positive, growing heterogeneity of the Jewish population in Germany (like its national counterpart) and its developing maturity as a community that remains, however, plagued by growing pains that are often quite serious. Here the Jewish community mirrors Germany's and Europe's confrontation with the 'difference' of Islam and its own place in a Christian Europe. This parallel struggle with diversity in these two populations is often neglected, even as both confront issues of integration and assimilation. Whether this evolution for Jews in Germany can be productive for the health of the community is not clear since such internecine battles, especially when they are so emotional and divisive, may actually lead to further animus and disharmony. Some cynical observers even predict the breakdown or dissolution of the official Jewish community. One might wonder if the old saying, 'two Jews and three opinions', will be productive or destructive for a community that bears so much historical weight and has been revivified so quickly by a massive immigration of Jews from the former Soviet Union who are so different from pre-war German Jewry. It is clear that this new 'German Jewry' has no relation to the past one; openness, however, to a change in the signification of this loaded category – from German to Russian, Ukrainian and more broadly European – might alleviate some of the anxiety about recreating a tradition that was definitively lost with the Shoah. Ironically, the revitalization of the Jewish community in Germany by other European Jews from the former Soviet Union and the rejection of many as 'Jews' because they are not *halachically* Jewish, on the one hand, and the problems prompted by this dramatic change, on the other hand, is only another complication in this highly charged new scenario. As a critical observer of the situation, I would welcome more flexibility and accommodation of difference both inside and outside the Jewish community.

But against this general backdrop, let me be more precise and enumerate some of the specific issues that are emerging at the beginning of 2007. Surely by the time this volume is published, additional events will have surfaced. However, many, if not most of these points I mention are symptomatic of deeper structural issues that remain flashpoints no matter what ignites tensions, such as the immigration from the former Soviet Union and its many repercussions. I want to address five major issues that will have ramifications for the future: (1) integration and representation of the Russian Jews in the official Jewish community; (2) Jewish life in Germany and its relationship to the German government and other minorities; (3) the Israeli–Palestinian conflict and its repercussions in Europe and the United States; (4) Jewish life in Europe in relationship to pan-European and national Jewish organizations and respective national institutions and governments; (5) Israel–Diaspora relations and Jewish identity.

(1) There is no deeper or more far-ranging issue than the integration of the Russian immigrants into the official community. Plagued initially by lack of a sufficient infrastructure to handle the overwhelming numbers, the problems now focus increasingly on power sharing and representation. With an overwhelming majority of Russians in the community and its representative bodies, the *Zentralrat der Juden in Deutschland* recently elected Charlotte Knobloch, the respected head of the Munich community, as its President. Serge Lagodinsky, a young Russian Jew active in Jewish affairs, wrote a stinging critique in the *Süddeutsche Zeitung* criticizing her election precisely because she did not represent the Russian community. While not all may agree with Lagodinsky's criticism, many feel it is time for a change or at least more attention to the immigrants. It remains to be seen in the future if a Russian Jew will lead the official German Jewish community. Knobloch is often publicly criticized for her statements that continue to represent a generation of German Jews whose vision is dominated by the Shoah. While many individual communities are completely made up of immigrants, the Central Council remains linked to the pre-war German Jewish identity that no longer dominates Jewish life in Germany. In Berlin these battles are often fought out by very publicly airing the community's internal political problems about leadership and representation. In addition, individual Russian figures such as Moshe Kantor, the creator and director of the World Holocaust Forum and president of the Russian Jewish Congress, as well as

Arkady Scheiderman, assume increasing power roles in Jewish affairs in Germany, not always with uniform acclaim. Clearly, the question of 'German' or 'Russian' dominance in the community is not about ethnicity or national traditions, but also about other religious, political, cultural and economic matters.

(2) The arrival on the scene of the World Union of Progressive Jewry (WUPJ), the Reformed movement, has raised specific questions of power sharing and representation within the religious sector. Long scorned by the official community, the WUPJ has slowly gained recognition. The fact that high-profile German officials have attended its meetings and called for its acceptance has helped its cause. The WUPJ now has approximately twenty congregations throughout Germany, but the differing standards for defining Jewishness by the Reform and the more traditional German Orthodox communities continues to separate these religious movements. On the other side of the religious spectrum is Chabad Lubavitch which has built a large new centre in Berlin and continues to attract many non-affiliated immigrants with its aggressive and appealing outreach programmes. Ironically, as the Jewish community diversifies, it becomes more complicated as to with whom the German government communicates. In short, who speaks for the Jews of Germany? The Central Council is wise to try to integrate these various factions under its central umbrella, but it will be cautious when issues of leadership and power are at stake. For the future questions remain as to how open and encompassing the Central Council can and wants to be. Further, as more effort is made to bring Jewish and Turkish elites together to discuss common 'minority' issues, such as the Central Council's initiatives and the Turkish–Jewish Dialogue of the American Jewish Committee in Berlin, it is not clear how well such groups will work together to combat the common prejudices of anti-Semitism and xenophobia. Secular Turkish organizations have now recognized that they have something to learn from the strategies of Jewish organizations.[1]

(3) The Middle East conflict between Israel and the Palestinians continues to be the single most pressing political issue which brings global conflict into Europe and Germany. From the Jewish point of view, the European Union and Europeans in general are seen to be pro-Palestinian and overly critical of Israel, even as they try as a member of the quartet to broker a Middle East peace accord. The so-called 'new' anti-Semitism in Europe – attacks on Jewish institutions or even the murder of Jews such as in France – are regarded as outbursts of Muslim

resentments towards Israel played out on the streets of Paris or Berlin on Jewish citizens of these countries. Such expressions of hostility towards French or German Jews are linked with ever new opinion polls that claim anti-Semitism is growing in Europe. For example, a recent Friedrich Ebert Foundation survey[2] showed that 17.8 per cent of Germans say 'the influence of Jews is too large'; 13.8 per cent say that Jews operate 'with nasty tricks to get what they want'. This was interpreted as anti-Semitism. Against this backdrop, however, Germany sent its navy to the Middle East in the wake of the Lebanon war, three rabbis (at the Abraham Geiger Reformed Seminary) were ordained in Berlin for the first time since the Second World War, and a new synagogue and museum were consecrated in Munich. These apparent contradictions may illustrate that official elite institutional attitudes towards Jews and Israel are out of step with those of the German people or it may show that Jewish life proudly continues even in the wake of such examples of anti-Semitism. However, it is clear that Jewish life in Germany, compared to its neighbour France, is still safer and less vulnerable to Muslim anti-Semitism which stems from its large Turkish rather than Arab population.

(4) European Jewish organizations are working towards building bridges and networks among themselves. The European Council of Jewish Communities, the European Jewish Congress, and the European Jewish Student Organization are primary players. European Jewry has long stood in the shadow of the dominance of the United States and Israel when Jewish matters are at stake. For many Jews outside of Europe, the continent where the genocide began and ended remains a bleak landscape for the future of Jewish life. Germany's Nazi past still looms large for many and the 'new' anti-Semitism that I mentioned above is still identified with long-held resentments by national non-Jewish populations or right-wing movements in various European countries. Yet, ironically, on the one hand, Jewish support of the nationalist Le Pen movement in France is strong since both are united by anti-Arab/Muslim feelings, and on the other hand, many Jews worry about neo-Nazi groups in Germany or the success of the right-wing NPD party which won seats in the Saxon legislature. Jewish populations in Europe need to be seen in their national contexts as well as according to pan-European and world Jewish affiliations and interests. In short, Jewish populations need to be differentiated by national and political affiliations as well as religious identifications. In the future the role of the European Union and other European-based institutions will have

an increasingly strong part to play as new countries with Jewish populations join the EU. Will these new political alliances help or hurt the Jews? Will minority rights provisions and anti-discrimination laws benefit Jewish communities and individual Jewish lives in Poland, Hungary or the Czech Republic, when within these countries national histories are not always successful in recognizing responsibility for collaboration against the Jews in the past or their own involvement in current anti-Semitic activities?

(5) Many observers claim that the relationship between Israel and the Diaspora is changing. Europe and Germany are central players in this shifting relationship of centre and periphery. These changes not only concern the German case which highlights the immigration of post-Soviet Jews to Germany rather than Israel or Germany and Israel's long-standing 'special relationship'. It also increasingly includes other Jewish voices in the Diaspora, most recently in Germany, Great Britain and the United States against the dominance of conservative Jewish communities or individuals who wish to silence and even condemn liberal or progressive Jews for criticism of Israel's political policies. The Lebanon War in the summer of 2006 seems to have heightened the pitch. In Germany, Rolf Verleger, the President of the Jewish Community of Schleswig Holstein, was removed from his position when he criticized the Central Council for being a mouthpiece of Israel's politics. In Great Britain a group of prominent Jews have spoken out forcefully against British Jewry's unfailing support of Israel. In the United States the publication of Professor Alvin Rosenfeld's article sponsored by the American Jewish Committee and published on its website with an introduction by its Executive Director David Harris brought coverage from *The New York Times* and an ongoing debate in the newspaper's pages and within Jewish progressive circles. In the latter case Rosenfeld, and implicitly Harris, criticize American progressive Jews for, in fact, contributing to anti-Semitism by their sharp jabs at Israel's policies. As in the American debate, in which most Republicans link the war on terrorism and the Iraq War, conservative positions on liberal Jewish criticism of Israel also lead far too quickly to conclusions about the relationship of support for Israel's politics and the questioning of the Jewish state's existence or anti-Semitism. Again, Jewish voices are not unified on any topic, even that of Israel. Furthermore, these controversies testify to increased self-assurance of diasporic Jews and potentially new bonds being established by diasporic communities with one another: for example, the interest of young North American

Jews in Berlin or the fledgling communities in Krakow or Vilnius. Globalization encourages this kind of restructuring of contact and the layering of new and changing identities among all Diaspora peoples between 'home' and 'exile'. However, these traditional terms no longer hold the same meanings now that we may speak of a more closely and intimately linked networked world where notions of place are virtual as well as real. Above all, such transformations are essentially about Jewish identity and its many, ever-changing forms in transnational and national communities where borders are far more flexible than ever before.

Notes

1. This has been discussed in some detail in Chapter 4 by Bodemann and Yurdakul in this volume.
2. O. Decker and E. Brähler (eds) (2006), 'Vom Rand zur Mitte. Rechtsextreme Einstellungen und ihre Einflussfaktoren in Deutschland', Friedrich Ebert Stiftung Survey.

Select Bibliography

Adelson, Leslie A. (2000) 'Touching Tales of Turks, Germans, and Jews: Cultural Alterity, Historical Narrative, and Literary Riddles for the 1990s', *New German Critique*, 80, pp. 93–124.
— (2002) 'Back to the Future: Turkish Remembrances of the GDR and Other Phantom Pasts', in Leslie A. Adelson (ed.), *The Cultural After-Life of East Germany: New Transnational Perspectives*, Washington, DC: American Institute for Contemporary German Studies (AICGS), pp. 93–109.
— (2002) 'The Turkish Turn in Contemporary German Literature and Memory Work', *Germanic Review*, 77, pp. 326–38.
— (2005) *The Turkish Turn in Contemporary German Culture: Towards a New Critical Grammar of Migration*, London, New York: Palgrave Macmillan.
Am Orde, S. (2002) 'Türken Fordern Vorschule für Alle', Die *Tageszeitung*, 21 February.
Anzaldúa, Gloria (1987) *Borderlands/La Frontera: the New Mestiza*, San Francisco: Spinsters/Aunt Lute.
Aviv, Caryn and David Schneer (2005) *New Jews: the End of the Jewish Diaspora*, New York: New York University Press.
Bagno, Olena (2006) ' "The Destination Does Matter": a Life-Long Openness Model of Political Socialisation Applied to the Study of FSU Jewish Immigrants in Germany'. Discussion paper prepared for the Graduate Conference, Haifa, Israel, 26 December.
Barthes, Roland (1977) *Roland Barthes by Roland Barthes* (Richard Howard, trans.), New York: Hill and Wang.
— (2001) 'The Death of the Author', *Norton Anthology of Theory and Criticism*, New York: Norton.
Beauftragte der Bundesregierung für Migration, Flüchtlinge und Integration (2000) *Einbürgerung: Fair, Gerecht, Tolerant* (2000). http://www.einbuergerung.de/
Becker, Franziska (2001) *Ankommen in Deutschland: Einwanderungspolitik als biografische Erfahrung im Migrationsprozess russischer Juden*, Berlin: Reimer.
Beer, Ingeborg and Reinfried Musch (2004) 'Soziale Stadt: Berlin-Kreuzberg-Kottbusser Tor', Berlin: Deutsches Institut für Urbanistik. http://sozialestadt.de/en/veroeffentlichungen/zwischenbilanz/2-berlin-english.shtml
Benjamin, Walter (1985) *Gesammelte Schriften VI* (Rolf Tiedemann and Hermann Schweppenhäuser, eds), Frankfurt: Suhrkamp.
— (2002) 'The Storyteller', in Howard Eiland and Michael W. Jennings (eds), *Walter Benjamin: Selected Writings Volume 3, 1935–1938*, Cambridge, MA: Belknap Press of Harvard University Press.
Ben-Rafael, Eliezer, Mikhail Lyubansky, Olaf Glöckner, Paul Harris, Julius H. Schoeps, Yael Israel and Willi Jasper (2006) *Building a Diaspora: Russian Jews in Israel, Germany and the USA*, Leiden: Brill Academic Publishers.
Berger, John (1975) *The Seventh Man: the Story of a Migrant Worker in Europe*, Harmondsworth: Penguin.
Berman, Paul (1994) 'Reflections: the Other and the Almost the Same', *The New Yorker*, 28 February, pp. 61–6.

Bernal, Martin (1987) *Black Athena: the Afroasiatic Roots of Classical Civilization. I: The Fabrication of Ancient Greece 1785–1985*, New Brunswick: Rutgers University Press.
Bhabha, Homi (1994) *The Location of Culture*, London: Routledge.
Biale, David (1997) *Eros and the Jews*, Berkeley: University of California Press.
Biale, David (ed.) (2002) *Cultures of the Jews: a New History*, New York: Random House.
Biller, Maxim (2001) *Deutschbuch*, München: DTV.
— (2003) *Esra*, Cologne: Kiepenheuer und Witsch.
Bodemann, Y. Michal (1996a) *Gedächtnistheater: Die Jüdische Gemeinschaft und ihre deutsche Erfindung*, Hamburg: Rotbuch Verlag.
— (1996b) *Jews, Germans, Memory*, Ann Arbor: University of Michigan Press.
— (2002) *In den Wogen der Erinnerun: Jüdische Existenz in Deutschland*, München: DTV.
— (2004a) 'The German Jewish Communities and the New Russian Jewish Writers', lecture presented at the conference Russian Jewish Diaspora after the Cold War, Brandeis University, 21–22 April.
— (2004b) 'Unter Verdacht: Parallelgesellschaften und Anti-Islamismus', *Süddeutsche Zeitung*, 20 November.
— (2005) *A Jewish Family in Germany Today: an Intimate Portrait*, Durham: Duke University Press.
Boyarin, Daniel and Jonathan Boyarin (1993) 'Generation: the Ground of Jewish Identity', *Critical Inquiry*, 19, 4, pp. 693–725.
Brann, Marcus (1963) 'Foreword', *Germania Judaica* I, Tübingen: J. C. B. Mohr, reprint.
Brient, Elizabeth (2000) 'Hans Blumenberg and Hannah Arendt on the "Unworldly Worldliness" of the Modern Age', *Journal of the History of Ideas*, 61, pp. 513–30.
Bronfman, Edgar M. and Cobi Benatoff (2004) 'Is Darkness Falling On Europe Again?' *The Financial Times*, 19 February.
Brouwer, Lenie and Marijke Prister (1983) 'Living in Between: Turkish Women in Their Homeland and in the Netherlands', in A. Phizacklea (ed.), *One-Way Ticket: Migration and Female Labour*, London: Routledge, pp. 113–30.
Brumlik, Micha (2004) 'Dies ist mein Land', *Jüdische Allgemeine*, 23 December.
Bundesamt für Migration und Flüchtlinge (BaMF)/Haug, Sonja (2005) *Jüdische Zuwanderer in Deutschland. Ein Überblick über den Stand der Forschung*, Working Papers.
Bundesverwaltungsamt Köln, Zuwandererstatistik 1991–2004, March.
Çağlar, Ayse S. (1994) 'German-Turks in Berlin: a Quest for Social Mobility', Unpublished PhD dissertation, McGill University.
Carlebach, Julius (ed.) (1992) *Wissenschaft des Judentums: Anfänge der Judaistik in Europa*, Darmstadt: Wissenschaftliche Buchgesellschaft.
Charim, Isolde (2007) 'Emanizpation der Diaspora', *Die Tageszeitung*, 6 March.
Çinar, Safter (2003) 'A Note to Mr. Brenner', *Jüdisches Berlin*, 6, 59, p. 4.
Cohen, Patricia (2007) 'Essay Linking Liberal Jews and Anti-Semitism Sparks a Furor', *The New York Times*, 31 January.
Craig, Siobhan (2000) 'The Collapse of Language and the Trace of History in Ingeborg Bachmann's "Simultan"', *Women in German Yearbook*, 16, pp. 39–60.
Cziesche, Dominik and Barbara Schmidt (2002) 'Schlag ins Wasser?: Deutsche Muslime distanzieren sich von Jürgen Möllemann', *Der Spiegel*, 24, p. 24.

Dannhauser, Werner J. (ed.) (1976) *On Jews and Judaism in Crisis*, New York: Schocken.
Decker, O. and E. Brähler (eds) (2006) 'Vom Rand zur Mitte. Rechtsextreme Einstellungen und ihre Einflussfaktoren in Deutschland', Berlin: Friedrich Ebert Stiftung Survey.
Der Spiegel (2004) 'Allahs rechtlose Töchter. Muslimische Frauen in Deutschland', 15 November.
Deutsche Welle (2003) 'German States Move to Enact Headscarf Bans', 25 September.
Dietz, Barbara (2003) 'Jewish Immigrants from the Former Soviet Union in Germany', *East European Jewish Affairs*, 33, 2, pp. 7–19.
Dietz, Barbara, Uwe Lebok and Pavel Polian (2002) 'The Jewish Emigration from the Former Soviet Union to Germany', *International Migration*, 40, 2, pp. 29–48.
Dörre, Andrei (2004) 'Transnationale soziale Lebenswelten jüdischer Zugewanderter aus den Nachfolgestaaten der UdSSR'. Unpublished diploma thesis, Berlin: Humboldt University.
Dundes, Alan (1991) *The Blood Libel Legend*, Madison: University of Wisconsin Press.
The Economist (2004) 'A Tragic Twist of the Scarf', 4 September, p. 40.
— (2007) 'Second Thoughts about the Promised Land', 13 January.
Elias, Norbert (1978) *The Civilizing Process*. Vol. I: *The History of Manners* (Edmund Jephcott, trans.), New York: Pantheon.
Elon, Amos (2002) *The Pity of It All: a Portrait of the German-Jewish Epoch, 1743–1933*, New York: Picador.
Emmerich, Marlies (2004) 'Berlin statt Israel', *Berliner Zeitung*, 2 December.
Erlanger, Stephen (2002) 'Small German Party Tries to Calm Uproar Over Slurs About Jews', *The New York Times*, 7 June.
European Forum for Migration Studies (2000) 'Beck Presents Report on the Situation of Foreigners in Germany', in *Migration Report: Chronology of Relevant News and Occurrences in the Area of the Institute's Work*, February: http://www.uni-bamberg.de/~ba6ef3/dfeb00_e.htm
Evrensel Daily Newspaper European Edition (2002) 'Yüksek mahkemeden kurbana vize çıktı', 16 January.
The Federal Government's Commissioner for Foreigners' Issues (2000) *Facts and Figures on the Situation of Foreigners in the Federal Republic of Germany*, 19th edition, Berlin.
Fleischmann, Lea (1986) *Dies ist nicht mein Land: Eine Jüdin verlässt die Bundesrepublik*, Munich: Wilhelm Heyne Verlag.
Friend, Bill (2004) 'Deferral of the Author: Impossible Witness and the Yasusada Poems', *Poetics Today*, 25, 1, pp. 137–58.
Garbolevsky, Evgenija, Sabine von Mering and Olaf Glöckner (eds) (2006) *Russian Jewish Emigrants after the Cold War: Perspectives from Germany, Israel, Canada and the United States*, Waltham, MA: Brandeis University.
Garloff, Katja (2004) 'The Emigrant as Witness: W. G. Sebald's *Die Ausgewanderten*', *German Quarterly*, 77, 1, pp. 76–94.
Gerstenberger, Katharina (2002) 'Difficult Stories: Generation, Genealogy, Gender in Zafer Senoçak's *Gefährliche Verwandtschaft* and Monika Maron's *Pawels Briefe*', in Stuart Taberner and Frank Finlay (eds), *Recasting German Identity: Culture, Politics, and Literature in the Berlin Republic*, Woodbridge, England: Camden House, pp. 235–49.

Gilroy, Paul (2004) *After Empire: Melancholia or Convivial Culture?* London: Routledge.
Goldberg, David Theo (ed.) (1994) 'Critical Multiculturalism', in *Multiculturalism: a Critical Reader*, Oxford: Blackwell, pp. 107–40.
Goldscheider, Calvin (2004) *Studying the Jewish Future*, Seattle and London: Washington University Press.
Göle, Nilufer (1986) *Mühendisler ve Ideoloji*, Istanbul: Iletisim.
Goody, Jack (2004) *Islam in Europe*, London: Polity.
Gorelik, Lena (2004) *Meine weissen Nächte*, Munich: Schirmergraf.
— (2005) 'Herr Grinblum, sie sind kein Jude!' *Aufbau*, 71, 1, January, pp. 20–1.
— (2007) *Hochzeit in Jerusalem*, Munich: Schirmergraf.
Görner, Rüdiger (2003) 'Im Allgäu, Grafschaft Norfolk. Über W. G. Sebald in England', *Text + Kritik* IV.
Graetz, Heinrich (1974) 'Judaism Can Be Understood Only Through its History', in Michael A. Meyer (ed.), *Ideas of Jewish History*, New York: Behrman House.
— (1975) *The Structure of Jewish History and Other Essays* (Ismar Schorsch, trans.), New York: Jewish Theological Seminar of America.
Greve, Martin (2001) *Das Türkische Berlin von A–Z*. Die Ausländerbeauftragte des Senats und Türkisch-Deutsche Unternehmervereinigung Berlin Brandenburg e.V., TDU., Berlin: Concept Verlag.
Grimm, Reinhold (1989) 'Nachwort', in Felix Pollak, *Vom Nutzen des Zweifels*, Frankfurt/M: Fischer, pp. 205–14.
Gross, Thomas (2003) 'Der Auserwählte Folk', *Die Zeit*, 31, 24 July.
Gruber, Sabine and Harald Rüßler (2002) *Hochqualifiziert und arbeitslos: Jüdische Kontingentflüchtlinge in Nordrhein Westfalen*, Opladen: Leske & Budrich.
Grundgesetz Article 116 par. 2, 'Information on obtaining/reobtaining German citizenship for former German citizens and their descendants who were persecuted on political, racial or religious grounds between January 30, 1933 and May 8, 1945', www.germany-info.org/relaunch/info/consular_services/citizenship/persecuted.html
Hall, Katharina (2003) 'Bekanntlich sind Dreiecksbeziehungen am kompliziertesten: Turkish, Jewish and German Identity in Zafer Senoçak's *Gefährliche Verwandtschaft*', *German Life and Letters*, 56, pp. 72–88.
Harris, David (2007) 'AJC Statement on Professor Rosenfeld Essay', *AJC News*, 1 February.
Heschel, Susannah (1998) *Abraham Geiger and the Jewish Jesus*, Chicago: University of Chicago Press.
Hess, Jonathan M. (2002) *Germans, Jews, and the Claims of Modernity*, New Haven: Yale University Press.
Hess, Rainer and Jarden Kranz (2000) *Jüdische Existenz in Deutschland heute – Probleme des Wandels der Jüdischen Gemeinden in der Bundesrebublik Deutschland infolge der Zuwanderung russischer Juden nach 1989*, Berlin: Logos Verlag.
Hestermann, Sandra (2003) 'The German-Turkish Diaspora and Multicultural German Identity: Hyphenated and Alternative Discourses of Identity in the Works of Zafer Senoçak and Feridun Zaimoglu', in Monika Fludernik (ed.), *Diaspora and Multiculturalism: Common Traditions and New Developments*, Amsterdam, Netherlands: Rodopi, pp. 235–49.
Hollinger, David A. (1987) *Postethnic America: Beyond Multiculturalism*, New York: Basic Books.

Hundley, Tom (2004) '"No Strikes, no Sit-ins" over France's Scarf Ban', *The Chicago Tribune*, 8 September, p. 6.

Hunt, Lynn (ed.) (2001) *The French Revolution and Human Rights: a Brief Documentary History*, Boston/New York: Bedford/St. Martin's.

Huntington, Samuel P. (2004) 'The Hispanic Challenge', *Foreign Policy*, March/April, pp. 1–16.

— (2004) *Who Are We: the Challenges to America's National Identity*, New York: Simon & Schuster.

Hürriyet Daily Newspaper European Edition (2001) 'Brenner: Ortak noktalarimiz var', 17 July.

— (2002) 'Hesabi Tutmadi', 10 June.

Huyssen, Andreas (2003) 'Diaspora and Nation: Migration into Other Pasts', *New German Critique*, 88, pp. 147–64.

Iyer, Pico (2000) *The Global Soul*, New York: Vintage.

Jacobs, Carol (1993) 'The Monstrosity of Translation: Walter Benjamin's "The Task of the Translator"', *Telling Time*, Baltimore: Johns Hopkins University Press.

Jonker, Gerdien (2002) *Muslime in Berlin*, Berlin: Ausländerbeauftragte Berlin.

Joppke, Christian (1998) *Challenge to the Nation State: Immigration in Western Europe and the United States*, Oxford: Oxford University Press.

— (2003) 'Multicultural Citizenship in Germany', in J. Stone and R. Denis (eds), *Race and Ethnicity: Comparative and Theoretical Approaches*, Oxford: Blackwell Publishing, pp. 359–67.

Jüdischer Kulturverein (2004) 'Vorurteile tanzend bekämpfen', *Jüdisches Berlin*, 7, 60, p. 15.

Judt, Tony (2003) 'Israel: the Alternative', *New York Review of Books*, 23 October.

Kagan, Robert (2003) *Paradise and Power: America and Europe in the New World Order*, New York: Atlantic Books.

Kaminer, Wladimir (2000) *Russendisko*, Munich: Wilhelm Goldmann Verlag.

— (2003) *Mein Deutsches Dschungelbuch*, Munich: Wilhelm Goldmann Verlag.

Kara, Yadé (2003) *Selam Berlin*, Zürich: Diogenes Verlag.

Kastoryano, Riva (2002) *Negotiating Identities: States and Immigrants in France and Germany*, Princeton, NJ: Princeton University Press.

Kepel, Gilles (2004) *The War for Muslim Minds: Islam and the West* (Pascale Ghazaleh, trans.), Cambridge, MA: Belknap Press/Harvard University Press.

Kermani, Navid (2004) 'Distanzierungszwang und Opferrolle', *Die Zeit*, 18 November.

— (2006) 'Was ist deutsch an der deutschen Literatur?' *Süddeutsche Zeitung*, 21 December.

Kessler, Judith (1989–2004) 'Mitgliederstatistik Zuwanderer, Berlin 1990–2004', Frankfurt/M: Zentralwohlfahrtsstelle der Juden in Deutschland, Mitgliederstatistik der Jüdischen Gemeinden.

— (1995/1997) *From Aizenberg to Zaidelma: Jewish Immigrants from East Europe and the Jewish Congregation Today*, Berlin: Die Ausländerbeauftragte des Senats.

— (1998) 'Jüdische Migration aus der früheren Sowjetunion seit 1990. Resümee einer Studie mit 4000 Zuwanderern aus der früheren Sowjetunion in Berlin', *Trumah*, 7, pp. 140–62.

— (1999) 'The Search for Identity and Subculture: Experiences of Welfare Work in the Jewish Congregation', in Julius H. Schoeps, Willi Jasper and Bernhard Vogt

(eds), *Ein neues Judentum in Deutschland: Fremd-und Eigenbilder der russisch-jüdischen Einwanderer*, Potsdam: Veralg für Berlin-Brandenburg, pp. 87–100.
— (2002) 'The Cultural and Religious Self-image of Berlin Jews: Results of the First Congregational Survey', Berlin: Umfrage.
— (2002/3) 'Analysis of a Questionnaire in the Jewish Community of Berlin', *Jüdisches Berlin* (in German).
— (2003) 'Jüdische Migration aus der früheren Sowjetunion seit 1990. Beispiel Berlin', *Hagalil Online*, 23 February. http://www.berlin-judentum.de/gemeinde/migration.htm
— (2004) 'Foreigners in Wonderland? A Critical View of the Expectations and Experiences among Jewish Immigrants from the Former Soviet Union in Berlin', paper presented at the conference Russian-Jewish Emigrants after the Cold War, Brandeis University.
— (2004) 'Klezmerfreie Zone oder Jewish Disneyland', in Wiltrud Apfeld (ed.), *Klezmer. Hejmisch und hip*, Essen: Klartext Verlag, pp. 100–4.
Kirschenblatt-Gimblett, Barbara (1994) 'Spaces of Dispersal', *Cultural Anthropology*, 9, 3, pp. 339–44.
Konzett, Matthias (2003) 'Zafer Senoçak im Gesprach', *German Quarterly*, 76, pp. 131–9.
Körber, Karen (2005) *Juden, Russen, Emigranten: Identitätskonflikte jüdischer Einwanderer in einer ostdeutschen Stadt*, Frankfurt: Campus.
Krieger, Hilary Leila (2004) 'Germany to Limit Immigration of FSU Jews', *The Jerusalem Post*, 19 December.
Kymlicka, Will (1995) *Multicultural Citizenship*, New York: Oxford University Press.
— (2001) *Politics in the Vernacular: Nationalism, Multiculturalism, and Citizenship*, New York: Oxford University Press.
Landesarbeitsamt, Statistisches Landesamt (1997) *Arbeitslosigkeit bei Türken Statistik*. www.tbb-berlin.de
Laurence, Jonathan (2001) '(Re)constructing Community in Berlin: Turks, Jews and German Responsibility', *German Politics and Society*, 19, 2, pp. 22–61. (A different version is published as Laurence, Jonathan (1999) '(Re)constructing Community in Berlin: Of Turks, Jews and German Responsibility', *Wissenschaftszentrum Berlin*, Discussion Paper.)
Legge Jr., Jerome S. (2003) *Jews, Turks and Other Strangers: the Roots of Prejudice in Modern Germany*, Madison: University of Wisconsin Press.
Lerner, Barbara (2002) 'Don't Call Them Arabs', *National Review*, 30 January.
Lewis, Philip (2002) *Islamic Britain: Religion, Politics and Identity among British Muslims*, London: I. B. Tauris.
Lipset, Seymour M. and Earl Raab (1970) *The Politics of Unreason*, New York: Harper & Row.
Macey, David (trans.) (2005) 'Notes on the New Planetary Vulgate', *Radical Philosophy*: http://www.radicalphilosophy.com/print.asp?editorial_id=9956 (Original work published by Pierre Bourdieu and Loic Wacquant (2000) 'La Nouvelle Vulgate Planétaire', in *Le Monde Diplomatique*, May, pp. 6–7).
Mack, Michael (2003) *German Idealism and the Jew*, Chicago: University of Chicago Press.
Manji, Irshad (2003) *The Trouble with Islam Today*, New York: St. Martin's Griffin.
Marcus, Ivan G. (2002) 'A Jewish-Christian Symbiosis: the Culture of Early Ashkenaz', in David Biale (ed.), *Cultures of the Jews: a New History*, New York: Random House, pp. 488–516.

Markovits, Andrei S. (2007) *Uncouth Nation: Why Europe Dislikes America*, Princeton: Princeton University Press.
Mearsheimer, John J. and Stephen M. Walt (2006) 'The Israel Lobby and US Foreign Policy', *Middle East Policy*, 13, 3, pp. 29–87.
Mendelsohn, Ezra (1993) *On Modern Jewish Politics*, New York: Oxford University Press.
Migrantische Initiative gegen Antisemitismus (2003) 'Antisemitizmle Her Yerde Mücadele', *Jüdisches Berlin*, 6, 59, p. 4.
Mosse, George L. (1975) *Toward the Final Solution: a History of European Racism*, New York: Howard Fertig.
Nadas, Peter (1997) *A Book of Memories* (Ivan Sanders, trans.), New York: Farrar, Straus & Giroux.
Nora, Pierre (ed.) (1993) *Les Lieux de mémoire*. Vol. 1: *Les France: Conflits et partages*, Paris: Gallimard.
Oz, Amos (2004) *A Tale of Love and Darkness*, London: Harcourt.
— (2004) *Aidez-nous à divorcer! Israël Palestine, deux états maintenant*, Paris: Gallimard.
Oz-Salzberger, Fania (2002) 'Europe Should Step In and Look Israelis in the Eye', *The International Herald Tribune*, 29 March.
— (2003) 'Europe Forgets Israel's Origins', *International Herald Tribune*, 27 June.
Peck, Jeffrey M. (1998) 'Turks and Jews: Comparing Minorities in Germany After the Holocaust', in Jeffrey Peck (ed.), *German Cultures, Foreign Cultures: the Politics of Belonging*, Washington, DC, Georgetown University/AICGS, pp. 1–16.
— (2002) 'The "New Anti-Semitism" in Germany', *American Institute for Contemporary German Studies in the Johns Hopkins University*. www.aicgs.org/c/peckc2.html
— (2006) *Being Jewish in the New Germany*, New Brunswick, NJ: Rutgers University Press.
Pessoa, Fernando (2003) *The Book of Disquiet* (Richard Zenith, trans.), New York: Penguin.
Peters, Edward (forthcoming) ' "Settlement, Assimilation, Distinctive Identity": the Historiography of Medieval German Jewry, 1902/3–2002/3', review article of Alfred Haverkamp (ed.), *Geschichte der Juden im Mittelalter von der Nordsee bis zu den Südalpen. Kommentiertes Kartenwerk. Jewish Quarterly Review.*
Pinto, Diana (2002) 'The Jewish Challenges in the New Europe', in Daniel Levy and Yfaat Weiss (eds), *Challenging Ethnic Citizenship: German and Israeli Perspectives on Immigration*, New York: Berghahn Books.
— (2004) 'Zukunft Europa. Wie die Juden sechs grundsätzliche Herausforderungen meistern können', *Jüdische Allgemeine*, 52, 4, 30 December.
Pogge, Thomas W. (2003) 'Accommodation Rights for Hispanics in the United States', in W. Kymlicka and A. Patten (eds), *Language Rights and Political Theory*, New York: Oxford University Press, pp. 105–22.
Protokolle der Repräsentantenversammlung der Jüdischen Gemeinde zu Berlin, 2004.
Rabinbach, Anson (2005) 'The Challenge of the Unprecedented: Raphael Lemkin and the Concept of Genocide', *Jahrbuch des Simon-Dubnow-Instituts/Simon Dubnow Institute Yearbook*, 4.
Rabinovici, Doron (1999) *Suche nach M. Roman*, Frankfurt: Suhrkamp Verlag.
Ramadan, Tariq (2003) *Western Muslims and the Future of Islam*, New York: Oxford University Press.

Räthzel, Nora (1995) 'Nationalism and Gender in West Europe: the German Case', in H. Lutz, A. Phoenix and N. Yuval-Davis (eds), *Crossfires: Nationalism, Racism and Gender in Europe*, London: Pluto Press, pp. 161–89.

Rauf, Feisal Abdul (2004) *What's Right with Islam: a New Vision for Muslims and the West*, San Francisco: Harper.

Remmler, Karen (2005) '"On the Natural History of Destruction" and Cultural Memory: W. G. Sebald', *German Politics and Society*, 23, 3, pp. 42–64.

Remy, Steven P. (2002) *The Heidelberg Myth: the Nazification and Denazification of a German University*, Cambridge, MA: Harvard University Press.

Rosenfeld, Alvin H. (2006) *'Progressive' Jewish Thought and the New Anti-Semitism*, New York: American Jewish Committee.

Roy, Olivier (2004) *Globalised Islam: the Search for the New Ummah*, London: Hurst & Co.

Rubin, Barry (2001) 'Turkey is Israel's Best Neighbour', *Jerusalem Post*, 11 July, p. 7.

Said, Edward W. (1993) *Culture and Imperialism*, New York: Alfred A. Knopf.

Schäfer, Peter and Gary Smith (eds) (1995), *Gershom Scholem: Zwischen den Disziplinen*, Frankfurt am Main: Suhrkamp.

Scheiber, Alexander (ed.) (1978) *Ignaz Goldziher: Tagebuch*, Leiden: Brill.

Schiffauer, Werner (2000) *Die Gottesmänner. Türkische Islamisten in Deutschland*, Frankfurt am Main: Suhrkamp.

Schirmer, Dietmar (2002) 'Closing the Nation: Nationalism and Statism in 19th and 20th Century Germany', paper presented at the German Studies Association Conference, San Diego, October.

Schoeps, J. H., K. E. Groezinger and G. Mattenklott (eds) (1999) *Menora: Jahrbuch für deutsch-jüdische Geschichte* 10, Berlin/Wien: Philo Verlag.

— (2005) *Menora: Jahrbuch für deutsch-jüdische Geschichte 15: Russische Juden und transnationale Diaspora*, Berlin/Wien: Philo Verlag.

Schoeps, Julius, Willi Jasper and Bernhard Vogt (eds) (1999) *Ein neues Judentum in Deutschland, Fremd- und Eigenbilder der russisch-jüdischen Einwanderer*, Potsdam: Verlag Berlin-Brandenburg.

Scholem, Gershom (1976) 'Against the Myth of the German-Jewish Dialogue', in Werner J. Dannhauser (ed.), *On Jews and Judaism in Crisis*, New York: Schocken.

Schröder, Gerhard (2004) 'Rede von Bundeskanzler Schröder zur Preisverleihung für Verständigung und Toleranz an Johannes Rau', 20 November. http://www.bundesregierung.de/Reden-interviews-,11635.748232/rede/Rede-von-Bundeskanzler Schroed.htm

Schütze, Yvonne (2003) 'Migrantennetzwerk im Zeitverlauf – Junge russische Juden in Berlin', *Berliner Journal für Soziologie*, 13.

Sciolino, Elaine (2004) 'Ban on Head Scarves Takes Effect in a United France', *The New York Times*, 3 September, p. A9.

Sebald, W. G. (1996) *The Emigrants* (Michael Hulse, trans.), New York: New Directions.

— (1998) *The Rings of Saturn* (Michael Hulse, trans.), New York: New Directions.

Senoçak, Zafer (1992) *Atlas des tropischen Deutschland*, Berlin: Babel Verlag.

— (1998) *Gefährliche Verwandtschaft*, München: Babel Verlag.

— (2004) 'Vernunft und Religion', *Tageszeitung*, 22, November.

Shavit, Ari (2001) 'Our Good Mother Medea', *Haaretz*, 28 December.

Shaw, Stanford J. (1991) *The Jews of the Ottoman Empire and the Turkish Republic*, New York: New York University Press.

Sheffer, Gabriel (2005) 'Is the Jewish Diaspora Unique? Reflections on the Diaspora's Current Situation', *Israel Studies*, 10, 1, pp. 1–35.

Shell, Marc and Werner Sollors (eds) (2000) *Multilingual Anthology of American Literature: a Reader of Original Texts with English Translations*, New York: New York University Press.

Silbermann, A. (1997) 'Participation and Integration of Jewish Immigrants from the Former Soviet Union: a Case Study in the Synagogue Community of Cologne', unpublished manuscript (in German).

Statistisches Bundesamt (2000) *Ausländische Wohnbevölkerung nach ausgewählten Staatsangehörigkeiten von 1997–2002*. Available at: http://www.integrations beauftragte.de/download/datentab2.pdf

Statistisches Bundesamt and the Türkischer Bund Berlin Brandenburg (2003) *Einbürgerungen in Deutschland*. http://www.tbb-berlin.de

Stern, Frank (2003) *Dann bin ich um den Schlaf gebrach: Ein Jahrtausend jüdisch-deutscher Kulturgeschichte*, Berlin: Aufbau Verlag.

Sutcliffe, Adam (2003) *Judaism and Enlightenment*, Cambridge: Cambridge University Press.

Swales, Martin (2004) 'Theoretical Reflections on the Work of W. G. Sebald', in J. J. Long and Anne Whitehead (eds), *W. G. Sebald: a Critical Companion*, Seattle: University of Washington Press.

Swidler, Ann (2002) 'Cultural Repertoires and Cultural Logics: Can They Be Reconciled?' *Comparative and Historical Sociology Newsletter*, 14, 1, pp. 2–6.

Taylor, Charles (1994) *Multiculturalism: Examining the Politics of Recognition*, Princeton, NJ: Princeton University Press.

Tibi, Bassam (1995) *Krieg der Zivilisationen*, Hamburg: Hoffmann & Campe.

— (2002) *Islam Between Culture and Politics*, New York: Palgrave Macmillan.

— (2002) *The Challenge of Fundamentalism*, Berkeley: University of California Press.

Tulgan, S. B. (2004) 'Geliebtes Istanbul', *Jüdisches Berlin*, 7, 60, p. 13.

Türkischer Bund Berlin Brandenburg (1997) 'Arbeitlosigkeit bei Türken. Statistik'. www.tbb-berlin.de

— (2003) 'Einbürgerungen in Deutschland'. www.tbb-berlin.de

Turkish Daily News Electronic Edition (1999) 'Israelis Concerned over PKK Revenge Attacks', 18 February.

'Ungebetene Hilfe' (2005) *Jüdische Allgemeine*, 1, 5, 6 January, p. 20.

Vertlib, Vladimir (1999) 'Der zwanzigste April', *Golem*, 1.

— (1999) *Zwischenstationen*, Vienna and Munich: Deuticke.

— (2003) *Letzter Wunsch*, Vienna: Deuticke.

Virchow, Rudolf (1886) 'Gesamtbericht über die Farbe der Haut, der Haare und der Augen der Schulkinder in Deutschland', *Archiv für Anthropologie*, 16, pp. 275–475.

Weiss, Karin (2004) 'Zuwanderung und Integration in den neuen Bundesländern – zwischen Transferexistenz und Bildungserfolg', in W. Woyke (ed.), *Integration und Einwanderung*, Schwalbach/Ts: Wochenschau Verlag.

Welsh, Christine (1993) 'Women in the Shadows: Reclaiming a Metis Heritage', *Descant*, 24, pp. 89–103.

Wieseltier, Leon (2002) 'Against Ethnic Panic', *The New Republic*, 27 May.

Wolf, Immanuel (1974) 'On the Concept of a Science of Judaism', in Michael A. Meyer (ed.), *Ideas of Jewish History*, New York: Behrman House.

Wuttke, Michael (2005) 'Deutschland: Diskussion um jüdische Zuwanderer', *Migration und Bevölkerung*, 1, 5, February. http://www.migrationinfo.de/migration_und_bevoelkerung/artikel/050101.htm

Yehoshua, Abraham B. (2004) Lecture presented at the Third General Assembly of the European Council of Jewish Communities, Budapest, Hungary, 21 May.

Yilmaz, M. (2004) 'Keine No Go Areas in Kreuzberg', *Jüdisches Berlin*, 7, 60, p. 12.

Young, James E. (2004) 'Variations of Memory: Berlin to New York after 1989', lecture presented at the conference (Re)Visualising National History: Museology and National Identities in Europe in the New Millenium, University of Toronto, 3–5 March.

Zenith, Richard (ed. and trans.) (2001) *The Selected Prose of Fernando Pessoa*, New York: Grove Press.

Zentralrat der Muslime in Deutschland (2002) *Islamische Charta*.

Zentralwohlfahrtsstelle der Juden in Deutschland, Mitgliederstatistik der Jüdischen Gemeinden, 1989–2004, Frankfurt/M.; Bundesverwaltungsamt Köln, Zuwandererstatistik, 1991–2005.

Zilcosky, John (2004) 'Sebald's Uncanny Travels: the Impossibility of Getting Lost', in J. J. Long and Anne Whitehead (eds), *W. G. Sebald: a Critical Companion*, Seattle: University of Washington Press.

Zohar, Zion (2004) 'Oriental Jewry Confronts Modernity: the Case of Rabbi Ovadiah Yosef', *Modern Judaism*, 24, pp. 120–49.

Index